W9-BQJ-232

Illinois Central College
Learning Resource Center

the Private Eye,
the Cowboy
and the Very
Naked Girl

......the Private Eye,
............the Cowboy
and the Very
...........Naked Girl

Movies from Cleo to Clyde

...........by Judith Crist

**Holt, Rinehart
and Winston**

★ ★ ★ ★ ★ ★ ★ ★ Chicago
New York · San Francisco

Published simultaneously in Canada by Holt, Rinehart
and Winston of Canada, Limited.

Library of Congress Catalog Card Number: 68-24757

Most of the reviews in this book appeared in the
New York *Herald Tribune* and the *World Journal
Tribune*. The following reviews were first published
in *Vogue*: "A Trade Like Any Other" (*The Thief of
Paris*); "The Legend of Bonnie and Clyde" (*Bonnie
and Clyde*); "Hold That Tiger!" (*The Tiger Makes Out*);
"Chills, Thrills and Jitters" (*Games, The Penthouse,
Our Mother's House*); and "Three Loves of Bathsheba"
(*Far from the Madding Crowd*). "Against the Groin"
originally appeared in *The Journal of the Producers
Guild of America*.

Published, October, 1968
Second Printing, November, 1968

Designer: Robert Reed
SBN: 03-072495-3

Printed in the United States of America

For my parents

and my menfolk

Contents

Introduction

Were this book about my professional life, it would be titled *Loew's Paradise Regained*; it is, however, about my professional preoccupation, about the movies, about the private eye, the cowboy and the very naked girl, the beasts and breasts and thousands of dead extras who populate the shadowland in which my generation has done its unreal living and learned the ersatz facts of the life we faced thereafter in the glare of daylight beyond the lobby and past the marquee. And this introduction is about the person, and the professional, preoccupied with the movies.

I am of the post-nickelodian pre-television generation, the children of Loew's Paradise—that rococo archetype of the movie palace, complete with niched statuary and a ceiling of star-filled sky across which clouds flitted. My earliest memory of movie*going*, in fact, involves my mother tapping at my shoulder to note that what I was supposed to be watching was in front of me and not overhead. (Janet Gaynor and Charles Farrell were in *Seventh Heaven* on the screen, I learned later, but thanks to those clouds the first movie*seeing* I remember, and always with total recall, is

The Gold Rush.) The movie palace was for special times, however; the small neighborhood theater was our habitat in those Depression-ridden days, when for a dime before five and fifteen cents
thereafter you could see a double-feature, a featurette, a newsreel,
a cartoon and your fill of coming-attractions and, piece by piece,
collect a set of dishes on the side. There were Saturday matinee
serials to hook us, horror shows at midnight, vaudeville on week-
ends and a truant officer in the aisles if you happened to have
scraped up a quarter and made the 9 A.M. show at the Paramount
instead of your first class. Until we began growing up with World
War II, what we learned of our historical past and present, of our
sociology and standards, of world situations and of human relations (including our fleshly ones: our first kisses were in the balcony, that haven of the sophisticates), came from that screen that
was still predominantly silver. (Would that I could report that
the first color film I saw struck me as a thing of cinematic wonder;
actually it was *The Trail of the Lonesome Pine* and my critical sense
was already active, I'm afraid.)

But movies were our secret life. In "our" circle our parents
went to the movies rarely and selectively and our teachers officially went never. There was somehow a perpetual edge of guilt to
exiting from a weekday movie in broad daylight, whether it was
from having filched the admission price from a parental purse,
from having cut school, from having to provide an alibi for the lost
hours or most of all from the conviction held (and instilled) by
parent and educator that time was better spent in developing the
mind and body anywhere but in a moviehouse. But the edge of
guilt didn't touch on the wonderful (and if not wonderful at least
never worthless) world of movies, so we hoarded the dimes or
filched them or tolerated companions with the price of two tickets
and we took a firm grip on our textbooks or wetted our tank suits
in the drinking fountain to support alibis involving the library
or swimming at the Y. And we assuaged our guilt with the conviction that nothing in the outside world could provide the intellectual
and emotional equivalent of Fredric March, his holiday over, en-
folding Rochelle Hudson in his Death's cape or Sally Eilers being
separated from the true love of James Dunn by walls of gold.

And we dreamed that impossible dream of going to the movies legitimately as a critic in broad daylight, on company time yet, and telling the world the truth that we alone understood and perceived and gleaned from the screen—and, fantasy of fantasies, getting paid for doing so.

The impossible dream came true for me twenty years later, when movies had suddenly come into their own a mere two "youth" generations after mine. The world we had wallowed in was suddenly rediscovered and truth and beauty and trash all bollixed up retrospectively. Movies suddenly became "film" and "cinema" and "art form" and terribly terribly chic. And the impossible dream came true overnight for those facile enough to latch on to a good and going thing, and film criticism became the means whereby a stream of young intellectuals could go straight from the campus film society into the professionals' screening room without managing to get a glimpse of the real world in between.

It took me twenty years to become a film critic not only because I had a lot of living and learning to do in preparation but also because the kind of critic I hoped to be was not one the then mass media were prepared for. The waiting time wasn't a waste: teaching on a high school, then college, then Air Force level, completing graduate studies, working as a general-assignment reporter on that sporadically great but consistently newspaperman's newspaper, the New York *Herald Tribune*, specializing first in education and then in the cultural areas with feature stories, serving a critical-training period as handmaiden to God (i.e. second-string to Walter Kerr, the *Tribune*'s impeccable theater critic); and then becoming the first editor of its newly created "Lively Arts" section, which later became part of the *Tribune*'s now independent *New York* magazine.

All is preparation: general assignment reporting for a New York newspaper, in the days before television-dominated journalism, provided not only a super-liberal extra-arts education but also the romance, believe it or not, that my shadowland education had promised—even though few fedoras and whiskey bottles were to be seen in the city room and the vast majority of my colleagues were good union men who commuted to suburbia and domesticity and none of us solved a murder a day or even got on the phone to the boss himself and said, "Chief, hold Page One—stop the presses—I got a scoop—here's the headline and here's the story."

Top stories—exclusives—page-one scoops—journalism prizes—and she's married and has a son, yet—and why in heaven's name does she want to turn to movie reviewing and bury herself in a "fringe" department of the paper? Wasn't the associate drama critic job (an after-hours extra) a pacifier from 1959 on? The more perceptive editors, whose primary interest went beyond holding on to a working reporter, would simply say, on the movie-critic question, "It's not your time." It wasn't. Newspaper movie criticism was and still largely is in an abysmally low state, as the few first-rate critics who tried it discovered to their sorrow and/or compromise. There is not one paper, good-and-gray as well as cheap-and-yellow, with a clean slate as far as the integrity of its film critic has been concerned. The reason is simple: movie advertising is a seven-day-a-week every-day-of-the-year source of revenue and movie moguls are in the high places where publishers find friends. During my reporting days at the *Herald Tribune* one good movie critic bit the dust and another simply had to bow out. But in 1960 John Hay Whitney bought the paper and began an era of critical freedom that had not and has not been equaled. By 1963 it was my time.

Critics may be born; for public and professional purposes they are made by being given their voice. The voice I had sought was in the mass media. I am, I suppose, a teacher and a preacher at heart and I am not interested in converting the converted, in chatting with fellow specialists and intellectuals via the high-of-brow and low-of-circulation "little" publication or an esoteric FM station. I'd long discarded the notion that popularity indicates middle-brow status or that anything that is good, let alone great, must of necessity appeal only to a chosen few (and guess who's going to do the choosing!). And it is a simple logical progression for the passionate reformer (the teacher-preacher bit) to choose to speak to the millions, in the hopes of being heard by hundreds of thousands and listened to by tens of thousands, rather than to the thousands among whom there are hundreds who've either heard it all before or could speak it out for themselves. In short, I am a journalistic critic with no pretensions to esoterica; I speak for the movie-lover rather than the cineaste, for the audience rather than the industry.

I am, admittedly, a severe critic ("severe" is the polite word that has been applied to me; "acerbic" is the usual one, and a triple-S rating, as a "snide, sarcastic, supercilious bitch," is the most glorious epithet I've gotten from an industry man). But the notion that the severe critic "hates" movies is, of course, idiotic. No one is going to be masochistic or suicidal enough to devote his days to something he hates at the rate of some five hundred films a year. The critics who love are the severe ones, setting a standard and dreaming that dream of perfection, suffering with each disappointment, exulting in the rare realization of the dream. Like parents, we carp and criticize and pick away at the flaws; like lovers, we go to passionate heights and depths in our reactions; like true friends, we know our relationship must be based on honesty.

Well, go try that on your old mass media—or so my own pre-sixties reaction would have been, because honesty doesn't win popularity contests; you don't find any standing monuments to that kid who said the emperor was naked, and advertising is the life's blood of the mass media. The first men to try it, in my own career, were Fendall Yerxa, a former *Tribune* man, and his superior, Jim Hagerty, at the American Broadcasting Company during the first "long" city-wide newspaper strike in 1962, using me daily as theater and film critic on both the 11 P.M. and 7 A.M. newscasts on New York's Channel 7. Viewers, so used to hearing only-the-facts-ma'am from the newscasters and nothing but laudatory superlatives from the folk in commercials, were stunned by even the mildest of negative comments by a critic; once they recovered, however, they liked it. All the stations got into the newspaper-critic act, and thereafter, of course, criticism became an established area of television journalism.

When the strike was settled on April 1, 1963, I returned to the *Herald Tribune* (print was my primary medium, after all), where Jim Bellows, the executive editor, asked me to become the paper's film critic. I did and proceeded in a matter of months to lose us ads by deriding *Spencer's Mountain* and the Radio City

Music Hall wherein it played and to have the temerity to be negative about 40 million dollars worth of movie labeled *Cleopatra*. The rest is history, movie-style. Overnight I became famous (if not rich and beautiful in true Hollywood tradition). Those eighteen years of newspapering and four of theater criticism were never noticed; I sprang full-blown into public being as a film critic and an "honest" and "courageous" one at that.

The achievement—or fault—was not mine. The credit—or blame —goes to a handful of editors, publishers and a television producer who could give me a mass media voice and did with no strings attached. Jim Bellows and Jock Whitney gave me access to the *Herald Tribune*'s 400,000 readers (ultimately 700,000 in the *World Journal Tribune*, its short-lived successor); later in 1963 Al Morgan, producer of NBC-TV's network *Today Show*, turned me loose and scriptless before 7.5 million viewers as both film and theater critic; in 1966 Merrill Panitt, editor of *TV Guide*, gave me my say on network movies for his close to 30 million readers. And *Look* and *Vogue* kept me in print on contemporary film after the newspaper died until I resumed my post as film critic for the *New York* magazine, which was revived early this year.

These are the courageous ones, not I. Messrs. Bellows and Whitney (himself an investor in films) were hit where it hurts when negative reviews caused loss of ads, but their instinctive and prompt response—heralded across the nation by the wire services—was an editorial declaration of critical freedom. (The ads in question came back but over and over movie companies tried to punish the *Tribune* even for my *Today Show* influence and my bosses never backed down.) Al Morgan, who gave me my first national outlet (as well as that showbiz glamor), has a cool way with the pressure boys and a rubber-stamped "Bullshit" for their correspondence. Merrill Panitt simply plays it with an "objection noted" and needling-luncheon-session brand of coolth. Pretty gutsy guys, those, when they're stuck with a critic who strikes straight at the roots of the republic with her lack of enthusiasm for *The Sound of Music* or Elvis Presley and Doris Day movies even on television and couldn't flip over any multi-million-dollar super-spectacular since *Gone with the Wind* until the Russian *War and*

Peace came along. It is men like these who make "honest" and "courageous" film criticism possible for the critic and available to the public at large.

I have subscribed to the James Agee premise that film criticism is a conversation between moviegoers; I relish agreement but I think quite frankly that my immediate goal is to keep the conversation going, to stimulate my listener into a response, whether it involves a reappraisal of his own opinions or an affirmation of his disagreement. Ours is the age of the expert, where we sit and wait to get the word from on high, to operate on a consensus of what the ephemeral "they" think. If I can prod a person or two into just thinking for himself, let alone organizing his thought into opinion form, let alone even articulating that opinion—critical mission practically accomplished.

The prodder, the bald-fact stater, the illusion shatterer, the conscientious truth-speaker, as noted, doesn't win popularity contests, but I have learned that he can earn respect. While I have been touted (and treated at times) as the critic most hated by Hollywood, the Motion Picture Association nevertheless asked me to write its guide to movie reviewing for high school students. Artists, truly creative people, of course, can be hurt beyond the pocketbook level and the recovery time is a long one. I have lost the friendship of a number of professionals as a result; my consolation is that I've gained the confidence of a much greater number thereby. Through it all, I've tried to stick to Margaret Leighton's thesis that though one may, the better to judge an omelet, go into the kitchen to learn how it is made, one need not kiss the cook thereof. It's not easy: I'm a fan from way back and I do regret not being able to do a bit of culinary cuddling backstage.

The front-stage sparring has its zest. In this volume you will find three reviews that won prizes, of *Cleopatra, The Sandpiper* and *Hurry Sundown*. The reactions of their makers to the prize awards is, I think, of interest. You'll note that each review is severe, to put it mildly, and you might also agree with me that it is our negativism and not our positive raptures that win us public notice.

Twentieth Century-Fox and other film companies traditionally buy tickets for the New York Newspaper Women's Club benefit dinner-dance at which the prize awards are made. When it was announced that I was to receive one for the *Cleopatra* review, Twentieth Century canceled its ten-ticket table and demanded its 250 dollars back. That was publicized, but what wasn't was that Joseph L. Mankiewicz, who wrote and ultimately directed the film, sent the club his personal check to compensate. I had met Martin Ransohoff, producer of *The Sandpiper*, several months before it was released, because he wanted to discuss in person my negative review of his earlier film, *The Americanization of Emily*. The second pan—and more of the same since—hasn't flawed our very pleasant friendship. It earned me instead a fan letter from his father. And when I was about to receive my prize for the review of Otto Preminger's *Hurry Sundown*, I was handed a telegram from the ineffable Otto offering "Congratulations on your night of triumph from the man without whom all this would not be possible." The last word, as usual, was his.

And it is the last-worders, the lovers, the detractors and the defenders and, above all, the reactors and the respecters who ultimately make the critic that editors, publishers and producers create. My pride is in Alfred Hitchcock's response to Jim Bellows' query as to whether he thought me blunt, "Not blunt, sir, but very sharp," in Dick Watts' declaration that while he admired my skill with the stiletto he admired much more my way with words of praise, in the friendship and education I've been given by both major and minor movie men and women. And my pleasure lies equally in readers who thank me for leading them to something of value or speaking what they have left unsaid, and in readers who thank me for my guidance because, as one put it, "I've learned to shun like the plague anything you recommend and dash off to revel in what you detest." And that's what makes for sprightly conversation.

You'll find no theories about theories of film criticism here. That's for the growing armies of cinema scholars and the next century's academicians who may have some literature, some backlog and some perspective on the various phases of this brand-new medium, child of our century, this largely industrial product that now too often bears the label of "art form," though it has increasingly less form and only on rare occasion even an inkling of art.

We didn't see an art form back at Loew's Paradise; we saw movies—and we're still seeing them to our heart's delight.

This volume, subtitled "Movies from Cleo to Clyde," consists of selections from my writings during five years of film criticism. The time span has several bases. One is that 1963's *Cleopatra* is typical of the multi-million-dollar fiasco that Hollywood alone can create, while 1967's *Bonnie and Clyde* represents the brilliant creativity and artistic achievement of which American moviemakers are capable. Another is that these five years have been the more crucial ones in the revolution in movie-making that has been going on during the sixties and has made film the most exciting and satisfying medium of our time. And perhaps the most important reason is that they span the years of my association as film critic with the New York *Herald Tribune*, a newspaper whose ultimate greatness lay in its respect for both its writers and its readers and its honoring the intelligence of both. I would hope that the reprints from it do it honor in turn and serve as a tribute in gratitude for my association with it as reporter, editor and critic during its last twenty-one years.

For the selection and preparation of my articles my primary thanks go to Dave Paley, a dear friend and a *Tribune* editor with that rare gift of never putting pencil to a writer's copy without improving it. He not only edited and headlined these pieces originally for the paper but proved his fortitude, and love, by rereading them a number of times in preparation for this volume. Bob Cornfield, of Holt, Rinehart and Winston, has also been an invaluable editor, working with Dave to rescue me from that inescapable infatuation with the sight of one's own words and calmly coping with my newspaper-bred deadline-hogging habits. And finally, my thanks to Ted Bernstein, of the New York *Times*, who furthered my respect for language immeasurably in my journalism-student days at Columbia, and continues to do so; he proved himself the ultimate prof by providing the ultimate headline—the title for this book.

J.C.

New York City
May, 1968

the Private Eye, the Cowboy and the Very Naked Girl

☆
☆ ☆Part I
. . . . .From Cleo
. . . . .to Tom

Piety, Prurience
and Teen-agers
May 19, 1963

Nobody in his almost-right mind (right minds are at a psychiatric premium these days) would accuse Radio City Music Hall of showing dirty movies. But at the moment—thanks to the dearth of quality American movies—it happens to be housing a film that for sheer prurience and perverted morality disguised as piety makes the nudie shows at the Rialto look like Walt Disney productions. The movie is *Spencer's Mountain.*

Why carp at free enterprise? The Music Hall, like it or not, is one of our major tourist attractions and lesser national shrines, where hundreds of thousands of devotees come to worship the Christmas and Easter stage shows and millions pay admission between times. It's the biggest movie house in creation, with seats for 6,200, and during a "good" week close to 150,000 have entered its portals.

Spencer's Mountain, outstanding for its smirking sexuality, its glorification of the vulgar, its patronizing tone toward the humble, its mealymouthed piety, was specifically selected for its appeal to American youth. No fooling. A spokesman said that now is the time that high school seniors throughout the country are making their class trips to New York with the Music Hall among their meccas (indeed, 100,000 advance tickets had been bought by groups of this kind) and *Spencer's Mountain* was booked with them in mind.

Well, I don't choose to sell our teen-agers that short, even when it comes to entertainment values, let alone interests. This film involves a poverty-stricken mob of semiliterates clustered in the Grand Tetons of Wyoming. Neither Paw Henry Fonda nor his eight brothers—their age range seems to be from mid-twenties to the mid-forties—have completed high school (and their provincialism would indicate they all dodged the draft), but their reverence for "book-larnin' " is something to see, if not believe.

Paw Fonda and Maw Maureen O'Hara are a pair of parental stereotypes that even television is abandoning: Paw is a cussin', gamblin', whiskey-drinkin' nonchurchgoer with a heart of gold, ready to blackmail other folks into going to church; Maw is cute and perky and God-fearin', toleratin' Paw with a lovin' heart. When they're not worrying about family finances, they're carrying on a public fanny-slapping flirtation worthier of pubescent twelve-year-olds than of the mature (at least sexually mature) parents of nine children.

When the Spencers aren't hymn-singin' and prayin', they're playing around with propagation in mind or watching a bull and heifer play around with the same idea. Ostensibly, though, the film's concern is with Clayboy, the eldest offspring and the first of his clan to get through high school, and the family's efforts to finance his college education.

Their efforts in this direction are rather naïve, not to say archaic; they—and even the minister (newly arrived, mind you) and the schoolteacher—seem to have carefully avoided contact with newspapers, radio or television; despite the presence of a quarry and a mill, the sources of local employment, they ain't even got phones, the way Clayboy has to race cross-country on foot to get a doctor or other help when disaster strikes. Shucks, Clayboy, from the looks of it, could have got a track scholarship to the college of his choice!

Let us, since the Music Hall has teen-agers in mind, take a look at Clayboy and Claris, the quarry manager's daughter. Clayboy isn't stupid; during a brief summer vacation he masters a year's worth of college Latin—or so the minister testifies to the college dean, who finally accepts Clayboy and agrees with his secretary that it is such college admissions that make his life worthwhile.

Clayboy is as American as apple pie, resenting taking a younger sister to the toilet interminably (we're with you, Clayboy, on that), being embarrassed by his father's drunkenness, learning about life from the animals and finally permitting Claris to rape him. (The rape is off camera, but on camera it is preceded by endless scenes of pudgy smooching and teasing with Claris in command and followed by Clayboy's anointing himself for a bad case of sunburn on chest *and* back.)

In contrast, Claris is a sophisticate; she rides a horse, looks fresh from the advertisements in *Vogue,* and goes to a big-city boarding school where the major cultural pursuit is looking up "dirty" words in the dictionary. Claris spends her summer vacation pursuing Clayboy in a manner that makes the word "shameless" seem not pre-Victorian but prehistoric; they don't throw it around like that in the meanest dive in Hamburg.

I won't swear that the average high school senior who has heard of Radio City Music Hall has heard of sex; I'll just suspect that the boys will find Clayboy slightly retarded in the boy-girl department, while the girls will find a rather insulting contemporary prototype in Claris. If they empathize with the screen couple's goings-on—well, all the *Sturm und Drang* concern about the morals of American teen-agers seems to me justified.

But it is the concept on the part of the film's maker—Delmar Daves wrote, directed and produced it—that this is a "wholesome" film, that its emphasis on equating human and animal sexuality is counteracted by the singing of hymns, that its glorification of the vulgar is justified by the trite aspirations of the vulgarians and the suggestion that these are indeed the American dream, that is deplorable.

The cheap, tasteless, patronizing tone of the film is epitomized not merely by the seemingly endless singing of every verse and variation of "America, the Beautiful" at the high school graduation while the camera scans the tear-soaked faces of the Spencers et al.—but the fact that the singer is a Negro. Since this attractive young lady has no other function in the film, since there is no other Negro face or family in the community, we can conclude only that she dropped from heaven for the occasion—so Mr. Daves could prove fashionably what a true-blue, red-blooded, tolerant America he is depicting. How he resisted putting a banjo on her knee and a tambourine in her hand we'll never know.

We can hope that the visiting high school seniors will be accompanied by faculty advisers to set them straight on a few human and patriotic values. And we can hope too that, afflicted by a shortage of quality American films as they may well be, the Radio City Music Hall's bookers will pause to consider their responsibilities.

Hud:
Unpackaged Reality
June 2, 1963

In this lovely land of corrugated cartons and plastic bags, we want our entertainment packaged as neatly as the rest of our consumer goods: an attractive label on the outside, a complete and accurate detailing of contents there or on the inside, no loose ends, no odd parts, nothing left out.

Thus the Hollywood movie tradition, wherein the bad ones get it in the end, the good ones triumph and the joys provide the proper balance for the tears. Not that we are unsophisticated— particularly in the face of competition from foreign films that have had the temerity to suggest that life, unlike the good things therein, does not come in small packages or packages of any size; that though the sun sets daily, it does not do so solely as a happiness-ahead backdrop for lovers, and that the not-nice people can have it as good as and frequently better than the very nice ones.

I am not here concerned with the pseudo-sophistication that has led too many of our moviemakers to nothing beyond vulgarity

film and the public appreciation of it indicate that we're getting out of the lollipop stage at last.

Cleopatra:
A Monumental Mouse
June 13, 1963

Long months—if not years—ago, I suspect, the majority of movie-goers made up their minds either to see *Cleopatra* no matter what or to avoid being caught dead in its vicinity. It's for the un-decided minority, therefore, that I must report that this film is at best a major disappointment, at worst an extravagant exercise in tedium.

It depends, of course, on what you have been waiting for. Certainly if you want to devote the best part of four hours to look-ing at Elizabeth Taylor in all her draped and undraped physical splendor, surrounded by elaborate and exotic costumes and sets, all in the loveliest of colors, this is your movie. And if you are able to adjust your focus from time to time, you will get two fine per-formances by Rex Harrison and Roddy McDowall, the lilting speech of Richard Burton and a couple of parades and divertisse-ments that Flo Ziegfeld or Busby Berkeley might well have mas-terminded.

But I think a bit more has been expected of this 1958–1963 *Cleopatra* under the aegis of Walter Wanger, with script and direc-tion by Joseph L. Mankiewicz. We were led to anticipate a fresh and sophisticated character-oriented approach to the story of Caesar, Cleopatra and Mark Antony, courtesy of Mr. Mankiewicz's past performances; a spectacular epic to take the breath away with panoramic scope and eye-filling extravaganza, courtesy of the thirty-four-million-dollar production cost; a vital history of turbu-lent times, alive with the excitement and fever of the politics and passions that framed them, courtesy of Mr. Mankiewicz's coauthors' researches and the breadth Todd-AO can give to near-global events. But *Cleopatra* is none of these.

And I might note at the outset that an even greater disappointment awaits those whose interest has been titillated almost exclusively by the Taylor-Burton real-life parallel to their Cleopatra-Antony romance. They should be warned that Mr. Burton does not appear for the first hour and twenty minutes; that another hour and fifteen minutes elapses before their first embrace and that, beyond much love talk and soulful ogling, their physical encounters are scarcely five degrees warmer than the Caesar-Cleopatra liaison—and that's a cool one. Perhaps the sexy bits ended up on the cutting-room floor.

I should prefer, in fact, to blame much of the film's inadequacies on the fact that it was cut from six to four hours. This might well account for the choppy incoherence of the action (at times we have to search for columns and hieroglyphics and uniforms to discover whether we're in Rome or Alexandria), for the sketchy portrayal of the pre-Cleopatra Antony (we know him only as a besotted, vain weakling—scarcely a man whose dying "should be shouted from the corners of the earth"), for the strangely abbreviated spectacle of the battles on land and sea and even of the "orgy" aboard Cleopatra's barge.

But cutting would not account for the level of the film's dialogue, provided principally by Mr. Mankiewicz, hitherto one of our most adult and literate screenwriters. Certainly he faced stiff comparison with Shaw and Shakespeare—but the resultant mélange of clichés and pompous banalities is unworthy of him. "Nothing like this has come into Rome since Romulus and Remus," Antony remarks of Cleopatra's spectacular arrival; "A woman that cannot bear children is like a river that has run dry," Cleopatra notes, adding, "I will bear many sons—my breasts are filled with love and life."

Time and tides, the characters keep telling each other, are either running out or waiting for no one; "One world, one people, one nation" is Cleo's political plea, apparently making her a World Federalist at heart; "The way to prevent war is to be ready for it," she assures her generals. "Antony—what has happened?" "To me? *You* have happened to me."

And you want to weep for Rex Harrison—or, at least, to get some of Shaw's *Caesar and Cleopatra* lines into his mouth. He is so good an actor, however, that in spite of the script he manages to make Caesar the larger-than-life creature he must be to be believed. Slightly amused, always superior, steadily approaching the ultimate ambitions that would destroy him, he conveys both the intelligence and the stature of an emperor, particularly in the subtle suggestion that, though he might succumb to her charms and ambitious chatter, he still regards Cleopatra as not too much more than a serviceable doll.

And Miss Taylor makes little more of her than that, her accents and acting style jarring first with those of Harrison and later with those of Burton. She is an entirely physical creature, no depth of emotion apparent in her kohl-laden eyes, no modulation in her voice, which too often rises to fishwife levels. Out of royal regalia, *en negligee* and *au naturel*, she gives the impression that she is really carrying on in one of Miami Beach's more exotic resorts rather than inhabiting a palace in ancient Alexandria or even a villa in Rome. And strangely, in the course of this eighteen-year history, she seems to reverse the aging process, looking a well-groomed thirty-plus when she rolls out of the rug at Caesar's feet and a lovelorn twenty in her death throes.

Miss Taylor's costumes are nothing short of sensational and her doing without any at all in a couple of scenes is equally impressive. But the fallacy is, alas, that neither her costumes nor her performance leaves anything to the imagination. We have on hand a rather unsubtle siren, a blatantly ambitious beauty in search of a man to conquer the world for her, with not even the illusion or suggestion of that eternally mysterious woman whose fascination would outlast the centuries.

With the mystique of Cleopatra missing, Antony loses heroic stature and winds up as a pathetic Caesar-ridden sot, given to occasional pangs of conscience, but a ninny. There's nothing grand about his passion for Cleopatra and no grandeur in his destruction. There is grandeur in Richard Burton's way with a line and a fit of remorse, but the monotony and inconsequence of his role limit this very able actor.

As Octavian, however, Roddy McDowall does bring to

Caesar's heir an underlying shrewdness and strength under an impassive exterior that is fascinating. Kenneth Haigh is briefly interesting as Brutus, but of the other "names" scattered in the cast Hume Cronyn seems oddly uncomfortable as Cleopatra's adviser and Pamela Brown is strictly from Fu Manchu as her high priestess. There's the usual hodgepodge of accents, as in all made-abroad spectaculars, with the ludicrous achieved by the small boy, depicting Caesar's and Cleopatra's son at the age of four, who bursts out with a ripe Italian dialect.

While there are the thousands of extras, the hundreds of Nubians, the dancing girls, the barges, the palaces, the statues, the sphinxes, Mr. Mankiewicz's heart is obviously not in the large-scale action that a film of this subject and physical scope demands. Aiming above, as he has put it, "the *Taras Bulba* crowd," he has attempted to emphasize the main characters rather than the panorama. But so grand and grandiose are the sets that the characters are dwarfed, and so wide is his screen that this concentration on character results in a strangely static epic in which the overblown close-ups are interrupted at best by a pageant or dance, more often by unexciting bits and pieces of exits, entrances, marches or battles.

Mr. Mankiewicz frustrates the requirements of the wide screen by reducing the naval engagement of Actium, after a few disjointed clips of the actual fighting, interrupted by static close-ups of his various characters, to a moving around of models on a map by Cleopatra's admiral aboard her barge. Given, at the outset, magnificent views of the battlefields at Pharsalia and Caesar's camp after the battle, we hunger for more than the brief clash, clatter and fireworks at Moongate, the mere marching of legions, even Antony's abortive one-man attempt against Octavian's legions.

We are cheated of a sense of size and power in the Roman Senate; Caesar's assassination is downgraded by having it splotchily seen through the augury fires set for Cleopatra by her priestess, and not even his funeral pyre on the Forum steps, with Romans throwing what look like old pieces of furniture on it, achieves significance.

The orgies? A bit of wild dancing aboard the barge, with a suddenly drunken Antony joining in, is strangely skimpy—and not helped one bit by having one of the dancing girls decked out as a double for Cleopatra. We should not be reminded that other girls can look just like Elizabeth Taylor, particularly when she is trying to portray the Queen of Queens.

Certainly Cleopatra's multimillion-dollar parade into Rome does beat the advent of Romulus and Remus; it's a mishmash of cavalry, burlesque-show girls and Ballets Africains—*Hot Mikado* performers, topped by Cleo and son, in cloth of gold, riding an arch-high sphinx on wheels. Unfortunately, the climax is dimmed for us by the unnerving but not illogical expectation that somewhere a tenor should burst out with "A pretty girl is like a melody."

The Queen's barge is impressive on the outside, what with pretty girls playing boatswain and lookout and all—and it's deceiving, because inside it's like the whole Hotel Manhattan laid out on one floor. And the banquet! Flaming shish kebab the Ambassador East never dreamed of, whole stuffed and fully feathered peacocks—"Fabulous feast," says Antony. "One is so limited when one travels by ship," replies Cleo.

A painstaking attention to tiny details makes it all too obvious that nothing has been spared on the sets and costumes. There are indeed some beautiful and impressive photographic effects, with transitions made by having faded frescoes slowly brighten into a live scene or a scene freeze and dim into a fresco. But the sets themselves never create an illusion of permanence. The cardboard and paint are there. Even in their most dramatic moment, when Cleopatra and Antony are slapping each other around in her tomb, one's most immediate image is of Miss Taylor and Mr. Burton having it out in the Egyptian Wing of the Metropolitan Museum.

All is monumental—but the people are not. The mountain of notoriety has produced a mouse.

Cold Brilliance of *8½*
June 26, 1963

Federico Fellini's *8½* ranks among the most brilliant cinema works of our time, an intellectual and artistic exercise of the first rank.

Of its importance there can be little question: it is a master-work of one of the great filmmakers, his obviously definitive statement of creative doctrine. But it is an "in" movie, a strangely cold and uninvolving one for the nondevout. Dazzled by the technique and the mind in control of it, we watch and listen with fascination, captives for the duration. And at the end we are instantly freed by the sudden realization that the heart has not been touched or the spirit moved.

8½—so titled because, in addition to three "half" contributions to omnibus films, it is Fellini's seventh full-length movie—is highly autobiographical. It tells of a film director unable to proceed with his next project, taking a rest cure at an infernolike spa, badgered by all his associates and hangers-on, visited by his wife and mistress, pushed and pressured through the purgatories of memory and fantasy until, simultaneously, inspiration and resolution are achieved. For the devout, the cultists who are intimates of Fellini's personal and professional history, the film is obviously a total revelation of the master. For those of us who are but admirers of his work, it is as if we are eavesdropping on the psychoanalysis of a comparative stranger—and hearing nothing that makes us care very much about him.

This is no denigration of Marcello Mastroianni's impersonation—nay, creation—of the director or of Fellini's great achievement in putting on film a man's troubled mind, in blending memory, fantasy and reality with a matchless artistry.

Anselmi, the director, is caught in a traffic jam—but caught within his car, whose windows and doors refuse to open; suddenly he soars, free and clear, only to find that a rope is on his ankle and he is being pulled, kitelike, to earth; the lines of health-seekers at the spa parade like the damned—and how much of the illness is feigned? Memories crowd in—childhood on a farm, the wine festival and children's bath; a boyhood induction into sex by a haggish harlot, the degradation of punishment, and a mother's rejection, a return to the harlot, who suddenly is beautiful, singing sweetly by the seashore. The foolish mistress arrives, to be secreted in a lesser hotel; the too-knowing wife arrives with her entourage to question and remain unanswered.

In what is perhaps the wittiest and yet most human sequence, Anselmi, at a terrace table with his wife and sister-in-law, sees, to his annoyance, his mistress arrive at a nearby table; his wife is only too aware of the situation. He raises a newspaper in front of his face; suddenly his sister-in-law has vanished; his wife approaches his mistress and they talk as old friends and then dance charmingly together; Anselmi is suddenly lord of a harem, in impresario hat, with bullwhip and toga, coddled and cared for by all the women of his desires, past and present, with his wife the willing hausfrau and houseworker for them all.

Throughout there is the dream girl—unmasked as a comparatively dull actress on the make; there is the Church, seen in childhood as an instrument for humiliation, encountered now as a Cardinal whose answers are enigmatic; there is the producer, urging action and compromise, and the writer, cynically nipping inspiration in the bud. And above all there are, as always with Fellini, the stunningly highlighted faces, the fleetingly glimpsed evils and virtues of the world as they pass in parades of human experience.

And, as always, the sophistication of Fellini sparkles in the finale, as the director realizes the wealth of his experience, the human involvement of his years. All the people in his life descend from the huge film set (a skeletal gantry for the scheduled science-fiction film he was to have made) and Anselmi orders them all to join hands and dance, and he and his wife join the circle too, as a pathetic circus band, led by a boy, pipes out the beat. Easy to say that the artist can function only as a part of humanity and as an active participant; cynical to say that life is a circus and, like it or not, you join the dance.

The final message, embodied in the dance and the little circus

boy, makes one remember the Perugino-angel girl at the end of
La Dolce Vita—was she the virtue Marcello could no longer recognize or was she, Lolita-like, another lure for the jaded man? That
child and all the worldlings in that vast contemporary life embodied in *La Dolce Vita* linger long in memory; it is Fellini's
technique and intellect that impress in his new work.

"Little" Films:
How To and How Not To
July 28, 1963

One of our traditional summer heroes is the kid with the bent pin
on the end of a string who keeps hauling in whoppers while the
man with the compleat outfit from Abercrombie & Fitch sits by
with nary a nibble.

For moviegoers the equivalent hero would be the man with
the hand camera and fifty-dollar spot cash who comes up with a
cinematic work of art that's coincidentally a box-office bonanza,
while the moguls with the corporate assets sit weeping among
their multimillion-dollar flops. It's all part of the era of our ad-
vocacy of the little guy (and our cherished rags-to-riches theme)
and a comparatively late awakening to the fact that size is not its
own justification. But while this latter realization has brought us
an appreciation and development of, for example, the compact
car, we've yet to master the art of the compact, or "little," movie.

By "little" I don't mean solely the nonspectacular or the non-
two-hours. I mean the independent film done on a low budget by a
group of filmmakers who have something to say that has to be said
on film in their own terms. I think of these movies much in the
same terms as of a certain segment of the off-Broadway theater,
where the experimental, the too-intimate-for-a-Broadway-house
play or the noncommercial (i.e., not for mass consumption) theme
can be explored.

Let's face it. Just as the Broadway producer considers profit and loss, let's say, "along with" rather than "ahead of" art for its own sake, so the major film producer ponders box-office prospects along with cultural contribution. And how far would you get—especially without Doris Day and Rock Hudson—with a story about two crazy, really crazy, mixed-up kids? And on the other side, who wants the moguls mucking up art? And so certain men with a movie in mind have turned to off-Hollywood, to far-off places or to their own back yards.

And with small exception, they've mucked up their own art and dashed our expectations. Certainly John Cassavetes' *Shadows*, Morris Engel's *Weddings and Babies* and similar "small" movies proved to a fare-thee-well Joseph L. Mankiewicz's apt comment that "unfortunately great ideas cannot be ad lib by either *nouveaux precieux* with shaky hand cameras or actors with deep feelings and limited vocabularies. . . ." And if we'll agree to look elsewhere for "great" ideas, we still will not find these folk spitballing either art or entertainment.

Two current films demonstrate the extremes of quality achieved by the independent makers of "little" films. What differentiates them is professionalism, talented performers and something to say on the one hand, and amateurism, mediocre performers and vacuity of intellect on the other.

David and Lisa is, of course, on the first hand. Made by a group of independent professionals in and around Philadelphia for about one hundred and eighty thousand dollars, it has so far earned more than one million dollars on its first-run showings in New York and other cities before starting its second-run stand. A box-office bonanza, certainly—but a work of art? Not quite.

But one can quarrel with success, wishing for the perfection that was possible. On the debit side, *David and Lisa* has many of the hallmarks of the "little" picture, a certain overall shoddiness, the distracting ineptitudes of passersby in the on-location shots, a studied artiness (no one ever sat in front of a window that did not look out on a Japanese-type branch arrangement, for example) and an overworking of symbolism. The adults are shallow in depiction; the dialogue is pedestrian. And the ultimate shoddiness is the ending, not only with the symbolism of clasped hands shoved at us again but also with an all's-well-so-it's-into-the-sunset-for-everybody upbeat, utterly unworthy of the subtlety and honesty that went before.

But the film as a whole has assets rare to the "little" film. First come its two stars, relative unknowns, Keir Dullea and Janet Margolin, portraying a near-psychotic boy and a schizophrenic girl who find each other in an institution for disturbed youngsters. These two actors show a sensitivity and grace that illuminate the film—and their own futures. And its equally great asset is that *David and Lisa* has something to say in its exploration of troubled adolescents, that it recognizes and probes the wounds of the mind and the heart and the power of love to penetrate even the most private of worlds.

Our eagerness to seize upon an independent venture by non-company men willing to gamble on themselves and their concepts has led to the enthusiasm or, at worst, tolerance with which too many critics have greeted *Greenwich Village Story*, the newest "little" movie to reach a local screen and a prime example of all that pretentious amateurism can produce.

Noting that this is a first film for Jack O'Connell, who wrote, directed and produced *Greenwich Village Story*, the film's publicist reports that O'Connell "turned his back several years ago on his successful Madison Avenue career and went to Italy to work directly with the leading Italian feature producers and directors." O'Connell "was an observer with Fellini on *La Dolce Vita* and was assistant director to Antonioni on *L'Avventura*."

"As a result," the press agent continues, O'Connell's film "is probably the first feature film made here by a native American which brings to the screen the definite hallmarks of Italian film style and technique." The publicist continues, "It is a 'film first' for almost the entire cast of new faces and for many of the technical crew as well, most of whom, in the Italian style, doubled as actors in the film, including the director and his assistant."

This kind of talk can really louse up international relations. Say what you will about the Italians in general—or the dropped names in particular—their cinematic hallmarks are scarcely ineptitude and banality. Where Mr. O'Connell is culpable is in his muffing a fine opportunity to make a knowing, understanding and sensitive film about Greenwich Village, to tell us something perceptive and illuminating about a segment of our society, something that would echo the sincerity of the teemingly authentic location shots of Village activity. Instead, he has written a soap-opera version of *La Bohème* about a struggling writer and a ballerina, updating it with beatnik clichés, ban-the-bomb references and a fatal abortion to replace fatal consumption. With nothing to say, Mr. O'Connell has given us a Greenwich Village that went out with Edna St. Vincent Millay's double-ended candle—and given it to us in cheapjack, sleazy unprofessional terms and techniques that make you wonder how he managed to spend as much as the one hundred and twenty-five thousand dollars the film reportedly cost.

But doesn't our heart go out to a man who abandons the lush but crass life of Madison Avenue ease to sit at the feet of the Italian masters, to struggle through to create his own masterwork? I'm sure the hearts of Mr. O'Connell's sixty-five backers did—and personally, so does ours. The result of all his endeavors is indeed a "little" movie—in every sense of the word.

Grand Hotel,
Nursery Style
September 29, 1963

One Hollywood formula has Ponce de León and his shoddy little aspirations beat hollow. Eternal youth? That's for the kids, strictly Peter Pan stuff. What Hollywood has is retrogression, a formula guaranteed not only to keep the public at large from growing up but also to get it back to the nursery level.

Keep the cotton wool around us, light the nursery fire and let Nanny tell us how the good children get the dessert and the naughty ones get their deserts (just, that is) and the almost-naughty-but-still-intact ones are allowed some goodies too, provided, of course, they say they're sorry. Thus the nursery morality that Hollywood insists on, and come hell, high water or "adult" films by the dozen, the insistence continues that the princes are charming, the maidens pure, the ending for all of them happy.

Don't let the rare film like *Hud* or even on a lower level the occasional *Toys in the Attic* or *The Stripper* mislead you. And don't get false notions about life from all that naked-under-the-sheets (and sometimes over them) stuff the Europeans are flooding us with. Life against the elements is lived in sleek, simple-minded tidiness on *Spencer's Mountain,* domesticity is love-love-love with time out for comic misunderstanding in households headed by Doris Day or Janet Leigh or Shirley Jones and life among the mighty is just one Cinderella story after another for *The V.I.P.'s.*

The standard is sustained whether American films are made here or abroad; it's the American way. Jean Seberg, for example, has made a series of films about an American *jeune fille* learning about life (i.e., sex) in Paris and winding up a sadder and wiser girl. That's how her French films left her, but in her most recent American-made *In the French Style,* she winds up sadder, wiser and en route to marry a successful American surgeon who knows and forgives all. And even the British playwright Terence Ratti-gan, who has given us the bitter with relatively little of the sweet in *Separate Tables,* for example, has gone all-American in providing *The V.I.P.s* for Elizabeth Taylor and Richard Burton and M-G-M and us.

The V.I.P.s exemplifies the retrogressive back-to-the-nursery tenet of our slick moviemakers, particularly with the realization that the M-G-M that brings it to us is the Metro-Goldwyn that back in 1932 presented us with *Grand Hotel.* For though by this jet age Vicki Baum's plush cosmopolitan hostelry has given way to London's semiplush cosmopolitan airport, the story structure is the same. But where once, in a romantic melodrama, we were allowed to see that unloveliness and heartbreak touch the lives of some, today we are permitted only the triumph of love and the pursuit of happiness—and the cotton wool is tucked around us cozily.

The *Grand Hotel* formula has served moviemakers (and playwrights) well through the decades, with a variety of folk from all walks of life brought into brief conjunction to love a little, suffer a little, gag it up a bit and then part, each to his own reward. We've encountered these little cross sections at bus stops, aboard ship, on doomed planes, in lonely inns, at the mercy of the elements, gunmen or the clock.

Rarely has this chance-encounter formula attained the level of *The Petrified Forest* or *Stagecoach.* More often it is another (and lesser) version of the Baum original, which was a straightforward melodrama involving a variety of well defined and engrossing characters. But never has it been employed by a cast comparable to *Grand Hotel*'s, with Garbo as the ballerina, John Barrymore as her baron lover, Lionel Barrymore as the doomed worm that turns, Wallace Beery as the vile financier, Jean Hersholt as the little desk clerk, Joan Crawford the little stenographer, even—unless my 20-20 vision is off—Charles Boyer in a bit role as the majordomo.

And Lewis Stone portrayed the cynical doctor who—amid the manslaughter, gambling, high finance, jewel robbery, tragic love affair and human comedy that have made and broken the lives of all—remarks from time to time that "people come and people go and nothing ever happens in the Grand Hotel."

The formula calls for such a soothsayer and in *The V.I.P.s* it is the airline official who shepherds the Very Important People into their very own lounge, coddles them through red tape and butters them up. And after each has played his little drama in the film, he's busily preparing to wet-nurse still another batch.

The batch Mr. Rattigan has provided us with is a far and much smaller cry from the spirited and admittedly romantic company Miss Baum provided. The poetic love-hungry ballerina, the baron-turned-thief, the vile industrial leader, the gentle mouse-into-lion have yielded to presumably more prosaic people, a love-starved wife and her too-busy-for-affection millionaire husband, a self-made businessman risking his honor for the sake of his employees, a grandiose movie mogul intent on tax evasion, a sweetly comic duchess seeking servitude vile (as assistant social director in a Florida hotel) to get money to retain her ancestral home.

Certainly these are contemporary characters, tinged with

topicality. And this is grown-up stuff: the love-starved wife, our luscious Miss Taylor, is eloping with a notorious gigolo-playboy because he "needs" her and she turns down all impassioned pleas from her suddenly articulate husband, our brooding Mr. Burton, firmly sticking to her beau, the infatuated Louis Jourdan. And the self-made businessman has risked all, gambling that he will get funds in New York to cover a worthless check he has written to save his business. And on the side the impresario mistreats his "protégée" and consults with his accountant, and the duchess doses herself with pills in preparation for the flight.

The fog closes down and the flight is delayed for twenty-four hours and everyone's problems get critical. And guess what? The impresario rents the duchess's home for a movie set so she doesn't have to make her trip and he marries his "protégée" to save his taxes (the naughty boy gets his deserts); the self-made man is saved by his plain-Jane secretary and realizes he loves her rather than his gold-digging girl friend. And guess what else? Miss Taylor learns Mr. Burton plans suicide without her (i.e., he "needs" her) and returns to him and naughty wife-stealing Jourdan is left flat.

Is not, by nursery standards, Miss Taylor a naughty girl? Heavens, no—because whether you believe it or not (and even Mr. Burton expresses his doubts on screen) she and Mr. Jourdan, who propose to live in unmarried bliss in New York, have indulged only in some teen-age necking during their three-month romance and their night in the airport hotel, and Mr. Rattigan has provided lots of awkward dialogue to get this notion across. Prospective adultery? Sí! Actual adultery? No!

Thus the prince charming and the princess are pristine-pure and happiness-bound; Cinderellas are rampant and the naughty boys get theirs. The trouble is nowadays that when you're relegated to the nursery, you find some of the oddest people acting as our storytelling nannies.

Hankering for a Hankie
October 13, 1963

Anybody here remember when that slip of a girl, Danielle Darrieux, took that broth of a boy, Charles Boyer, into her arms in *Mayerling* and murmured, in haunting heart-touching tones, *"Ah, mon amour—comme tu souffres!"?*

Forget—if you crassly can—its context and the suffering Prince Rudolf and his lovely Marie Vetsera, and consider it as one of the key phrases that serve as touchstones for each of us, depending on the catholicity of our cinematic tastes. A key phrase—yes, because we too suffered and the tears flowed and hearts throbbed through the theater. Far away and long ago. And in recent weeks a number of readers have confirmed my growing suspicion that although movies may well be better than ever, a good three- two- or even one-handkerchief movie is getting rarer and rarer. *Ah, mon amour, nous ne souffrons plus!*

It didn't have to be Austrian royalty. There was Claudette Colbert breaking her heart over the pancake batter in *Imitation of Life*; Margaret Sullavan taking those fatal steps across the room in *Three Comrades*; Leslie Howard moaning "Moonyeen—Moonyeen" as he followed the specter of Norma Shearer in *Smilin' Through.*

My comments on the nursery-level sentimentality of *The V.I.P.s*, an upstate reader reports facetiously, "moved me to purchase a bag of chocolate-covered marshmallows, a caramel-fudge bar and a box of creams to take with me to the Shadowland Theater when, wrapped in my new autumn-colored coat, I returned to the classic, luxuriant suffering of the poor rich who have not made an appearance on our screens since the passing of Joan Crawford's middle age and Shirley Temple's childhood."

But she is not, the lady hastens to note, seeking to recapture her "lost, pimply-faced, plump-as-a-partridge youth," when the goo in the mouth matched the goo on the screen. She is, rather, suddenly aware of an emotional aridity in our post-World War II screen fare: "The movies have made me dis-enjoy the protagonists' suffering, a suffering so real that only the salt of popcorn can assuage its anguish. Popcorn-sated, I have watched the meaningful, intelligent, artistic films offered by our adult moviemakers, and my soul cries out for the sweets of the golden thirties, when I could enjoy, without qualm or quibble, someone else's suffering."

The enjoyment was post-facto, we old hands know, as, red-rimmed eyes blinking against the lobby's glare, uneaten candy bar melting against the tear-damp hanky finally tucked away, we heaved that satisfying sigh of emotional purgation and felt the peace of sorrows shared. And they were shared not with the tinsel-thin coloraturas of soap operas that constituted "women's pictures" then as now. They were shared with larger-than-life but filled-with-life creatures who could make you care—a race fast fading from the screen.

They flourished in those golden thirties. Golden they were indeed. On but one hooky-playing day in 1939 an equally movie-mad friend and I started out with *Gone with the Wind* at the Capitol, proceeded across Broadway to the Rivoli for *The Grapes of Wrath* and wound up at the 42nd Street Apollo (then one of two or three "art," or foreign-film, houses in the city) with *Grand Illusion*. And how we suffered with Melanie and Ashley and even, ultimately, Scarlett; the Joad family tore at the heart, and the tears flowed for Pierre Fresnay's white gloves and Von Stroheim's last flower.

Why the lachrymose nostalgia? It is prompted by the re-release of *Wuthering Heights* (another 1939 product—what a vintage year!): For here is a classic, William Wyler at his directorial best, a work of art in its fidelity to the wild, haunted mood of the moors, a larger-than-life romantic drama of tormented souls, souls bared in the darkness of Olivier, the depths of Merle Oberon's eyes, the agony of longing in Geraldine Fitzgerald's quivering voice, the resigned anguish of David Niven.

But the lump in the throat precludes the consumption of sweets. The absorption in romance is complete. And afterward comes the realization that we do have tears and we are prepared to shed them—but for whom today? The schoolteacher in *Winter Light*, Patricia Neal in *Hud*, the transient lovers of *The L-Shaped Room*, the martyred boys in *Lord of the Flies*, Richard Harris in *This Sporting Life*? For their brief moment, yes—before the frost of their surroundings penetrated.

How cold, how chilling, how ultimately forbidding are the serious dramas of our screen—simply because at their best they make a demand upon our intellect and none on our heart. There is no caring, implied or inferred, to warm the brilliance of *8½*.

Must we turn to another time, another place, for catharsis—for the empathy of heartbreak, the fellowship of tears? Ah yes, we moviegoers suffer, but most often because we are left with only the popcorn salt to rub into our wounded intelligence.

That Jones Boy
October 20, 1963

Somebody out there's listening.

We've been brooding for months about the state of the movies, about how sex isn't funny anymore, sentiment is sadly lacking and the little remaining talk rarely to any point. And then along comes *Tom Jones*.

Let cynics say this British film is the exception that proves the rule; I'll settle for understatement and call it exceptional. For indeed it follows the rule of fine moviemaking, with a story to tell and a comment to make, and a perfect collaboration between writer and director, actors and camera, to transmit both. And as a result *Tom Jones* emerges as a rollicking, civilized, utterly joyous and literate celebration of the human comedy in all its aspects.

Age—215 years, at that—hasn't withered the bloom or the bite of Henry Fielding's gay satiric comment on the manners and morals of eighteenth-century England's town and country, an age of vicious class lines and social injustice, with venality and gross

materialism thinly disguised by fraudulent piety and frippery.
Above all, it was an age of lusty living—with its lust for women,
for food, for the blood of the hunt and for the hangman's noose.
But it was also, as Fielding's work attests, an age of wit, of sense
and sensibility, that took full measure of itself.

All of these have been captured in the film in its fidelity to
the spirit and story of *Tom Jones*. This is a movie whose visual
delights complement its intellectual pleasure, whose panorama
teems with characters and caricatures to delight the soul.

John Osborne's script and Tony Richardson's direction have
made high comedy and social comment meet in purely cinematic
terms: a silent-movie-melodrama takeoff to introduce the melodrama of Tom's foundling status; stop-action to freeze a scene
that simply cannot proceed without bursting our laughter seams;
speed-ups to hone the Keystone Kop edge of a chase to end all
bedroom-farce pursuits in confusion and comedy; sudden asides to
the audience, whose sensibilities are protected right down to Tom's
covering the camera eye with his tricorn before embarking on an
intimacy; sight gags and slapstick to tickle the ribs—and an inter-
scene narrative to please the mind. Here's a movie which provides
the sex comedy, the sentiment and the good talk that we've been
missing—and that so many movies have missed.

No, sex isn't funny in *Tom Jones*—it's hilarious, in haystacks,
wooded dells, wayside inns and elegant boudoirs as Tom and
Squire Western have their way with willing wenches and/or
equally willing ladies of fashion. And its hilarity lies in its openhearted lustiness, the frank bawdiness that allows for no sleazy
hinting or coyness and never slides into prurience.

Watch Squire Western wolf his food and guzzle his drink,
greasy hands to be wiped on flowing locks; watch the wildness of
the hunt over farm and field, horses spurred to spurts of blood,
barnyard fowl crushed beneath pounding hooves until the gory
stag is held up in triumph; look at the teeming slums of London,
the pining prisoners at Tyburn, the avid crowds surrounding the
gibbet that Tom is soon to mount.

Watch the goodwives of the countryside in royal battle in the
churchyard with the poacher's sluttish daughter—and watch the

elegant ladies of the town scheme a small matter of rape to secure Tom's Sophia for a bumbling nobleman and secure Tom for their own pleasure. And feel the pulse of the era.

Sentiment? Seldom has the playful nonsense and ineffable tenderness of young love been captured to sweeter (and less cloying) effect than in the courtship scenes between Tom and lovely Sophie Western. And with no disruption of the overall brawling fun of the film, we are allowed a clear view of Tom's deep loyalty to his foster father and our own moment of feeling as he leaves the home he loves to make his way in the world. How wonderful to loathe those sanctimonious villains who conspire against Tom at home, to hold our breath as he faces barehanded the sword of a foul abuser of womanhood, to root for Sophie as she fights off the advances of a lecherous lordling! What fun to care about all these marvelously vital creatures—Albert Finney's goodhearted but all too human Tom, Susannah York's spirited and lovely Sophie, Hugh Griffith's Rabelaisian Squire Western, Dame Edith Evans' positive and positively wrong-headed but right-hearted Miss Western—and to revel in the matching performances of all their colleagues.

For all these pleasures, our thanks to the *Luther* boys, Messrs. Osborne and Richardson, author and director of that play on Broadway (in which, by the way, Mr. Finney and Peter Bull and John Moffat, the villainous Thwackum and Square of *Tom Jones*, win distinction). It's of particular interest, in the light of *Luther* and their earlier collaboration on *Look Back in Anger*, of Mr. Osborne's *The Entertainer* and Mr. Richardson's *A Taste of Honey*, that two men who have come to us with laurels for starkly contemporary and impassioned work should have such brilliant success in so frankly romantic, rollicking and lighthearted a frolic as *Tom Jones*.

You're Dead Without Sex
November 10, 1963

"Maybe," the distributor's man said, "maybe we should have had a nude scene, or the boy and girl on, if not in, a bed. Maybe that's what we need. As it is, we're just not making it at the box office."

The film in question (and maybe with our all-American hit psychology I shouldn't even name it, because we true-blues just wouldn't be seen at something that wasn't a box-office smasheroo) is Ermanno Olmi's *The Sound of Trumpets*, an Italian movie that every critic in town has greeted with what the coolest minds would term "rave" reviews. It's a beautiful film, for truth is indeed beauty, and its truth is in its quiet story of a boy's application and testing for a job in a large corporation and his becoming a cog in the machine that absorbs so many of us.

Boy meets girl—but as a minor part of the film and in the fashion of youth, wherein a couple talks hesitantly during an intermission in the examination day, spends a lunch hour wandering idly and meets at the end of the day before she catches her bus and he his train. They meet again when successful applicants are gathered for their assignments; their jobs separate them. He waits for her in vain several times, sends her a Christmas card through the house mail, meets her accidentally in a corridor. They chat of the company New Year's Eve dance; he attends, but she fails to appear. We do not see her again.

This is the way it happens—but it's not the way, apparently, you sock 'em in at the box office. We're pretty hip to box office around here. And that's why though hundreds of thousands of young Americans take National Merit Scholarship and College Board exams annually and hundreds of thousands more are plugging away in educational and industrial competition, no American filmmaker could possibly see any drama in such situations. Let Gidget and Tammy epitomize young America, and *Beach Party* and *Palm Beach Weekend* describe its aspirations. There's b.o. in them thar dream worlds.

Yes, Olmi's young couple, it seems, should have steered clear of the coffee bar and bus stop and headed for the nearest bed or bushes. Or at very least the ads should show the girl near-nude (regardless of the non-nudity in the film, let's make the best of a bad job) saying with succulent leer to the preferably bare-chested boy, "You're an old-fashioned boy, aren't you?" This would pack 'em in—and the quote at least is correct, if only because the girl does say it, as a city girl impressed by the gentle courtesies and simplicity of a small-town lad.

Distributors with the taste to select fine films for us will just have to learn—although anyone who has managed to remain ignorant of our infantile sexual preoccupations in moviegoing just hasn't checked the box-office returns or read his Krafft-Ebing lately.

The makers of *A New Kind of Love* have. First off it is packaged in Technicolor, with title song by Sinatra, guest appearance by Chevalier, fashion shows from the hautest of couture houses, camera-crew-garnered shots of Paris by day, night and Baedeker—and something for everybody, particularly the sexually deranged.

Now, "sexually deranged" may be a bit strong, and I'm not being blue-nosed about the Paris stripteasers in endless nightclub footage, or Paul Newman's incessant wenching in the role of a satyr-sportswriter. But it seems to me that mental health rather than prudery is in question when we are presented with Joanne Woodward as a heroine who, bruised by an unsuccessful romance, hates men so much that she dresses like one, to the point of being accosted by a streetwalker. Big joke. Us transvestites understand. But the bigger one is yet to come. St. Catherine (not a psychiatrist, mind you, but far more tastefully a statue of the patron saint of unmarried girls in France) analyzes her problems and recommends beauty treatments and high fashion. We're not quite sure if the *New Kind of Love* boys had this in mind, but thereafter Miss Woodward, plastered with paint, swaddled in chic and with a blond wig similar to the one Norma Shearer wore in *Idiot's Delight*, winds up looking like T. C. Jones at his most modest. And whaddaya know, but Newman, that old satyr of the Seine, suddenly thinks she's the nuts.

But it's not the T. C. Jones look—which may just be my reaction. Heavens no, we're coming to the nubbiest joke of the whole 110-minute orgy. Little Robert Clary is a pimp, and he palms off Miss Woodward as a very high-priced whore. Doesn't that just kill you? What marvelous comedy, what giddy romance, to have Newman in torment because, while Miss Woodward supplies him not with her personal services but with endless tales of sexual orgies as material for columns that are winning him international fame—he is falling in love with her. Why, he even drags her to a priest in the hope of reforming her and then in disgust passes her on to a casual acquaintance. . . . It's enough to make you roll in the aisles—and don't tell me you don't need derangement to still be in the vicinity of an aisle at this point.

You will note that Miss Woodward is physically intact throughout; shucks, this is an American movie and we don't allow no sex acts here—just lots of sex talk and such. Matter of fact, when she finally strips down to her undies in Newman's apartment (that old rogue has discovered the boyish virgin beneath the wig by then), the scourge of the boulevards tells *her* that they're going to get married before they hit the hay.

Well, it's *A New Kind of Love* and an old kind of moviemaking and, my, my, but the rubes are supposed to wallow in it. And the nonrubes? Well, apparently they too are not interested in the good and the beautiful so long as it hasn't a bit of bed and body for flavoring—or so the fate of *The Sound of Trumpets* indicates. At this rate we'll all be feeding from the same trough—and the only one in town.

Back to the Essence of Comedy
November 24, 1963

The question before us is, just how mad can you get on the subject of American comedy, let alone the world. Well, now that Stanley Kramer's gone quadruply mad, we have the essence of the Hollywood comedy that Hollywood has been ignoring for much too long.

The Kramer formula—made public via *It's a Mad, Mad, Mad, Mad World*—is ridiculously simple, so much so that it's simply ridiculous that apparently only a man hitherto dedicated to the making of socially significant and serious movies would cook it up. It's a case of back to the classics.

For American movie comedy the classics are, of course, the products of the golden days of silents and of comedy-star two-reelers. Their hallmark is the chase, its concomitants being confusion, crash-bang devastation and full exploitation of the individual talents of the comedian. Stupidity, venality, pomposity, dishonesty, hypocrisy—the human vices and frailties are taken to pieces along with the furniture and the masonry.

Mr. Kramer has got himself a chase of superclassic proportions, on land and in the air, by a variety of cars, trucks, planes, helicopters—even kiddie bike; one suspects that a very good hunk of the eight million dollars this Cinerama orgy cost went to pay for all the lovely vehicles that go slam-bang-crash, sink to the bottom of river or canyon or smash through obstructions with epic ease; that still another big chunk went for the stuntmen who provide the chills, spills and thrills and still another for all the breakaway structures that are demolished—and I mean demolished—in the course of it all.

But mathematically the suspicion is wrong. Because all the eight million dollars must have gone to the comedians—as only a partial payment, in fact—for Mr. Kramer, in his wisdom, has got himself a collection of talents that money can't buy, and having got it he has let each talent fulfill itself, ultimately meshed, by the Bill and Tania Rose script and Mr. Kramer's directional hand.

It's a comic's field day. We haven't seen such a salute to the gift of lunacy for decades. Mr. Kramer has, of course, gone in for the Mike Todd-originated "cameo"—the Three Stooges at the ready as firemen; Jack Benny as a passerby; ZaSu Pitts as a switchboard operator, and many others. Then he has supercameos, with Jimmy Durante sublime as the dying gangster whose last words about buried treasure set off the chase; Jim Backus as a blueblooded alcoholic; Paul Ford as a befuddled ex-major talking-down a plane; Peter Falk and Rochester as conniving cab drivers; Arnold Stang as a gas-station attendant—and many more.

But for his leaders of the chase that proceeds under the watchful eye of Spencer Tracy, as an honest cop whose honesty has a breaking point, Mr. Kramer has taken nine first-rank entertainers and given their comic talents full rein. Not since the days of Harold Lloyd's two-reel or W. C. Fields' feature-length domesticity has anyone come up with a family group to match that headed by a nonsinging, pratfalling Ethel Merman as a nonstop loudmouth; Dorothy Provine as her mother-ridden daughter, dreaming of wealth enough to enable her to retire into a convent; Milton Berle as her pill-gulping cringing son-in-law, and Dick Shawn as her superathletic beatnik son who weeps at the very word "Mom." It's genius of a sort to team Buddy Hackett and Mickey Rooney as a pair of empathetic gagwriters, to let Phil Silvers swindle his way toward the loot, to have Sid Caesar as a dentist driven to desperation by greed, Terry-Thomas as an American-hating cactus collector and Jonathan Winters as a mindless muscular fall guy.

Like a master puppeteer, Kramer keeps any number of old "meanwhile, back at the ranch" side adventures going as the mob heads for the loot; a small boy misleads Silvers through crag and stream to a side road, Shawn and Barrie Chase twist euphorically as a vital phone call goes unheeded, Rooney and Hackett freeze at the controls of a rocketing plane, Caesar and Edie Adams are trapped in a 1916 biplane with Ben Blue at the controls, and Winters takes time out to wreck a gas station with a thoroughness not seen since Laurel and Hardy went their most berserk.

The best of the sight and speed gags of the Keystone-Chaplin-Keaton (yes, Buster shows up briefly) days are duplicated here with a gag-laden script and all the expanses of Cinerama. And here lies the rub in the latter-day trimming, for the economics thereof calls for a "full" show, three and a quarter hours of mad, mad, mad fun—and even with a fifteen-minute intermission after two hours it's a bit much in the madness department. The hilarity—and there is a good two hours' worth—is dissipated by the merely funny, and even that becomes attenuated; we have too much—albeit of a good thing.

How's that for ingratitude? Call it, rather, perfection-seeking. The cheers are not only for Mr. Kramer's *It's a Mad, Mad, Mad, Mad*

World but basically for his having appreciated and reminded us of the fundamentals of pure American comedy and of the glories of exploiting true comedians. And after the dreary cinematic years that have neglected such talents as Durante's, Danny Kaye's and even Bob Hope's and left Jerry Lewis, Jack Lemmon and leers to epitomize movie comedy, it's a joyous reminder of our heritage.

The Crash of Symbols
December 1, 1963

Anybody seen any significant white horses lately?

It dawned on me only recently that even the lay, or non-Western-oriented, moviegoer has to be a horse fancier, or at very least a watcher of fancy horses. I mean, I've seen black and white horses in Bergman films and known that they were indeed steeds of a different color for a purpose—but it seems you can't catch them all. Recently a passionate film fan was recalling with me the artistry of the Polish segment of the omnibus *Love at Twenty*. We shared an admiration for the story and performances and the subtlety of direction. Then he said, "The white horse—now wasn't that magnificent? It gave the entire ideology of the film." The white horse? Oh—did he mean the white bears in the zoo, where the middle-aged workman rescued the child and thereby aroused the transient passions of the young woman? Ah no—hadn't I noticed that white horse just fleeting against the horizon—a masterful political symbol?

Well, I hadn't. I missed it (and its historic reference to a Polish general); I saw only a brilliant and bitter anecdote of the cruel self-absorption of the young, of the lack of loving understanding between generations. But no white horse.

Now, mind you, I don't wear blinders. I spotted that white horse in *Muriel*, all right, with the young Algerian war veteran astride. But all I saw was a troubled, haunted youth seeking surcease in a ride along the cliffs of Boulogne, natural enough, since

horses were available in the stable below his studio. Yet any number of my critical colleagues knew immediately that this white
horse was a symbol, and they all complained bitterly that it was
a symbol they could not understand. (Nor, I suspect, could the
film's director, Alain Resnais—who's a mean man with a symbol
but scarcely a fanatic. Resnais, in fact, confides that he used a
white horse because that's what the stable had for rent on the day
the scene was shot.)

The neigh of horses typifies rather than dominates the current
crash of symbols heard by "earnest" moviegoers, whether they were
intended or not by the moviemakers themselves. Oh, that knife
play is phallic as all get-out in *Knife in the Water*, but how about
the Crucifixion bit? (You didn't spot it—when the boy is stretched
out on the deck, arms extended, a coil of rope sort of above his
head? Shucks—You thought it was just still another shot of him
sunning himself?) And that battered-up crow that her husband
tosses at Simone Signoret's feet in *Naked Autumn*—man, you can
mull that one over to a fare-thee-well-Freud!

While the cineastes are doing the symbol-spotting and inter-
pretations for us (and for many of the directors), any number of
moviemakers are doing their bit—allegedly for art, actually for
redundancy and ultimately for banality. At the top of the scale
we get the "parallel" symbol, which obtrudes by its very nature.
I cite the careful but unnecessary underlining of the heroine's entrapment by provincial life in *Thérèse* through the endless netting
of wild pigeons by the county clods—all very artistic, but we can
get the point without it or with just a hint, at most.

I have a particular fondness for the symbols our more "subtle"
moviemakers use for the heights of sexual passion, a fondness that
dates from that desert rendezvous of Ronald Colman and Claudette Colbert in *Under Two Flags*. Barely had they embraced before the camera discreetly turned to the sky and stayed there, to
return only when the lovers were remounting their horses. Ah,
what a sky was there!

Plus ça change. . . . Jules Dassin turned up with fire and water
in *Phaedra*, as Melina Mercouri and Tony Perkins merged their
profiles. First the camera explored the fireplace, roaring away, and
then it went on to the window, rain-slashed and wind-pounded.

Obviously double is better than nothing; let's have the symbol if we can't have the act. And the Poles give us a sail fluttering in the breeze for sex at sea in *Knife* and in *An Affair of the Skin* Ben Maddow gives us a pair of bare shoulders rolling around with upside-down heads lolling (a case of *Hiroshima* revisited but undigested), and *Under the Yum Yum Tree* simply settles for a tomcat trotting after Jack Lemmon while he leers and peeps and lusts for women.

We rightly credit the great filmmakers for their potent use of symbols—and yet, recalling the great films, we rarely remember the symbol. For that is the wholeness of art, where all is meshed in theme and mood, dimensions blended for a purpose, details interwoven. It is only in brooding retrospect that one can dissect and analyze; when our eyes readjust from the brilliance of *8½*, we can see the machinations of Fellini's mind in each cogent element; when the joyous laughter of *Tom Jones* is hushed, the details of technique come to mind to enhance our satisfaction.

It is this age of psychoanalysis and one-upmanship among the cultists that has led to the demand for the "in" detail on one hand, the oversupply of symbolic gimmickry on the other. A father's simple concern about his daughter's college career in the light and laughing *Take Her, She's Mine* is apparently not enough; it has to carry a note of incest in some viewer's book. But how can one keep Freud out of mind when noting in *McClintock!* that both mother and teen-age daughter yield to their beloveds only after both males have soundly thwacked their bottoms with coal scuttles?

And so we are symbol-sotted on both sides of the screen. It used to be in the eye of the beholder, but now it's strictly in the mind. Thus one almost finds relief in the elementary purity—let alone the nostalgia—of the symbolism in Grigori Chukhrai's *Clear Skies*, a film some notches below his *Ballad of a Soldier*. There's a grand moment when a young man comes to tell his family, "Stalin is dead," and after everyone has registered glum and silent surprise, the camera moves on to show us the ice breaking, brooks bubbling, freshets springing up all over. That's the kind of symbolism you can't quarrel with—especially in films made under the Khrushchev regime.

We needn't go back to this sort of banality, but it is time to realize that we're a little off the track in our movieviewing and have reached the point where we can't see the cinema for the symbols.

87th Precinct—
Japanese Style
December 8, 1963

The trouble with the Japanese moviegoer—and it was a gentleman from Japan speaking—is his insistence on "prosaic detail." One course does not make a meal for him; he wants the menu complete, and he wants to see every morsel consumed, every *sake* bowl emptied.

"It lets the Japanese identify, it makes him feel it is real, but how very boring it must be for the Americans," Masahiro Ogi noted.

The Japanese film critic, described by his compatriots here as the most influential in his country via television and a weekly publication, was interested primarily in learning, during a brief visit, Americans' reactions to Japanese movies in general, in discovering whether his dissatisfactions with the "mass" product and its audience were shared, in finding how American critics acted as "tastemakers," in indicating that Japanese movies don't begin and end with Akira Kurosawa and Toshiro Mifune, the director and star who epitomize Japanese film art for many of us.

Mr. Ogi's timing was unintentionally right. We have just been treated to the latest Kurosawa-Mifune product, *High and Low*, which is very much to the point of our discussion. For Kurosawa has taken an American whodunit, right out of the 87th Precinct series—Ed McBain's *King's Ransom*—and made it entirely on his own. But first, back to Mr. Ogi.

The generalities were dealt with handily (with a very handy interpreter's help): agreed, we get the best products of the Tokyo studios here; technically, the Japanese stand first in the consistently breathtaking beauty of their color films; relatively, the language barrier is greater than for other foreign films, despite the improved subtitles. For that reason, perhaps, the samurai stories have been the most effective for us—the triumph of beautiful and exotic costumes and scenery, clear-cut characters and motivation and simple action over semantics. But even with the fairytale beauty of *Chushingura* still lingering, perhaps we have had the samurai bit for a while, at least until *Harakiri*, a stunningly beautiful and great drama we were privileged to preview at the New York Film Festival, is exhibited here.

Many of the modern, or nonsamurai, Japanese movies—*Fire on the Plains, The Happiness of Us Alone, An Autumn Afternoon* (another Festival film)—did indeed suffer from the major fault Mr. Ogi finds with his countrymen's films: detail upon detail, piled on to soap-opera proportions.

"This is what the women want," Mr. Ogi said. "The women are the moviegoers; they pick for themselves and for the men. The women are very conservative, even the young ones. Ah yes, Doris Day—you see, she is the ideal housewife for them, too—and they want to see everything, every detail."

Details—the bane of the movies, stretching them to marathon length. But what of Kurosawa's details? "Ah, these are for his art," Mr. Ogi said. "This is the artist at work, inserting the detail—not to please those who want to know each course of the meal, but for his artistic effect. It is difficult for Americans, is it not?"

Yes, it is difficult for "Americans"—but the total effect and the ultimate reward are there. *High and Low* is a fascinating case in point, because the artist has taken over where the whodunit writer merely began. In *King's Ransom*, McBain posed a fascinating moral issue: a tycoon who has mortgaged himself to the hilt to make the stock takeover of his life is suddenly notified that his son has been kidnapped and is being held for five hundred thousand dollars' ransom. He is ready to pay off pronto.

Then comes the twist: he and the kidnappers learn simultaneously that they have taken his chauffeur's son by mistake—but the kidnappers hold to their terms. Thus the issue: will the tycoon pay off, ruining himself and his family, to save another man's child?

Much to the distress of McBain's humane cops, the American tycoon refuses. His wife leaves him, taking their son; the cops scorn him—but he cannot, as a self-made man, destroy himself. Finally, with a suitcase stuffed with newspapers instead of money, he goes off to the rendezvous. Simultaneously, however, the wife of one of the kidnappers has had a change of heart and turns informer. The tycoon is saved, the goodhearted criminals escape, and we suspect that the errant wife will be wooed back.

Now Kurosawa, posing the same moral issue, takes an entirely different tack. His tycoon, portrayed with wracked soul but outward stolidity by Mifune, pays the ransom in a thrilling railroad-train sequence, with the police on hand to see the perfection of the kidnapper's plan. The child is saved, the tycoon ruined, and the lone criminal, whom we have encountered, has the fifty million yen. And now the police take over.

Detail piles upon detail as Kurosawa proves himself far more the painstaking novelist than the author of the original fiction. The endless reports of the teams of detectives who come upon one blank wall and one dead end after another are given in endless fashion; the clues that lead nowhere are followed as painstakingly as those that ultimately lead to the criminal. For this is detection without glamour, suspense created by reality, a slow pacing. And the tycoon's creditors hounding him, the chauffeur's enormous sense of guilt and frenzied attempts to gain clues from his child, the emergence of the criminal's character as the chase threatens him—all form a tapestry of crime, detection and punishment, with vivid vignettes of various strata of society, haunting moments on the waterfront, in an all-night saloon, in an opium den, right down to the confrontation between victim and criminal in the death cell.

It is two hours and twenty-three minutes of character and suspense drama, with no detail of frustration or personal sorrow or social morality omitted. We go beyond good guys and bad guys to consider the motives of both—in detail. This is the Japanese approach—a bane in the hands of lesser men, a work of art in

☆
☆ **Part II** ☆
........**From Tom**
...........**to Mary**

The Strangelovian Age
January 30, 1964

Dr. Strangelove, Or: How I Learned to Stop Worrying and Love the Bomb is one of the most cogent, comic and cruel movies to come along in many a year, and one of the best. Don't miss it—provided that you have the wit and stamina to withstand a savage satire on any number of our society's untouchables, the courage to hear a howl of outrage at the supersonic supersecurity idiocies of our time and the readiness to share Stanley Kubrick's realization that ironic laughter and ferocious caricature are the only possible responses of a sane man to the insanities of the international race toward nuclear self-destruction.

In this age of superautomation there has been the general suspicion that fool or madman could trigger the atomic holocaust on whose brink we hover; Kubrick has chosen to have it triggered by a madman—General Jack D. Ripper, of Burpelson Air Force Base, who sends a missile-laden wing of Strategic Air Command bombers off to attack the Russians, declaring his own war against the triple-pronged threat of communism, fluoridation and sex. "Well, boys, I reckon this is it—nuclear combat toe to toe with the Ruskies," drawls the airborne wing commander, Major T. J. "King" Kong, swapping his flight helmet for a Stetson as the Red Alert Go-Code is transmitted—and off they go into the big-boom yonder.

And there's not a thing anybody can do to stop them—not

with all the supersecurity, chain-of-command, automated secrecy that is the order of the day. And there's not a facet of the civilian and military involvement in this order on which Kubrick does not cast a scathing eye as Ripper's war sets off an American counter-attack on Burpelson, international intrigue in the Pentagon's War Room and intercontinental defensive plotting to have the Russians destroy the planes before they reach their targets.

For there are fools, bigots and madmen in high places, Kubrick points out, and men of goodwill are at their mercy and at the mercy of the pushbutton scientific know-how that controls our future. And so a well-intentioned President Muffley copes with a besotted Premier Kissof on the hot line ("Now, then, Dimitri, you know how we've always talked about the possibility of something going wrong with the bomb—the bomb, Dimitri, the hydrogen bomb . . . "); General "Buck" Turgidson urges a follow-up on Ripper's attack ("It is necessary to choose between two admittedly regrettable but nevertheless distinguishable postwar environments: one where you've got twenty million people killed and the other where you've got one hundred and fifty million people killed"); Ripper's executive officer, arrested by Burpelson's conquerors as a "deviated prevert [sic]," is finally allowed to phone the President with the Stop-Code, only to find that he hasn't the right change for the toll call—and Kong's plane, sole survivor of the mission, goes bravely on, dodging missiles and radar detection, heading for its target in the grand tradition, because "There's folks back home is a-counting on you, and, by golly, we ain't about to let them down."

Know-how, something that "bunch of ignorant peons," the Russians, haven't got, Turgidson points out, will undoubtedly en-able Kong to get his disabled plane through to target, and that will trigger the Russians' Doomsday machine. And here, emerging in pure admiration of the nihilism of this ultimate weapon, comes Dr. Strangelove, the "kraut" scientist with the artificial arm that has a will of its own as it swings to a Nazi salute or gropes for its owner's throat. Strangelove has the scientist's sunny hope for the future, for the survival of several hundred thousand people, care-fully selected, of course, in some of the country's deeper mineshafts, with males polygamously repopulating an earth that would be fit for human habitation in about a hundred years. . . .

For this is the way the world will end, in a welter of mechanical failures, human bloopers, jargon and gobbledygook. And the sheer insanity of it all bubbles forth as Ripper babbles on about the purity of life fluids, a gum-chewing Turgidson grapples with the camera-clicking Russian ambassador ("Please—gentlemen—you can't fight here—this is the War Room," the President protests), an officer who has blasted his way into an Air Force base questions the propriety of breaking open a soft-drink machine and Kong's crew cheerfully checks survival kits, from pep pills to tranquilizers to a combination Russian phrasebook and Holy Bible.

And behind the flashing needles and knives that Kubrick wields against the sacred cows, there is a gripping suspense thriller, sharply unfolded, tightly told, neatly cut from climax to climax. And beyond the laughter and the tension there is as bitter a little morality tale for our times as we have had to face in a long time, neatly tucked between the opening bars of "Try a Little Tenderness" as an airborne B–52 is refueled, and a grand finale of "We'll Meet Again (Don't Know Where, Don't Know When) . . ." as mushroom clouds fill the sky.

Kubrick earns further distinction as a model of self-discipline in his triple roles as co-author, director and producer, maintaining a fine balance throughout the film's taut ninety-three minutes. He has, of course, a superb cast at hand. Peter Sellers tops his past record for versatility in three diverse roles, as Mandrake, Ripper's British aide, embodying understated sanity in the face of madness; as President Muffley, a man made neither fool nor hero but simple and decent, and as Strangelove, the fascist supreme feeding on even the possibility of annihilation. Sterling Hayden, as the pleasantly paranoid Ripper, and George C. Scott, as the military mind of Turgidson at large in a civilian world, are perfection, and Slim Pickens, as Kong; Keenan Wynn, as the officer hunting "preverts," and Peter Bull, as the Russian ambassador, are outstanding.

Dr. Strangelove is irreverent to a point of savagery; it is funny and it is engrossing. And it's heady stuff for moviegoers, for Kubrick, boy genius that he is, assumes that we're grown-up enough to share his bitter laughter.

The Cry of Silence
February 4, 1964

The Silence is a symphony of despair, a harrowing harmony of the unspoken anguish and the unheard lament of the loveless. And it is, perhaps, the most psychologically complex and symbol-laden of Ingmar Bergman's movies and one of his most demanding.

Certainly it has been the most talked about in his homeland, with controversy raging throughout Sweden over its depiction of sex. Let me say at the outset that unless we are being treated to an expurgated version (and the local distributor testifies that we are not), one wonders what the fuss is about; the glimpses of nudity and of sexual activity are inherent to the frankly adult narrative and are integral to the theme. Those who go to see *The Silence* with prurient interest are in for a disappointment; those who find its sexuality offensive are suffering from a major case of *honi soit.*

But make no mistake: *The Silence* is not for the prudish. It demands maturity and sophistication from the viewer. The drama is of character; the plot is barely incidental. But every action, every verbalization carries a variety of implications. To each his own inference.

This is the burden Bergman places upon his audience, and it must be borne with intellectual patience while he fascinates the eye and touches upon the emotions.

We meet three travelers, two women and a boy, riding on a train at snail's pace. One of the women is ill and they break their journey at the next stop, to stay in a rococo hotel in a grim city where only the roar of the tanks rumbling through the streets and the wail of air-raid sirens break the silence in their suite. The country is nameless, the city unknown, the language strange. Ester, the cough-wracked elder sister, takes to her bed; Anna, the younger, bathes and rests, and her son prowls the corridors of the deserted hostelry that is almost literally a child's garden of Freudian symbols.

Slowly the seething souls of the women come to life, almost humming with the desperation with which they feign compatibility. Anna, anointing herself with feminine care and consciousness, her cold catlike glance a cruel contradiction to the sensual droop of her lips, goes out to prowl the unknown streets to find release in a sexual encounter. Ester, coolly blond, curtly tailored, but with dark eyes glittering with torment, turns first to self-gratification and then to self-pity and is rescued, finally, in a state of physical and alcoholic collapse, by an elderly hotel waiter.

The sisters cannot talk without sullen rage from Anna and quiet suffering from Ester. Ester's attempt to mitigate her involvement with her sister with alcohol and intellect is placed in pathetic juxtaposition to Anna's flight into vengeful promiscuity and mutual degradation. But their ultimate achievement is only self-torture, never communication.

Only to her transient lover can Anna talk of Ester and take her ease. "How nice—how nice that we don't understand each other," she murmurs. And only to the elderly waiter, who responds to her sign-language request for food but merely smiles kindly at her speech, can Ester probe her own rejection of heterosexuality and her ensuing loneliness. "We try out attitudes—and find they're all worthless."

All has been lonely and loveless and hopeless, even for the boy, who has rewarded the elderly waiter's attempted friendliness with a mean and childish prank by hiding his family mementos and has played with a troupe of performing dwarfs and seen the passion of his mother's embrace with a stranger and the frightening vulnerability of his aunt's face in sleep. There is little more than a physical relationship between mother and child, and even that seems transient. And when Ester is left behind, to die or survive, and the boy and Anna resume their train journey, Johan's words to his mother are drowned out by the roaring wind as she opens the window to bathe her face in the driving rain.

They have come from a trip to nowhere and they are going nowhere. The streets are filled with drearily dressed workers and soldiers, and there is little traffic beyond a giant tank and a horse-drawn cart overloaded with household possessions. The hotel is deserted, the dwarfs the only apparent guests besides the travelers, but the café across the street is crowded, with frenzied couples glimpsed dancing in the rear, and in the loge of an upstairs vaude-ville house a pair of lovers writhe as the dwarfs perform onstage.

Obviously—and ultimately—there is a surfeit of symbols, a weight of gratuitous innuendo, of action and reaction in almost psy-choanalytical terms. But gratuitous though these seem, they in no way distract us from the fascination of Ester, of whom Ingrid Thulin makes a heartbreakingly beautiful and powerful figure of sorrow, the sorrow of the solitary aware of the limbo in which she is lost. Miss Thulin brings a reality and depth to much that is ir-relevant in Bergman's penchant for the rococo, the macabre and the shocking (but actually naïve) symbol. She succeeds in making the human agony supersede the director's lapses into artiness.

Bergman's is a tale told purely in cinematic terms, with the camera providing as much—or as little—as the viewer chooses to find. These are strangers, travelers—without roots, twisted in an-guish, struggling toward surcease, if not self-knowledge. And this, perhaps, is life, the life of quiet desperation that *The Silence* embodies.

No Tickets
to Paradise
February 9, 1964

Love in New York isn't what it used to be, not for moviegoers. There are actually people walking around who can look at the Empire State Building and not see Charles Boyer up there waiting for Irene Dunne, who's just been crippled for life in a cab acci-

dent en route to their rendezvous, or pass an unremodeled East
Side whitestone and not expect a beminked Katharine Hepburn
or Carole Lombard to pop from mansion to limousine in pursuit
of some nonmillionaire beau like Henry Fonda or William Powell,
or not recognize all the little boys on the Lower East Side who are
going to grow up to be Spencer Tracy, John Garfield, Clark Gable,
George Raft and Humphrey Bogart and in love with upper Fifth
girls like Myrna Loy and Rosalind Russell.

It isn't just that these people don't remember how it was
when you'd hear Dick Powell and Alice Faye caroling away from
the interior of one of those Central Park hacks, or how when any
big-time gangster finally got the works at the Criminal Courts
Building you knew he was taking the rap for the prosecutor's
wife whom he and the prosecutor had loved in the good old
Gashouse days on the West Side—or how Broadway was just paved
with broken hearts even though Ruby Keeler or Eleanor Powell
could be counted on to come out of the chorus to replace the star in
a pinch and get the hero in a clinch after the curtain fell. No. It's
not nostalgia or failing memory. It's just that things aren't what
they used to be in New York lovewise in the movies.

It's all become Iowa, if you know what I mean—and I cast
no aspersions on Iowa. The magic is gone from the Empire State
and the Central Park hacks, and the Staten Island ferry isn't the
aphrodisiac it once was. It's all become real—and if it's not real-
sordid it's real-Hollywood, and however you slice it or black-and-
white or Technicolor-widescreen it, it might as well be Cedar
Rapids.

You can't go by appearances. Let them have Sinatra blowing
his horn in a posh East River Drive pad, or Steve McQueen ro-
mancing Natalie Wood on the corner of Thirty-fourth Street and
Seventh Avenue, or Viveca Lindfors and Kevin McCarthy guzzling
champagne at dawn in the environs of the Fulton Fish Market.
Alas. It's all exterior. When you get right down to love, love, love—
it might as well be anywhere, because it's all in the never-never
land of movie morality, no matter how you sex it up for the teen-
age trade.

You get Sinatra living it up all over town and teaching his

kid brother how to be a man-about-Broadway type, with girls for
the asking and for the having in his twelve-by-twenty-acre flat;
but the girl Sinatra loves isn't even allowed past the bedroom
door, and Sinatra is solidly shocked at her suggestion that she join
the procession of playgirls. Ah, but that's all in gorgeous color and
strictly for laughs and the drive-in trade, and only a carper would
suggest that there be any big-city sophistication when it comes to
s-x. Let's get down to the stark realism of the movies that were
really shot around this city, that deal with true-blue Manhattanites.

For now we have a big New York love affair, *Love with the
Proper Stranger*. Big? Bubie baby, it's like Marty never imagined!
You stick to Cinderella; me, I'm for the notion that for every
Macy's salesgirl there's a Steve McQueen (for every Macy's salesgirl who's Natalie Wood, that is), and that everyone in his or her
twenties in this town is strictly a first-generation American, offspring of real comedy characters with vaudeville accents and
quaint old-country ways. Don't stop to think that the children of
the Cohens and the Kellys ought to be pushing sixty and wondering about their grandchildren's intermarriages, because then you'd
do us out of that batch of Italian-dialect comics who claim Wood
and McQueen as their delightful post-teen-age progeny; and don't
stop to think about how the McQueen, Wood and even Tom Bosley
mamas in this film behave like Molly Picon or Gertrude Berg, simply saying "mama mia" instead of "oi vay," because then you'd sort
of shatter the melting-pot illusion.

But let's get right down to love itself in all the just-folks aspects
of this film. It seems that Manhattan is no island unto itself; boy
meets, hates and loves girl and doesn't get sexy with the girl he
loves just like anyplace else in the U.S.A. Oh, don't let the fact
that right at the start of the movie Miss Wood is pregnant courtesy
of McQueen throw you. Golly, he didn't even like her much during
their one night together at a resort hotel and he can't even remember her face or name several months later—so illicit sex is okay for
them at that point. And he's really very unfond of her as they go
through hell getting hold of an abortionist (they don't know how
easy it is downtown, like in *Greenwich Village Story*, you see—her
being a sheltered salesgirl in the pet department of the world's

biggest department store and him being an innocent trumpet player, a member of Local 802 and bedmate of a nightclub stripper).

They finally get together with the abortionist, a strictly-from-Transylvania-type hag, in a condemned slum flat (does the Department of Buildings know about this kind of thing? Let's get the cops back on the condemned-dwelling beat!), and if there's anything to inspire love in a man's heart, it's this. McQueen not only saves his girl from the hag but proceeds to pursue her—and he chases her until she catches him, in true Hollywood tradition—and, mama mia, the cultural pattern remains unpolluted and it's enough to stop traffic at Thirty-fourth Street and Seventh Avenue—and it does.

Because this is love in New York cinematically this year—abortions and adultery notwithstanding. And the love stories are just as silly the farther they get from Fifth Avenue and the deeper they get into all those construction sites. Ah, well, it's the jet age, and all the idiocies of amour are taking place in Paris or on the Riviera or in Stockholm, I suppose, and New York City gets left with the slice-of-slum realism. Me, I liked it better when Madeleine Carroll and the Ritz Brothers pranced around the Plaza and Paul Muni and Sylvia Sidney provided love in the slums with a social conscience.

But one moves with the times. What, after all, do new generations know of romance even off the screen, these young who have not played hooky with a true love to make the 9 A.M. show at the Paramount or stolen a kiss 'neath starry skies in the second balcony of Loew's Paradise? I mean, you gonna neck with a girl in a five-hundred-seat art house with a Fellini film staring you in the face? These days, love in New York is from nothing, cinemawise.

Medieval Chess Game:
King and Bishop
March 15, 1964

You can't kid me, the lady said, Felix Aylmer is the Archbishop of Canterbury.

The remark, made anent *Becket*, is both a tribute to the venerable British actor and a comment on the type casting that goes on both in the making of movies and the viewing thereof. Mr. Aylmer has, in fact, played England's leading cleric only once before on screen, in Olivier's *Henry V*, but sound the call for Canterbury in a costume drama, and be surprised only if Mr. Aylmer does not appear.

In *Becket*, however, the two top roles are not type cast, even though two actors of the range of Peter O'Toole and Richard Burton can be typed primarily, if not exclusively, in the physical sense. One would somehow have envisoned Burton, sturdy of frame, rugged of face, as Henry II, the uncouth Norman baron whose heart has been ineradicably marked by love for a man of fine perceptions who has chosen a higher dedication. And that man and future saint, Thomas à Becket, could well have been embodied by O'Toole, tall and slender, ascetic of face, a man of grace. Instead, we have O'Toole as an almost fragile King, bringing a shrill petulance of frustration to what might have been a bellow of befuddlement for his inability to understand the friend who puts the "honor of God" before that of the King. And Burton, purse-mouthed and stolid of stance, is an immutable Becket, unswerving and seemingly empty of heart in his service first to the King and finally to God. This Becket is a rock of a man, against whom the King first leans for the comforts and enrichment of friendship and then blasts with the princely prerogative that temporal domination commands; this King is a changeling among his boorish barons, a sly jester aware of ironies, a man of sensitivity beyond Becket's teachings but a man to writhe with the wracking tortures of unrequited love without being deterred from waging a cold-blooded battle for power.

And both men are fascinating individuals. O'Toole and Burton are masters of the spoken word; the lines flow, the eyes glint, the gestures are firm and to the point. But amid the crude baronial splendors, royal panoply and church ritual of twelfth-century England, are the characters to the point? Playwright Anouilh's original point was of two men with different needs—Henry's for Becket's intellectual stimulation and Becket's for a spiritual commitment—caught in apposition, placed despite themselves in mortal conflict, Henry to defend the supreme power of the King, Becket that of the Church. But the irony of Anouilh dominated—even in Becket's devotion to "the honor of God," in the ramifications of the contest within the Church itself, in Henry's ultimate political ploy of advocating the martyred Becket's canonization. The playwright made of *Becket* a medieval chess game, king and bishop reduced to pawns.

The screen version is a spectacular; but again, just as *Becket* has interestingly reversed our thinking in terms of type casting, so it changes it in terms of type moviemaking. For while there are handsome moments of spectacle—a victorious army's entry into a French town, a breathtaking ritual of excommunication, sober and beautiful panoramas of medieval architecture and countryside—the power of the film is in the close-up, the concentration on the two protagonists. And what is so fascinating in this exploration is that Burton and O'Toole provide no ultimate answers for each other or for us.

On Broadway, Laurence Olivier, first playing Becket to Anthony Quinn's Henry and later in the same season playing Henry to Arthur Kennedy's Becket, showed us the many facets of each role. And yet O'Toole and Burton present still others for our choice. Is there indeed, as the Queen suggests, an "unnatural" side to Henry's affection for Becket, or is it only a lonely man's infatuation with the one man who extends the hand of friendship, or the clod's reaching out for the embodiment of a civilization he cannot aspire to himself? Is Becket's dedication and stern sense of duty to God only another application of the same devotion he gave in

his earlier assignment to the King; is this the shell of a man suddenly—and inexplicably—infused with a spiritual dedication, or is
this a personal vengeance upon the King, who was too ruthless in
his exercise of prerogative? Pick what explanation you will, and
reading it against the background of two men whose purpose and
interests were once the same but who can no longer linger even
briefly side by side, you have the seeds of tragedy. But neither the
burning eye and twitching lip of O'Toole nor the cold dispassion
of Burton's glance will give you the easy answer.

Nor is an answer given to the conflict between Church and
State beyond its historic context of Becket's seeming victory in
his martyrdom and Henry's taking an initial, albeit abortive, step
toward the separation that would come in centuries. In dramatic
context we are presented with a political move—Henry's appoint-
ment of Becket as the new Archbishop of Canterbury—a move that
turned into a personal tragedy because the monarch did not know
his best friend. It was a human error, not a stupid one, and it became a spectacular one because of the men and times involved.

There's intellectual content here that seems to have been the
keynote of more than the usual quota of films so far this year.
A year that starts out with such perpetually discussable films as
The Silence and *Dr. Strangelove* has set its sights high—and sustained them with France's *The Fire Within*, a haunting, introspective study of a futile love-seeker, and the sheer entertainment of *Seven Days in May*, a perfectly tooled political thriller.
If *Becket* is, by any chance, an indication of spectaculars to
come— But stay. Let's get out of cloudland and back to shadowland, where the dead extras barely outnumber the courtesans and
types are types and Felix Aylmer is you-know-who.

Two Men in a House
March 22, 1964

A moviegoer's version of not judging books by their covers might well be an adage about not judging films by their directors' statements of intent. We've been burned too often by the promises of an "intellectual" spectacular, a "grown-up approach" to sex, a "human comedy"—all of which have variously insulted the intelligence, attained the adult level of the titillated teens or presented neither humanity nor comedy.

The seasoned film fan tends, therefore, to follow the fashion of readers who prefer to scan the introduction after they've finished a book. And he can then find either enlightenment or food for speculation in comparing what he has seen with what the film's creator claims to have set forth. Rare indeed is the noncommittal creator; Harold Pinter will long stand as a model of restraint for his replying, to all the speculators and seekers of the esoteric, that in his play *The Caretaker* (known on film as *The Guest*) he was simply writing about three men in a room.

I wonder if, after one emerged from *The Servant* and sought Mr. Pinter's concept—for he wrote the screenplay, adapting it from a Robin Maugham novel—the young British playwright would reply simply that he was writing about two men in a house and leave us to our complex complexity-seeking for the subsurface implications of this fascinating and superbly performed film.

But *The Servant* is a movie, and this is the day of the director, and so it is Joseph Losey who has chosen to issue "a note on the film," to put his intent on record. An American who has long been involved in the theater and in movies here and abroad and currently in England, he has had a minor "cult" following but no major acclaim before this film. Mr. Pinter has already won the British Screen Writers' Award for *The Servant*, adjudged the best screenplay of 1963.

And it is, to repeat, a "fascinating" film, one from which it is virtually impossible to turn our eye or our attention, for we are watching a snake at work, a poisonous worm of corruption disguised as a servant and brilliantly played with a vicious servility by Dirk Bogarde. And his work is concentrated on the decaying core of a man, blond and beautiful on the surface, effete and empty-souled within. The suave, well-bred young man hires a manservant to help him decorate and then run his newly acquired eighteenth-century house in an elegant square; slowly, surely, catering to every vanity and exploiting every weakness, the servant expands his power, drives away the young man's last link with decency—a fiancée who has tolerated too much too long—and becomes the master of his master and the household.

No facet of corruption is left unexplored: there are overt suggestions of homosexuality, even as the servant Barrett arranges for the master, Tony, to seduce the servant's "sister" (we see her go from Barrett's bed to Tony's) and then have the master discover, in his fiancée's presence, that the "sister" is the servant's mistress too; Barrett plays the role of "nanny," then becomes a playmate, then a "pal," with liquor and drugs and an orgy of seducers and seductresses. The dregs are tasted in a shattering finale by the fiancée, lured to the house by Barrett and his doxy and almost hypnotically introduced to the orgy; she offers herself trancelike into a revolting embrace with Barrett in an agonized attempt to evoke the remnant of man from Tony—and indeed there is a shudder and leap before collapse, the death throes before the human yields to the slime. Slowly, meditatively, she emerges from shock, stares speculatively at the triumphant Barrett and slaps him viciously across the mouth. There is the cringe, then the automatic responses of seeing a lady out the door—but as she runs from the house in hysterical reaction, the servant slides the bolts, turns out the lights and walks past the blob that was his master to the room where his mistress waits.

The eye hasn't wavered as the slow process of dehumanization takes place, for Losey is a lover of shadows, infatuated with reflections in endless mirrors, preferably in rococo frames and concave for distortion. He has spared no suggestion of the illicit thrill, no attitude of the face and body in sexual throes, no hint of perversion. And Bogarde's smooth villainies are in counterpoint to the blandly vacant amenities of James Fox as Tony, with Sarah Miles the Lilith-Lolita as Barrett's accomplice and Wendy Craig the cold taunt of conventional reality as the fiancée, all to the aphrodisiac blues of Cleo Lane singing "All Gone" on a record played over and over and over.

Mr. Losey has held us with his glittering camera eye, with Pinter's half-muffled exchanges of banalities and suggested thoughts half spoken, with performers who never flicker out of character— and then we stop to think. What has been said? That the Devil can steal a man's soul? But Faustus had a soul worth stealing; our Tony was an idler, a wastrel, petty, peevish, sexually ambivalent, babbling about projects in Brazil but quick to add "there's no hurry" and sink into lethargic concentration on comforts and super- ficials. With Pinter's involvement—or merely a sociological turn of mind—can we see Tony as a decadent upper class, Barrett the lower class justifiably asserting itself? But both are so repellent, so obviously despised by their creator, that sociopolitical parallels lead only to nihilism.

Let us turn, then, to Mr. Losey: "Thematically *The Servant* is about the destructiveness of trying to live by obsolete and false standards—standards which one intellectually recognizes to be ob- solete but emotionally still tries to make a guiding code. It is about a young master who still lives in the eighteenth century behind the eighteenth-century terrace facade, but who nonetheless doesn't wish to and cannot accomplish the shutting out of the twentieth cen- tury. It is about a household he wants run 'just like his mother's and grandmother's,' by a servant just like the 'beloved old things.' The result is that he gets a servant who is just as fraudulent and spurious as the master, but a little more realistic, and therefore a little more vicious. This is therefore a film about people for whom servility is a way of life. In fact, the film might well have been entitled *Servility* (all kinds), or one can say it is about the rude collision of old ways and manners with new ways and manners that are recog- nized intellectually but ignored practically and ethically. If you like, it is also a kind of Dorian Gray tale, because it deals with the vain aspiration to eternal youth which leads instead only to age and death. It is also about corruption—and innocence ... " And so on.

Beyond the fiancée, there is little of innocence here—and she

is innocent only where Tony's character is concerned. Is it obsolete for a man to be a snobbish weakling interested in a well-
run household, or for another man to be a gentleman's gentleman? ("Except that you're no gentleman!" Barrett snarls at his
master.) And Dorian Gray was a pretty nice guy to begin with—
beyond the fact that our Tony is more interested in inertia than
in eternal youth.

No, Mr. Losey hasn't quite provided what is in his manifesto.
What is, in fact, missing from his film is the valor whose fall we
are asked to mourn, a man worth our caring and our sorrow, and
a theme worth the mulling over.

Why not, in fact, just borrow a leaf from the Pinter folio and
say that this is about two men in a house? Why not indeed? *The
Servant* tells their story in engrossing cinematic terms—and some
movies are, after all, made for watching.

Doing It Over
and Overdoing It
March 29, 1964

Somewhere in a deserted sound studio, I like to think, there is a
little old lady sitting by arc light embroidering spectacular samplers with mottoes for moviemakers to flourish by. There's one
aglow with Technicolor and sex symbols that advises, "If at first
you do succeed—try, try again"; another, with fluorescent forget-
me-nots, notes, "Anything anyone did, you can do bigger, slicker
or sicker"; and a third, with petit-point profiles of great lovers and
director-star combos, urges, "Don't break up the team."

That the lady has plied a profitable needle in Hollywood goes
without saying, and now we have fresh evidence that she enjoys
an international clientele as well. Money-grubbing, after all, is not
confined to the territorial limits of the U.S.A., nor to the lesser
lights of the film industry. Just try on for stellar size the names

of Karel Reisz and Albert Finney in England, of Vittorio De Sica, Sophia Loren and Marcello Mastroianni in Italy.

Reisz and Finney made their first mark (and that's an understatement) as director and star of *Saturday Night and Sunday Morning*. Thereafter Mr. Reisz produced, but did not direct, *This Sporting Life* and Mr. Finney has been proving his versatility as Luther and as Tom Jones. Perhaps in every director's heart there is a dream of out-hitchcocking Hitchcock, in every actor's a yearning to play a psychopath, a latter-day substitute for Hamlet for the non-Shakespearean performer. Perhaps Mr. Finney has been fascinated by the torment of the soul (which was so largely that of bowel in *Luther*) or merely challenged to go beyond the completely captivating surface aspects of his portrait of the Jones boy. Perhaps—and perhaps.

Messrs. Reisz and Finney decided to coproduce and serve respectively as director and star of *Night Must Fall*, a remake of the 1937 film version of Emlyn Williams' 1936 play, a movie distinguished by the taut suspense of John Van Druten's screenplay and Richard Thorpe's direction and, above all, made memorable by Robert Montgomery's baby-faced psychopathic murderer, the prototype of all the charming and boyish crazed killers to come. And no perhaps about it. That little old lady's samplers not only must have hung high in the coproducers' office; the mottoes thereon were graven on their arts.

In plot, *Night Must Fall* is a melodrama, its protagonist Danny, the egomaniac pretty-boy given to killing old ladies; called to account at the Bramson cottage for getting the housemaid pregnant, he charms the foolish and aged invalid, Mrs. Bramson; fascinates her suspicious niece-companion to a point of inertia, and even, as the police close in, commits his second murder. But above all, *Night Must Fall* is a psychological thriller, which simply means that it is not in the blood and gore and head-chopping that the titillation should lie, but in the suggestion, the nuance, in the sight of Danny's hatbox that may—that must—contain the head of his last victim, in our knowledge of the killer and the crime juxtaposed to the ignorance of his potential victims. But with a television writer's pedestrian script, with Mr. Reisz's directorial con-

viction that seeing is believing and Mr. Finney's aboriginal inter-
pretation of psychosis, we are subjected to round after round of
violence, sexual exercise and mental aberration to the point where
one begins to suspect that *Titus Andronicus* came from the pen of
Kate Douglas Wiggin.

The sleekly smiling, sneaky Danny has become a muscular
bit of the auld Welsh sod given to hot-rodding on a motorcycle,
getting his kicks out of cavorting with the housemaid in the bed
he has recently shared with the niece (elevated to daughter status
in this rehash) and in looking in his hatbox—not directly, but via a
mirror, for that added kick. In-between, he writhes in spasms in
a fashion that should bring the straitjacket crew on the run in even
the loony-bin atmosphere of the Bramson cottage—now a rambling
old house, with acreage galore. The daughter's a neurotic mess
and Mama is far past the dotty-old-lady phase and deep in hyper-
thyroid senility; the housemaid looks like a transvestite orgiast left
over from *The Servant*, and there's an idiot handyman around
just for the laughs he gives out with.

Beyond the peeking up, under and over stair railings and
through panes of glass that are hallmarks of his suspenseful ambience, Mr. Reisz has provided floods of sunlight (that's the good
clean world, you see) to contrast to flood-stage rainy nights and
half-empty moviehouses (that's the time of evil, natch). And beyond Mr. Finney's hacking away at his various victims (so Paul
Bunyanesque that one expects a cry of "timber!" as the head
tumbles), there are various fillips—typified by a skindiver, who, recovering from a pond the hatchet used in the first murder, doesn't
take it to his superior officer but stands neck-deep in mid-puddle
to twirl it over his head in a sort of wild weapon-worship rite.

"Psychological" thriller? Psycho is the word—and sodden the
art. But what a combo—big names, title to stir the nostalgia, a once-
successful plot to sex-up and sick-up. And that's how the money
rolls in.

The money has rolled in over the years for the De Sica-Loren
combo, which has proved its weight in platinum from the delightful pizza episode in *Gold of Naples* to the feature-length drama
of *Two Women* to the raffish raffle episode in *Boccaccio '70*. Salt

the gold mine by making a movie of three Loren episodes? Yes indeed—a two-hour movie, yet—and spice it with Marcello Mastroianni, more than something for the girls with *8½* clinching the appeal he set forth in *La Dolce Vita* and *Divorce—Italian Style.* And that's how a *Yesterday, Today and Tomorrow* comes to pass.

Miss Loren's physical charms can be denied by no one of any sex, nor can her personal charms be overestimated as she portrays variously a Neapolitan fertility goddess who blooms amid pregnancies and progeny, a wealthy Milanese who doesn't let love distract her from important things like cars and furs, and a Roman prostitute who can take time out from affairs of the flesh to keep a young seminarian devoted to the spirit. But when twenty-minute anecdotes are spun out unconscionably, when Miss Loren's body is the sole aesthetic offered us and sexual activity the only topic touched upon, when Mastroianni is the perpetual straight man, and a frustrated one at that—one begins to see, amid the sunsets and sunrises and Roman rooftops, the sheer venality of the creation, the cynical circus thrust upon us on the assumption that breasts and bodies and fornication are all that these leading lights of the Italian cinema need provide to keep us from baying at the moon.

There are still, of course, a number of creative minds at play and at work for our benefit. But the inherent disrespect for the moviegoer that something like *Yesterday, Today and Tomorrow* implies and the self-denigration involved in the making of the new *Night Must Fall* are disheartening signs of our movie times. For both are based on the premise that the star, the sexuality and the sickness make for the current box-office bonanza. And that's the motto on the sampler currently on the little old lady's embroidery hoop.

A Western with Togas
April 5, 1964

Spectaculars are geared for sight, but somehow it's the sound that lingers on. Aficionados of spectacular-talk have their favorites, hallowed perhaps to the point of paraphrase in recall. DeMille's Calpurnia to Caesar, "Please don't go to the Forum today—I had a terrible dream last night." Hercules, as the valiant Greeks row madly away from the isle of the Sirens, "Play us a tune, Orpheus." Orpheus, to the watchdog of Hades, "Down, Cerberus!" Mary to her sons, as they search for Jesus in Jerusalem, "There's that nice Mr. Iscariot, boys, perhaps he knows where your brother is."

But it is when spectacular-talk goes from the vernacular to the sublime that the true flavor of the form is captured—a flavor embodied in the current Upstairs at the Downstairs revue's "Unchain the Jewess; she has found favor in the eyes of Marcus Maximus." And if that doesn't conjure up every fond memory of praetors and proconsuls and legions and lions and Christians and such, right up or down to Claudette Colbert taking a milk bath and Kirk Douglas preaching socialism to the gladiators, you've flunked the audiovisual test.

The Fall of the Roman Empire will fill the gap, however, and replenish the quote pile. There's something close to immortal about Christopher Plummer's surprise at bumping into Sophia Loren: "Sister—and I thought you'd retired as a vestal virgin!" Or Miss Loren, as Marcus Aurelius' favorite offspring, and Stephen Boyd, his favorite general: "I am Caesar's daughter," she murmurs. "You are a woman. That is a much higher rank," he ripostes. Or Boyd, to the senators who have gone hog wild and hysterical in support of the mad emperor Commodus, "Honorable fathers of Rome—what have you *done?*" Or Boyd again, to James Mason, stone-cold dead in a village the nasty Romans have leveled by fire and strewn with corpses, "What happened, gentle Greek?"

What has happened is that Samuel Bronston has once again made a Western, his third, in the sunny and/or snowy hills and

plains of Spain. His first, a Lone Ranger liberation tale, was labeled
El Cid; his second, an Alamo-type siege story, he decorated with
late-Manchu spectacle and called *55 Days at Peking*. Now it's the
bit about the old cattle baron who forgot to put it in writing that
he wanted to disinherit his no-good son and have his true-blue
everlovin' foreman (who loves the baron's daughter) take over
the ranch (Part One, before the intermission) and how the no-
good son dissipates the estate, persecutes the homesteaders and
kills friendly Indians until even the loyal foreman's had it and,
after shooting it out on Main Street with the son, rescues the beautiful daughter from the stake where her brother has set her out to
burn with a lot of Indians, and walks out on the whole shmear.

But face it, folks, this man Bronston not only makes but also
thinks spectacular. So this time his Western is set in the second century, with the scene ranging from frosty Germany to rock-ridden
Armenia and lingering in Rome amid grandiose glories of architecture and decor. And he has jam-crammed it with thousands upon
thousands of extras doubling in brass, bronze, bearskins and togas
as Romans, Persians, Syrians, Egyptians, Armenians, barbarians
and just plain folks; stars of all nations (and national dialects)
in close-up and lavish costume; all the battles, parades, riots and
rituals and even chariot races that other large-screen historic-type
movies have aspired to—and lots and lots of philosophical pseudo-
political jargon, exceeded only by indications of mental aberration
to justify the rather psychoanalytical approach the screenwriters
have taken to the happenings of the time. And all of this Mr.
Bronston has grandiosely entitled *The Fall of the Roman Empire*—
subtitled, in my mind at least, "My Son the Crazy Emperor."

The old cattle baron is labeled Marcus Aurelius, his son is
Commodus, his daughter Lucilla, and his pet foreman is a general
he "raised like a son," called Livius. The first three people are for
real, but the youngster who thinks he can bone up on Roman history at this movie better have an encyclopedia handy when he
gets home. Aurelius, the stoic philosopher-statesman, was indeed
the last of the empire's "good" rulers, but scarcely (*à la* Mankiewicz's *Cleopatra*) the democratic World Federalist he is made
to appear. As to his kooky son Commodus—well, as H. G. Wells

put it in a comment I have long cherished for its restraint, "Commodus was a startling person for a good home to produce." We, however, in our generation, are not in the least bit startled to find that what with Marcus Aurelius busy all the time meditating and warring and emperoring, he didn't make a pal and confidant of his son and so the kid has turned out to be a nasty, jealous paranoiac with very peculiar feelings about his mother and his sister and dear old dad and the gladiator who claims to be his real dad, and getting to be emperor makes dementia praecox inevitable. And that, students of Spock and followers of Freud, is how an empire can begin to fall. (At the end of his 188-minute desecration of Gibbon, Bronston's narrator notes that we've only been through the beginning of the fall. We should, perhaps, await a sequel, something like *The In-Process Fall of the Roman Empire*— but are there extras enough or set-builders sufficient unto the ever-expanding vistas of Bronston spectaculars?

Fiction can be an awful lot more fun than fact, so let's take the scriptwriter's couch-dream over history, any day. And even so, in spite of all our pretensions to psychoanalytical sophistication, let's cling to the simple things of mind and life, like good guys and bad guys and the fate of millions hanging on virtuous Stephen Boyd getting villainous Christopher Plummer in the gut as thousands and thousands of Romans riot in the Forum—and just in time to snatch Sophia Loren from among the barbarians chained to stakes and already set aflame. It's wild and Western and one thousand percent American—and that's how we like our super-duper spectaculars, so much larger than life in their physical presentation and so minuscule in their intellectual validity that they sustain purely dream-world status. They are for the closed mind and the open eye—and the funnybone.

The Fall of the Roman Empire, costing sixteen million dollars, is half the price of *Cleopatra* but twice as tolerable because there's a complete lack of pretension, a childish innocence, about it. A fellow movie buff remarked, "It has more movies than *Hallelujah the Hills*"—and how right he is. You'll find bits and pieces of every spectacular, from the geopolitical parlance and vacuous philosophy of *Cleopatra* to the *Ben Hur* chariot race (wilder, woolier, with the chariots roaring and screeching and catapulting over the country-side), to even some pseudo-*Becket*, in the breakup of the Boyd-Plummer friendship over political philosophy, in Boyd's begging Plummer not to give him too much power, in Plummer's "I loved you, Livius—but now you must die; that's the sort of jokes the gods love best!" And over it all—deluging it, at times—is Dimitri Tiomkin music that's the granddaddy of all spectacular scores, stopping just short of "Jingle Bells" in the snowy encampment scenes, going in for Khachaturian-type tambourines as we move east to Armenia, surging and swelling and oozing with schmaltz to match the organ music that gives the titles real movie-palace-type stature and sets a reverential mood.

Ask yourself why ultra-Panavision and Technicolor came to pass. Once you could dive into Kirk Douglas' chin dimple; now you can count each of Miss Loren's eyelashes and see the studio arc lights reflected in those deep, dark, delicious blank pools. We've seen posses aplenty pop out from behind rocks in the old dry gulch—but six armies at a time, with loyal and disloyal Romans by the legions flooding out from behind crags and crannies in Armenia, is something else again. And where but in such a spectacular would the snow not snow on the just and unjust alike, even though they're standing within a few paces of each other?

What is even more impressive is that Mr. Bronston has turned Marcus Aurelius into Alec Guinness, Commodus into Christopher Plummer, the adulterous gladiator into Anthony Quayle, and so on. It can't all be Spanish (or Bronston) gold; Mr. Guinness may be fulfilling an urge to be paternal toward Miss Loren; Mr. Plummer, like Albert Finney, probably feels that any young actor of serious intent has to have a psychopath somewhere in his repertoire, and Mr. Quayle was probably enchanted by all that nice scar tissue the makeup man plastered over his face, gladiator style.

No, you have to hand it to Bronston for thinking and making it big—both in spectacle and silliness. The only question is how stoic a philosopher you are. Live life to the full, said Marcus Aurelius, but don't go to any extremes. Perhaps the question is how full you feel your life has to be of the stuff and nonsense spectaculars are made of.

Politics as Unusual
April 19, 1964

The time has come to talk of politics, moviewise rather than national-election-year-wise, because there are straws in the wind (if we can call three recent major movies straws) and trends in the making (critics can make trends out of one movie, let alone three).

Flying in the face of Lincoln's edict, Hollywood has long labored under the illusion that you can please all of the people all of the time, particularly when it comes to politics. But what has become peculiarly apparent in recent months is that several moviemakers are making political films that name names and set forth notions that are, *a priori*, going to displease a nice fat segment of the ticket-buying public. But strangely enough, box-office receipts indicate that either their displeasure has not kept them from buying those tickets or that the rest of the public is doubling its pleasure by increased patronage of these films.

We can, of course, sing songs of the social significance (let alone the political commentary) of the virtue-triumphant *Mr. Smith Goes to Washington*, the more pointed and wildly hilarious *The Senator Was Indiscreet* and the brilliantly sardonic *The Great McGinty*. These were giants in their day and in their way, which was, however, to emphasize that any resemblance to persons, etc., etc. And certainly there's a marvelously contemporary note to a report that the owners of some 325 theaters in Iowa and Nebraska had condemned and urged a ban of *The Senator Was Indiscreet*; this Nunnally Johnson-George S. Kaufman-Edwin Lanham-Charles MacArthur political burlesque about a bombastic, pompous senator (William Powell at his best) with presidential aspirations, they held, was "a reflection on the integrity of every duly elected representative of the American people" and "could be used as vicious propaganda by subversive elements in this nation as well as our enemies abroad."

If the film and the clipping reporting the exhibitors' reactions

were not sixteen years old, one might think the good folk of the
Midwest were waxing wroth about *Doctor Strangelove* or *Seven
Days in May* or *The Best Man*. They weren't, but an awful lot of
our contemporaries are, so much so that even the hardly radical
Motion Picture Herald took issue with them recently.

But we are not concerned here with the ultraconservatives
who just think national cows are sacrosanct and that things like
generals and statesmen and scientists can't be criticized, let alone
kidded. What is of particular interest is our own pleased surprise
that at long last some of the things that we have taken for granted
in books and in the theater are now showing up on the big screen.
(We're surprised—but not teen-agers; man, they've been reading
Mad magazine, so they dig *Strangelove* deeper than any of us.)

What is suddenly so impressive about the current crop of political films? Haven't any number of movies—let's add *State of
the Union* and *Born Yesterday* and, with the reservations that
latter-day Preminger productions provoke, *Advise and Consent*—
considered the body politic with a certain cynicism, caricatured our
legislators and faced the fact that all is not pure white and true
blue on Capitol Hill? They have indeed, but all has been in the
realm of fiction (despite lots of Washington location shooting), virtue has triumphed and the villains have got theirs in the end.

Thus the unvirtuous conclusion in *Strangelove*, the seemingly
only temporary and none-too-secure triumph of virtue in *Seven
Days in May* and the clear-eyed, cynical conclusion of *The Best
Man* provide us with the final discomfort of facing a few verities,
among them the notion that all is not necessarily for the best in
this not quite the best of all possible worlds. Strange words from
the screens of Hollywood moviemakers.

Strangelove is concerned with the fantastics on a military
and diplomatic level, but the other two movies walk right into
the realm of everyday politics. The stark actuality of the Pentagon
and the White House underline the plotting of *Seven Days in
May*, a superb suspense story of the discovery and aborting, by
the President and a handful of men, of a plot by the Joint
Chiefs of Staff to take over the government. But it is not their
leader, General Scott, or the chiefs or "even the very emotional,

very illogical lunatic fringe" who are the enemy, the President points out. It is the nuclear age that has given man a feeling of "helplessness, weakness, and from this—this desperation—we look for a champion in red, white and blue. Every now and then a man on a white horse rides by and we appoint him to be our personal god for the duration. For some men it was a Senator McCarthy, for others it was a General Walker. Now it's a General Scott."

Those are strong words, because you don't go tossing the name of McCarthy around in that kind of context and not in any kind of movie—as those of us know who ventured to praise *Point of Order*, an extraordinarily good dramatic documentary of the McCarthy-Army hearings. The late Senator's supporters are quick to take pen in hand.

Strong or not, however, what is even more important is that the references are to controversial contemporaries and not to men from, centuries past whose heroism or villainy has been long settled. It makes you wonder what dream worlds are coming to—and suddenly, you see them coming to a bristling no-pseudonyms-please topicality with *The Best Man.*

Neither as a stage play nor on screen does Gore Vidal's drama *The Best Man* pretend to be more than a comment on practical politics by way of a tense contest for the presidential nomination at a national convention. What distinguishes it is that here is a comment by a man of strong opinion who makes no bones about his political bias and principles and minces no words when it comes to remarks about politicians and ex-Presidents, living or dead, or persons and creeds to the right of the liberal. He even makes it clear that he doesn't idolize President Eisenhower and that he loathes segregationists. It takes no clairvoyant to see McCarthy in the methods and Nixon in the personal aura of Senator Joe Cantwell, the tough, self-made, amoral young man who doesn't know truth when he sees it and therefore sees no value in fair play when foul is more efficient. It's Cantwell versus Secretary of State William Russell, a man made hesitant by moral and ethical questions, who has Adlai Stevenson written all over him by being an intellectual and a wit. And there's the Truman image in the pivotal character of ex-President Art Hockstader, who knows that practical politics demand decisiveness and a knowledge of men, respect intellect though one may, and is the old pro who admits, "There is nothing like a dirty low-down political fight to bring the roses to your cheeks." And they're surrounded by the small talk and pertinent references and the wheeling and dealing that are the life-blood of national conventions—and a transfusion for movies.

Mr. Vidal's villain (and Cliff Robertson gives his best perform-ance to date as Cantwell) is undone, but so is his hero, and therein lies the validity of his tale. (And how's that for a Hollywood switch—good graying Henry Fonda not getting his heart's desire in spite of all his star credits?)

So let's call it all a trend, an indication that even an American movie can say something on a super-twelve-year-old level and make it at that old box office. Heavens, three movies are doing it right now. Trend? It's a landslide.

The Slice of Life:
Art and Diatribe
May 10, 1964

There's many a kiss of death at the box office, but the deadliest is undoubtedly the term "social document." And so when a great or a beautiful or a powerful one comes along, the movie blurbers will seize upon the adjectives alone and thank their stars for their stars, because if there's anything deadlier than deadliest, it's a social document without a big name in the cast.

We're *en garde* about these matters in the making of the few American movies that could be termed social documents by sig-nificance-seekers. We haul in star-studded casts and look for high-level suspense plotting if we're going to get down to the facts of our political life or the international race toward automated anni-hilation. We go for broke—or extremes. At one end we have social documentarians who douse their message in plotting and package it with sophistication; at the other we have the hand-held-camera crowd plugging away at a message to be pounded out in plain speech and plainer acting in such bald and forthright terms that only the converted will gather to listen to post-facto arguments for their conversion. From *Strangelove* we go whole hog across the board to *The Cool World.*

Not so the Italians, who at the moment seem to have captured the field of the social document as a work of art. The French are preoccupied with self in their more serious moments; the British have gone from the comic to the kitchen sink and are resting there; the Japanese, and that means Akira Kurosawa, clothe their comment in modern melodrama or historical perspective (and herewith a plug for *Seven Samurai* in Kurosawa's original uncut version—a magnificent film).

But the Italians have a rare ability for making a social document a human document, for seeing the shadings of a condition and the many facets of the man involved and stating a case with a subtle certainty that requires no black-and-white distinctions or diatribes. They know that tears can follow laughter and that the human tragedy and divine comedy are interwoven. And this they translate into terms of ordinary and undistinguished people who have no importance beyond their universality.

What Ermanno Olmi accomplished so beautifully in *The Sound of Trumpets* in detailing a youth's entry upon the treadmill of big industry, Mario Monicelli has done to broader and even more beautiful effect in *The Organizer*, the story of a strike.

Monicelli's story might be of a strike anywhere, at any time, wherever the oppressed have their first stirrings of social conscience and their first striving for self-betterment. He has chosen to tell it in terms of late-nineteenth-century Turin, where men, women and children were virtually enslaved in an eighty-four-hour, six-day week in a spinning mill until the hospital, the poorhouse or the grave claimed them. But above all, he tells it in terms of individuals, of the illiterate, the naïve, the cynical, the dreamers and the doers—and those who are a little of everything. He sees them as part of a tapestry, and if any figures stand out, it is because they are perhaps more colorful by character or more prominent by chance.

His star is not his hero, or anyone else's for very long, although he finally wins the affection of all. For the organizer—and only the credit sheet will tell you that Marcello Mastroianni is behind the shaggy hair and beard, the moonish spectacles, the stooped, starved frame in near-rags—is merely a man, a high school teacher hailed by illiterates as "professor," who is honest enough to admit that he has preferred organizing to teaching, that his wife and children are "somewhere" and that it is only the cause and the practical victory that fire his faith. And the strikers are simply men and women who know of family and friends and the bitter bread of poverty and are struggling only half-successfully toward a knowledge of principle. They become heroes by accident; they achieve dignity with difficulty; their striving is slow and painful and comical and heartbreaking. And Monicelli does not betray them by shouting the rights and wrongs of the issue (these filter through and are self-evident) or by offering a cheap and easy victory. The end of the strike is bitter, marked with the outer defeat and inner hope that has been the way of human progress.

It is strange, indeed, that American films have virtually ignored the story of labor in terms other than those of crime and corruption or glamorized immigrant-to-riches fables; there has been no laughing at industry since, perhaps, *Modern Times*. But Monicelli can find poignant laughter in an adult-education class, in a slick foreman's manipulation of a workers' committee, in a hunted man's avid appeasement of his hunger and his gauche gallantries to a benefactress.

Not so our singleminded social documentarians, who face our problems with a grim zeal and underline, emphasize and finally distort for the sake of their message. The prime example of this is Shirley Clarke's *The Cool World*, based on Warren Miller's brilliant novel about a boy in Harlem. All the humor and breadth of Mr. Miller's work, which was a touchingly universal story of a slum-ghetto child, has been deleted for a single-track indictment of the white world and a grimly bitter tale of tragedy. Only in part because she has used amateurs for her adolescent stars, the focus of Miss Clarke's film has somehow shifted from the boy who must touch our emotions to the passing faces of the crowds and to the garbage pails, the endless overflowing garbage pails of the Harlem streets. What would be a personal story and potential work of art ultimately becomes a polemic.

The bane of American moviemaking has been its perpetual big-think in larger-than-life terms. Certainly *The Organizer* sets a brilliant standard for big-think in human terms. Our hope would be that it set an example as well.

Film-Kidding Films
June 28, 1964

Who is kidding whom?

You never know these movie days, do you? Just as Broadway seems to have rediscovered Hollywood with a vengeance (two of the season's major musicals, *What Makes Sammy Run?* and *Fade Out—Fade In*, are devoted to satirizing the films of the thirties), so moviemakers seem to have latched on to the idea that a little bit of self-satire, a kid in the right direction, is, perhaps, a sign of maturity.

The only trouble is that in the heavier hands of Hollywood we're never quite sure on whom the joke is, or if, in fact, the joke is intentional. *What a Way To Go!* took time out to kid the "Lush Budgett Production" with the lushest production budget of the current comedy crop; *Paris When It Sizzles* had a patch-and-paste screenplay making fun of a patch-and-paste screenwriter. These jokes were intentional but the pie boomeranged smack into the jokester's face.

Since *Singin' in the Rain*, that gem of a dozen years ago, there hasn't been an American movie satire of note. Well—*Beat the Devil*, perhaps; I for one found, in its recent revival, that it was not the ten years ahead of its time that the ads claimed and that it isn't as funny as it was.

But the French, with their heretofore relatively humorless devotion to the American movies of the thirties, have hit the mark. In his previous films (*The Five Day Lover, The Love Game, The Joker*) Philippe De Broca was obviously warming up for *That Man from Rio*, which is the ultimate takeoff on the adventure-intrigue movie, from Pauline's perils through to those of James Bond. With Jean-Paul Belmondo as his hero extraordinary, De Broca leads us a mad and merry transatlantic trans-Brazilian chase after a birdbrained redheaded beauty and the buried treasure that lies behind the secret of the three ancient "Maltec" statuettes.

One admirer finds Belmondo pulling a Harold Lloyd; another sees him as a *Beat the Devil* Bogart. He's both, along with bits of Tarzan and every Hitchcock hero. Essentially, he's a pure, simple-minded guy whose aim is bad and whose karate blows leave villains unscathed, who will chase racing cars on foot, parachute into the alligator's jaws and dangle from tenth-story windows all for the love of a lady who insists throughout that his love for her is "just words." Bloodied and ragged one moment, he is impeccable and suave in evening clothes the next; one hairbreadth escape simply deserves another, and, above all, the ambience is made to match. When a millionaire suggests an "impromptu little party" for the out-of-the-jungle arrivals from Paris, we're plunged into fireworks and haute-coutured splendors; if Belmondo drops into a waterfront café it is crammed to the hilt with refugees from every waterfront-mayhem movie and more breakaway furniture than ever stocked the whole cinematic Western frontier. Near at hand, of course, are the deliciously dumb girl, the sinister natives, the double-dealing criminal mastermind, and always—breathtakingly beautiful—there are the landscapes, the near-surrealist nouveau architecture of Rio and Brasília and fantastic vistas for the chaser and the chased.

There is a flaw, however; De Broca is, if not merely mortal, his own coauthor and director, and he is very much infatuated with his own joke. And so the chase goes on and on, the joke is prolonged beyond its juiciest and *That Man from Rio* passes its peak of fun not too long after the first of its two hours. Alas for the lack of the cutting shears—the very pair that, used perhaps ruthlessly, could have made *It's a Mad, Mad, Mad, Mad World* one of the funniest American-made comedies of all time.

De Broca's intent is clear. I don't know what the makers of *The Long Ships* had in mind, but they've come up with one of the best spectacular-type jokes in ages. (*The Fall of the Roman Empire* just missed being a fine travesty; it wasn't quite bad enough.) It's a saga sort of story about those grand, brawling, sprawling Vikings, those highly civilized torture-crazy Moors and their competitive chase after the Golden Bell—"the one people call the mother of voices, as tall as three tall men and made of half of the gold in the world."

It's crazy, man, from the moment Richard Widmark, shipwrecked Viking Rover Boy extraordinary, escapes from the tower torture chamber of Sidney Poitier, Moorish sheik superb, and swandives *à la* Zenda into the sea some fifty stories below—and lives to lead another expedition in search of the bell. This time he's being chased by the Viking king whose daughter he has abducted (along with the king's ship), and this time he and all his merry men are shipwrecked again on the Moorish coast. It's back to the torture chamber—and the seraglio—and the slave market; then there's a Widmark-Poitier expedition for the bell again. And surprise, surprise, the bell does not turn out to be the bluebird of happiness.

There's all the carousing and gouging and battling away with scimitars and axes and spears and bow-and-arrow, and everyone is beaten to bits, only to rise and fight again. Fresh from the rack, the chain gang or the wettest shipwreck on record, those Vikings are battling away with each other or the "Allah Akbar" boys and wenching away with the nuttiest enthusiasm ever. And there's Poitier, straight out of the Arabian Nights, playing it dedicated-straight, and Widmark, right out of California, playing it with understatement—and all of it for the little boys of seven and seventy (the harem girls are for the latter group) and for anybody who wants to revel in the utterly silly simplemindedness of it all.

Don't tell me Jack Cardiff (the British director who did the fine *Sons and Lovers* and was cinematographer on *The Red Shoes*) didn't plan it all this way—the Vikings at play on their home grounds at a party their Thane gives for the king, a brawl that makes the *Taras Bulba* sprees Boy Scout affairs; the marvelous cacophony of dialect—Poitier's tight-jawed Oxonian-regal, Rosanna Schiaffino's ripe Italian tones as his favorite wife, Russ Tamblyn's Hollywood-juvenile accents as Widmark's brother; the shots of the harem girls at play or rest; the spectacular arrivals and departures in Poitier's capital city.

I choose to think all this was intentional, a straight-faced spoof of all the stuff and nonsense that mythologies are made of—so straight-faced that it can afford the occasional wisecrack, the here-we-go-again ending. James Bond—or Rolfe the Viking? It depends on the era in which you want to daydream.

Mirth and Murder
July 26, 1964

With the dog days yapping at our heels, the time has come to seek the coolth of crime, with the relaxing chill of murder available in hammock with paperback mystery or moviehouse with murder-for-laughs.

Murder for our pleasure is, of course, a movie staple, with murder for high comedy one of its rarer but more delightful aspects. The embarrassing or befuddling corpse or, preferably, corpses in the closet—or, better yet, in the open—have been high points of hilarity in a number of films, from *A Slight Case of Murder* to *Charade*. But much rarer is the comedy provided by the killer; the lesser criminal as clown can be a laughing matter (as the Europeans most often demonstrate in the *Big Deal on Madonna Street* or *Lavender Hill Mob* sort of story), but clowns are close to our hearts, and who, besides his mother, can love a murderer, let alone laugh at his on-the-job activities?

It has been done, of course, with such classics as *Arsenic and Old Lace* and *Kind Hearts and Coronets*—but there was the touch

of madness for mitigation. And now we are offered two comedies—
Monsieur Verdoux and *Nothing but the Best*—that offer us the
murderer as hero amid slapstick and social comment.

Verdoux is a classic that we are at last privileged to appreciate after its abortive debut seventeen years ago. Some say that
the cool reception accorded this Chaplin movie reflected the public's reaction against the great performer's private life and political
activities; others, claiming objectivity in separating the man from
the performer, feel that the temper of the times (of 1947, with
war wounds still fresh) was wrong for equating a Bluebeard who
murders to support his loved ones with a war hero—that the temperament and sophistication of the general public were not yet
attuned to the particular brand of satire and the relatively "sick"
humor of the plot.

Whatever the reasons for its initial failure, Chaplin's Bluebeard story is ours to revel in for the sheer brilliance of performance, the cinematic excellence of his direction and the simplicity
that shines in all its latter-day naïveté. The naïveté is clearer now,
for Chaplin's genius is as performer and creator of performance;
as ideologist he tends to oversimplify and to harangue. If only, one
wishes, he had constantly had in mind the absolute perfection of
the final scene between the tramp and the flower girl in *City Lights*—
a wordless scene, with the pantomime underlined only by music.
This would have precluded the endless harangue that mars the
conclusion of *The Great Dictator*, and in *Verdoux* it would have
led to sentences rather than paragraphs in the serious scenes.

If one can—well, not even quarrel—simply point to Chaplin's
writing as a flicker of a flaw in the jewel that is *Verdoux*, one can
proceed to the declaration that seldom has murder been made more
delicious in all its various stages—the exquisite courtship of a reluctant prospect, the single shot of the smoking furnace, the hilarity
of the attempted drowning of Martha Raye in the rowboat, the
insane sequence of switched peroxide bottles and wine glasses.
Has there ever been a comedy partner to compare with Miss Raye
in all her hideous bellowing vulgarity? Here indeed is a dame who
goes fishing with silver-fox stole and pompon chapeau. And the slapstick, the delicate timing of ringing doorbells and tinkling tele-

phones, the face after face of the venal grotesques who deserve all they are to get at the murderer's hand. And there's cruelty in Chaplin's making Verdoux's wife and child so romantically sweet—and the young refugee widow so openhearted—a cruelty whose calculation is just right, for the murderer has won our hearts through them and we become a part of his nightmare in all its fantastic comedy, its biting ironies (where is there a precedent for Verdoux's gentle, "What can I do for you?" to the priest who comes to his prison cell?) and its crushing social satire.

Monsieur Verdoux stands as a work of art—and as, perhaps, the prototype of the lovable-murderer comedy. The latest effort in this direction, a successful one, *Nothing but the Best*, does not have a "lovable" hero, only one who charms us completely because he's our kind of anti-Establishment success story.

The hero of this offbeat British film, Jimmy Brewster, is not an angry young man; he's just a horribly clear-eyed one with ambitions, who knows that in England's postwar society it's still the old school tie that counts, regardless of your inner talents and outer charm, when it comes to getting the "smashing" things of this world. So Jimmy sets out to make himself upper-U under the tutelage of a down-and-out but still teddibly upper-upper-U remittance man. But his tutor, alas, who has done a perfectly fine job on Jimmy, who's whizzing his way to the top, has had the bad taste to see Jimmy plain as one more "ambitious yob," and so, like anyone who has outlived his usefulness or has impeded Jimmy's progress, he's "got to go." But this time, instead of having the metaphorical dagger deftly stuck in his back, the victim is all too literally strangled by the old school tie and stuffed into his own old school trunk. "The trouble with living in digs is there's no place to put things," Jimmy remarks as he struggles sloppily down the stairs of his roominghouse to stow the trunk in the basement. And from this point on it's a case of body, body, who's got it and who'll find it—and when it does pop up, does it drag Jimmy down?

The answer is left in your lap, and if you like, you can decide that the most offbeat feature of this film is that it suggests that crime might pay—at least for Jimmy Brewster. You may even want it to pay for him, because the beauty of the film is that his various victims usually deserve what they get, that his invasion of the upper echleons succeeds because underneath their veneer the old guardsmen are just as venal and shrewd as Jimmy, and that all he's doing is playing their own game in their own style, albeit his style is acquired rather than inbred.

And the joy of this jazzy, stylish, dashing film is its ruthless satire on the Establishment Jimmy is joining—the university phonies, the gaping and hesitant young men who've been mannered into a near-catatonic state, the doting dowagers and their rapacious daughters, the stultified clubmen and the young set with a jargon and jive all its own. ("You've done something facetious to your hair," the playgirl sighs. "I've cut it," her fiancé explains.) It's all too obvious that once Jimmy has acquired the polish there's nothing that separates him and the elite—beyond the fact that Jimmy's handsomer, far more charming and the smartest of the lot. Get away with murder? Maybe yes?

A cooling thought—or is it chilling? Monsieur Verdoux walks in resignation to the guillotine and Jimmy Brewster is left preparing himself for the crucial test of his masquerade and we are left to ponder our affections for the murderers.

The Care and Feeding
of Love Goddesses
August 3, 1964

It's two years now since Marilyn Monroe's death, and the image-makers still haven't come up with a successor, despite all the sweat, strain and Carroll Baker that's being exhibited. The American Sex Symbol score still stands at two for our generation; we may well have to wait another twenty years for the third.

The magic of Monroe—and "magic" is as good a cliché as "mystique" or "indefinable something"—has survived and even trans-

Thus the psychological thriller has slowly but surely displaced the horror story and even the pure crime or suspense story. Television has taken over in the crime-and-punishment arena. In movies the fine clean-cut "What is the plot; will the good guys learn of it in time—and will they be able to save the nation" progression of a *Seven Days in May* or the clear "Will they pull off the impossible" of a *Topkapi* comes just about once a year. For nowadays moviemakers, including even the maestro, Hitchcock, are increasingly preoccupied with the psychoses and neuroses of criminals rather than the technique and suspense of the crime. We have, perhaps, only our own sophisticated tastes and the follow-the-hit propensities of producers to blame for the fact that the psychological thriller—from *Marnie* to *The Visit* to the remake of *Night Must Fall* to *Lady in a Cage*—has become all psychology and no thrills, with sadism the upcoming substitute for the latter, sympathetic psychoanalysis muddling the morality, and our own post-Freudian sophistication vitiating the suspense.

How long has it actually been since you experienced the engrossing, step-by-step entrapment-and-revelation unfolding of character and crime that we found in *Strangers on a Train* or *The Haunting* or *Diabolique* or—what? Pretty tough to make a more current list, isn't it?

Well, now we have *Seance on a Wet Afternoon*, and it stands by itself as not only a psychological suspense thriller but also a top-notch crime-and-detection tale and, above all, a horror film. For the horror lies in the hearts of Kim Stanley and Richard Attenborough, who are presented to us as a slightly seedy and undoubtedly phony medium and her rabbity husband who seem to be up to something in the overstuffed monstrosity of a rundown London house. What they are up to is revealed slowly, slowly—and even more slowly comes the revelation of what is in their hearts. Yet the film moves at breathtaking pace, with incident twisting the skein of suspense, challenging the intellect and setting the nerve ends atingle.

The fascination of the film lies, of course, partly in its ingenious plot (and I am not going to tell you a thing about it, lest I spare you a single held breath), partly in the brilliant photography, and in the subtle and exciting direction of Bryan Forbes, author of the screenplay as well—and not only author-director of such films as *The L-Shaped Room* and *Whistle Down the Wind*, but also author and a star of *The League of Gentlemen*, to give him his top-notch crime-thriller credit.

But the largest part lies in the talents of Miss Stanley and Mr. Attenborough, in their faces and in their hearts. For this care-worn, mundane, slightly shabby middle-aged couple—a drab, blowsy shrew, her mousy walrus-mustached mate—are clichés in our life, the gray people who surround us unnoticed. And then, slowly, slowly, we hear the edge to the woman's voice, the frightening insistence on something of no import, the suggestion of murder in her heart—and we see a softening sorrow around the man's subservience, then a glimmer of resistance subdued by a slavish devotion to the something of this woman that is unrevealed to us. They present enigmatically both a mysterious conflict and a tantalizing alliance in their relationship, and the human experience that is not revealed in its shattering totality until the final fadeout holds us in the grip of terror.

Between them Miss Stanley and Mr. Attenborough create the true monster of our time—the secret sickness of the soul—that is without season and ever present, an invisible horror lurking in familiar faces. And this is *Seance on a Wet Afternoon*—no masks, no tricks, only the treat of perfection.

French Filmflam
December 20, 1964

What, may we ask, is going on with foreign films in general and French films in particular? The French, after all—and the Russians—were responsible for developing our taste for and in the foreign film. Beyond the—well, let's reach for the politer adjective—beyond the ambitious *Hamlet* shown at the New York Film Festival, the Russians have offered us little of interest and nothing of note in the past year. And the French—well.

The Umbrellas of Cherbourg is not only officially representative but officially regarded as the apex of French cinema work of
the year. Winner of the Grand Prix at Cannes, it's France's entry
in this year's foreign-film Oscar race.

At any rate, the country that last year entered Louis Malle's
The Fire Within for the Oscar is now going all out with *Umbrellas*,
and a pure parallel might be that the Nobel Prize for literature, offered (albeit unsuccessfully) to Sartre this year, next year be
awarded to—well, let's not reach for someone of the stature of a
Harold Robbins or Mickey Spillane—let's just say the TV con-
tinuity writer for *My Living Doll*.

Umbrellas, in fact, doesn't quite achieve the level of sophistication to which television series have accustomed us, although it is,
in its stale and supersentimental plot, strictly an *opéra de savon*.
Stress the "opera," because the great cinematic advance that this
Jacques Demy movie has allegedly made is that its dialogue is entirely sung, one note per syllable, prosaic lyrics by Demy and
monotonous music by Michel Legrand, a kind of Gallic Lawrence
Welk with intellectual aspirations. Aurally, it offers proof positive
of Richard Rodgers' contention that "there is nothing so dreary as
trying to set a line like 'I'm going downtown to buy a bunch of
bananas' to music." Not that there are bananas in Cherbourg, but
there's endless talk—i.e., song—about the operations of a gas station,
unwed motherhood, the umbrella business, economics in general
and the high cost of living in particular.

Intellectually, it's girl loves boy, boy is drafted, girl suffers
Immediate Conception from their last night together, boy is bad
letter-writer, girl is very pregnant, girl marries rich salesman, boy
returns to take to drink and then be rehabilitated by ever-loving
plain Jane and fulfill his ambition to open a gas station. And then
comes the apex of French moviemaking: Christmas Eve, snow
flurries, boy's wife and son are off on last-minute window-shopping,
and up to the shiny new Esso pump, in a shiny new high-priced
car, swathed in mink, drives—okay. You take your imitation of life
and I will stick to mine. And the Esso pump— Scorn not the commercial; that's pop art, which Demy mixes in with all his pastel
cardboard backgrounds for a touch of Renoir here and a flash of

Matisse there amid the Cherbourg rain that falls on everything but the singing actors in midstreet. It is all so sweet, so sentimental, so artsy, so craftsy, so pretty, so pretentious, so abysmally simple-minded.

Because it you don't want to take to *Umbrellas* in pursuit of subinfantilism, you're faced with going to Godard for something for grown-ups. Whether it's *A Woman Is a Woman*, still another of his superuxorious concentrations on Anna Karina's admittedly pretty face, or *Contempt*, where the devotion is now to Brigitte Bardot's even more admittedly pretty rear-view nudity, we are still subjected to the banalities of film "in" jokes, the fake spontaneity that is supposed to cover up the plotless pointlessness of his work and the meandering literalness of his camera. On a bed, on a shaggy white rug, on a sun deck, there sprawls Barclot, as tangle-haired and sulky-mouthed as when she is fully clothed. In fact, the only thing this actress offers us in the way of a change is the constant covering up and uncovering of her charming derriere.

But even your own baby's, even on that shaggy rug, has limited appeal when he's squawling—and for an hour and a half Miss Bardot, Jack Palance and Michel Piccoli squawl at each other to no purpose. It's a tale of a nonintellectual wife's feeling contempt for her husband's undertaking to rewrite *The Odyssey* for a vile American film producer, and I have the fleeting impression that Miss Bardot tries at one point to droop her mouth even more to look contemptuous. But that backside ends up bemusing us, as it obviously has Godard—and bemusement leads to benumbment. And that's what we're getting from abroad these days. *Chacun a son goût*, as we Russians like to say.

1964:
Cream of the Crop
December 27, 1964

1. *Dr. Strangelove, Or: How I
   Learned to Stop Worrying
   and Love the Bomb*
2. *Seduced and Abandoned*
3. *The Organizer*
4. *Mafioso*
5. *The Fire Within*
6. *The Servant*
7. *Girl with Green Eyes*
8. *Seance on a Wet Afternoon*
9. *A Hard Day's Night*
10. *Mary Poppins*

Step aside, Sam, it's odious-comparison time. Out of my way with your continuing questions about where the laughs were in *Tom Jones* or what the hell *8½* was all about anyway. It's time to let go of last year's list, Sam, but don't go away mad. Stick around and you'll get madder than ever.

There is one reward in compiling a list of the ten best movies of most years and particularly of 1964. You realize, in reviewing the past twelve months, that amid all the sleazy, pretentious, venal, crude and, above all, dull moviemaking to which we've been subjected, there has been a surprising number of good movies. Beyond the Top Ten there are many "best of the rest" to be listed.

Picking the Top Ten is otherwise a frustrating pastime. You compare the noncomparable, splitting hairs and tipping balances with a wafer of whim; you force yourself to think of movies per se and not of The Industry. You put aside chauvinism and refuse to sweat over the national origin of a film and the international implications of your choices. You harden your heart in regard to the amateur and/or independent who deserves E for effort and I for integrity and Z for the total product. You remind yourself that great performances or fine photography or excellencies of script alone do not make a movie of quality. And you forget about the film as an Art Form and as an Opiate of the Masses and as an Educational Instrument. You think about Movies—and you make your list. Here it is:

Stanley Kubrick's *Dr. Strangelove, Or: How I Learned to Stop Worrying and Love the Bomb* is the incomparable—the year's best film, a masterpiece of moviemaking of a very American kind. With superb script, performances and cinematic techniques, Kubrick has triumphed in an area where few others have even ventured and none succeeded, the area of Swiftian satire. He wields the needle and the knife mercilessly in parody and pastiche with devastating wit and excruciating fun on the super-sacred cows of our military and political establishments. His is a comedy of our contemporary nightmare—of the slip and slide over the brink of atomic holocaust precipitated by fool or madman. His is the sane man's only possible response to the insanities of the international race toward nuclear self-destruction—that of ironic laughter and ferocious caricature. And he has created not only a nightmare comedy but also a top-notch suspense thriller that is a model of disciplined direction, of immaculate casting, of iconoclasm used with both sensitivity and sophistication. You need not "enjoy" his courageous irreverence, his refusal to settle for the specious, his glittering clarity of vision and ruthlessness of comment, but I defy you to remain indifferent. And that is the triumph of *Strangelove.* It has substance and argument, as rare as satire of our establishments, and its effect on American moviemakers will be—hopefully—far-reaching.

On the individual rather than establishment level, Pietro Germi's *Seduced and Abandoned* is also a comic nightmare, another meaningful funny film. Broadening the Sicilian canvas he used in *Divorce—Italian Style,* Germi is concerned with the crimes committed in the name of honor and of family pride, the inhumanities of man in defense of his public face and the two faces of man in his moral attitudes toward women. With a hand so skilled that it can handle slapstick and farce with the same ease brought moments later to searing drama and subtle wit, the Italian director reveals a universal truth amid the trappings of an engrossing and colorful regional comedy.

Still another universal story, of the struggle of the downtrodden, not merely for economic betterment but for self-respect and social responsibility, and of the selfless, near-faceless man who helps them toward their intimations of human dignity, is told in Mario Monicelli's *The Organizer*. It is a stirring and stinging social document, this story of a strike in turn-of-the-century Turin; but it is, more importantly, a human document, this tale without heroes but with men and women whose striving is slow and painful and comic and heartbreaking and whose importance is their universality. Its tone is set by its star, Marcello Mastroianni—bespectacled, stoop-shouldered, shaggy-haired, the unprepossessing man of faith and fire for a cause and a principle. Above all, it is perhaps the most beautiful film of the year, its time re-created in what could be called animated daguerreotypes, combining the lyricism of Atget with the realism of Brady in an all-pervading sense of place and people and period.

And finally—at least for the Italian entries on my list—there is Alberto Lattuada's *Mafioso*, a rare film in that it goes from comedy to horror and back to everyday life without a break. What begins as a pleasantly sophisticated domestic comedy suddenly turns into a chiller; the man in the button-down collar becomes the tool of Mafia terror, but life goes on in surface ease, and *Mafioso's* incidents are our recent headlines. The film retains pace and fascination with each switch, with Alberto Sordi's brilliant portrait of a modern man caught in a medieval ritual and the striking authenticity of its physical and psychological backgrounds adding to its distinction.

Louis Malle's *The Fire Within* is an epitaph for all the beautiful young men, the semi-intellectual "gilded mediocrities" who skim through their days to their doom unchanged save for a surface tarnish. A latter-day parable of a Dorian Gray, superbly acted and beautifully filmed, it gives no quarter—and demands no tears for Adonais—as it brings us to a haunting realization of a malaise of our time.

The British next take over our list with four selections. *The Servant*, made by the "exiled" American director Joseph Losey, is pure cinema, a brilliant and detailed exploration of corruption in stunning movie terms. *Girl with Green Eyes*, a beautiful and eloquent first directorial effort by Desmond Davis, made exquisite by Rita Tushingham as its heroine, is a story of a girl's first encounter with love that embodies all that is naïve and silly and noble and wonderful and heartbreaking and funny about being young. Bryan Forbes's *Seance on a Wet Afternoon* is a perfect psychological suspense thriller, with Kim Stanley and Richard Attenborough as the sick-souled nobodies at the core of a brilliant mystery story tinged with the macabre and warmed by human passions. *A Hard Day's Night*, Beatles and all, is an original film in many senses, with script, direction and camera capturing a contemporary phenomenon in such exciting, diverting and empathetic terms that the unexplainable (the Beatles and all) becomes not only understandable but thoroughly delightful.

And then back to the good old U.S.A. to list *Mary Poppins* as a charming, imaginative and technically superb movie musical, sparkling with originality, melody and magical performances by Julie Andrews and Dick Van Dyke and, through the triumph of Walt Disney's craftsmanship, offering uniquely cinematic entertainment.

There are the Top Ten—and now for what lies immediately below the top, some with only that hairbreadth of separation. We have first the enchanting *My Fair Lady* and Japan's *Harakiri*, a superb film that too few people had time to see during its brief release; add quickly *Seven Days in May*, *Woman in the Dunes*, *Becket*, *The Luck of Ginger Coffey*, *Cartouche*, *The Silence* and *Topkapi*. Go on to *Night of the Iguana*, *Marriage Italian Style*, *The Chalk Garden*, *The Best Man*, *The World of Henry Orient*, *That Man from Rio*, *Nothing but the Best*—well, it's fan's choice from there on in.

Two of the finest documentaries of the year were not in so-called commercial distribution: *To Be Alive!*, the Francis Thompson-Alexander Hammid eighteen-minute movie shown at the Johnson's Wax pavilion at the World's Fair, is not only a paean to the life we are too busy living to enjoy and appreciate; its use of a triptych screen for one, two or three images involves both conscious and subconscious absorption of the pictures and opens vast new artistic and technical dimensions for film. And George Stevens Jr.'s feature-length *John F. Kennedy: Years of Lightning, Day of Drums*, made by the USIA for distribution abroad, is a beautiful, stirring and utterly un-maudlin story of the Kennedy years and Kennedy policies.

Other feature-length documentaries that gave the year distinction were *Point of Order*, on the McCarthy era; *The Finest Hours*, a Churchill-centered story of our century, and Jacques Cousteau's beautiful and completely fascinating *World Without Sun*, the story of the colony he has established some forty to eighty feet below the Red Sea.

There you are, Sam, more than twenty movies that are first-rate in addition to the Top Ten. Aren't you glad you stuck around? What? *Strangelove* is un-American and where's *The Carpetbaggers*? And how come I haven't got Brigitte Bardot's— Okay, Sam. Better you should go away mad.

☆ Part III ☆
........From Mary
.........to Darling

Billy's Getting Wilder
January 3, 1965

Professional purveyors of pornography at least have the courage of their convictions; you don't find them trying to pass off smoker movies as satiric comedies of the American scene, cute romantic versions of best-sellers or adult comic strips. When they make dirty movies they sell 'em that way—and it's buyers' choice.

But if a big studio makes a movie that is given no seal by the Motion Picture Association—and the MPA rules demand that its members put forth sealed products—the big company just hands the movie over to its subsidiary or affiliate that is not an MPA member and then waits for the money to roll in, as in the case of *Kiss Me, Stupid*.

Kiss Me, Stupid is quite a case, and while focusing on it I don't want to overlook *Sex and the Single Girl* or certain aspects of *Goldfinger*. And countless films of the past months could provide further cases in point.

Billy Wilder's *Kiss Me, Stupid* bears probing because it is by a man of vast talent and vaster accomplishment. And what has happened to Mr. Wilder's movies in recent years is exactly what has been happening to the Hollywood movie. Some people like to sum it up in simple terms: our movies are forced to provide what television cannot—or at least so far does not—in the way of sex exploitation or, another simple term, are forced to compete with foreign films on the nudity-and-sex level; others think that our movies are simply becoming belatedly "adult." If so, let eternal childhood be ours.

Mr. Wilder's movie history is, in fact, being explored at the Museum of Modern Art at the moment. Sixteen films, dating from 1929 on, in which he has been involved as director, writer and/or producer collaboratively, are being shown on a two-a-week basis through February sixth. This week's attractions are *Five Graves To Cairo* and *Double Indemnity*; then we'll have *The Lost Weekend* and *Sunset Boulevard* and on through such glories as *Stalag 17* and *Witness for the Prosecution*. And then we get, for the last week, into the produced, directed and written with I. A. L. Diamond group, *Some Like It Hot* and *The Apartment*; *Kiss Me, Stupid* is in the group but not in the Museum series.

It is the group that is of interest, for it is in *Some Like It Hot*, made in 1959, that the smut starts to show. Seen it lately? All pretty cute and jazzy, with Marilyn Monroe a delight and lots of comedy kick-ups with Tony Curtis and Jack Lemmon masquerading as a couple of girl musicians in a twenties setting. Look at it closely again and you start to notice how for every raucous and/or ribald masquerade joke there is another that involves a transvestite leer, a homosexual "in" joke or a perverse gag. *The Apartment*, 1960? The big gag involves the key to the executive washroom, and there is some sheer-fun stuff in the lonely bachelor life, the button-down-collar rat race. Look again. Our hero is, in essence, little more than a climber who finds pimping the way to get ahead; the heroine is a tramp whom we are supposed to bleed for simply because her most recent and most permanent client refused to pay (payment involved divorce and marrying her). Small wonder that Mr. Wilder went from *The Apartment* to *Irma La Douce* (after a side foray into *One, Two, Three*) and took his hero and heroine, Jack Lemmon and Shirley MacLaine, with him for that merry tale of a prostitute and her pimp.

And now, *Kiss Me, Stupid*, which, unlike its predecessors, is a witless bore, with neither a smile nor a laugh to augment the smirk for the feebleminded. And now there are no bones made about Topic S, with lines that a burlesque show would reject as unfunny but consider reworking for their salaciousness, both sexual and scatological. Only the characters' clothes separate them from their counterparts in a stag movie.

Here in subtly named Climax, Nevada, we have a husband preparing to give his wife to a lecherous, alcoholic singer in the hope of selling the singer a song. The husband balks at the last moment (his wife has been preparing to celebrate their fifth anniversary by showering, opening up the bed and looking at their photo album as an aphrodisiac) and hires a prostitute, Polly the Pistol, no less, to pose as his wife, whom he has driven from the house by a staged quarrel. He balks again, however, at the thought of giving the singer the nice, dumb blond prostitute posing as his wife; so he drives the singer from the house and takes the nice dumb blond prostitute to his uxorial bed. Meanwhile the wife has gone to the local roadhouse, the cutely named Belly Button Cafe, to drown her sorrows and has passed out in the prostitute's bed. The singer finds refuge there, takes her for the prostitute and, since she doesn't enlighten him, takes her. And the wife winds up with five hundred dollars, the prostitute is happy, the husband sells his song, the singer makes it a hit—and when the husband looks a little dazed, the wife murmurs, "Kiss me, stupid."

Here is the prurience, the perversion, the sexual sickness that is obsessing the characters and plots of our films. *Goldfinger*, lacking the freshness, the action, the empathetic high-living and vicarious heroics of the two preceding James Bond films, turns to lesbianism, to Krafft-Ebing tortures, to unadulterated sadism for fillips. *Sex and the Single Girl* involves a marriage-counseling psychologist—named Helen Gurley Brown, a name bought, we presume, from Miss Brown along with the title of her best-seller—trying to prove that she isn't a virgin to a scandal-magazine editor out to prove that she is.

Grown-ups—real ones, not figments of distorted imaginations—are going to leave these movies flat through sheer boredom, if nothing else. But given nothing in the way of humor or satire or even imitations of reality to occupy their minds while watching these films, young people are going to get some pretty strange ideas of what is amusing, what is titillating, what is sophisticated.

I can't for a moment imagine they're going to pick up any moral values, even negative ones, but their idea of entertainment is going to be an odd one.

And through it all, trying to be a little more prurient than the last guy, a trifle more immoral than the next, these American moviemakers are going to cut their own throats. That's fine with us. But hopefully we won't have to sit and watch while they do it.

Pointing a Pinky
at the Negro
January 17, 1965

Let's stop already with the *Pinky* bit.

Every time anyone wants to know what Hollywood has been doing about the integration issue or the Negro's problems, up comes *Pinky*. That quondam social document, which in retrospect stands as a mild bit of soap-opera contention that a nice Negro girl who passes for white up North shouldn't try to come home again, came upon us in 1949, the year that also boasted *Lost Boundaries*, a semidocumentary about a Negro doctor and his family passing for white in a New Hampshire town, and the film version of *Home of the Brave*, which changed the focus of prejudice from the Jew of the stage play to a Negro in the screenplay. And then Stanley Kramer, in the years of his maverickdom, gave us *The Defiant Ones* in 1958; David Susskind and Philip Rose brought *A Raisin in the Sun* to the screen in 1961; Roger Corman, also on his own, came up with *The Intruder* in 1962, and Nicholas Webster made the movie of the play *Purlie Victorious* (called *Gone Are the Days!*) in 1963.

And there you are. Beyond the fact that the Stepin Fetchit servant is out (and why was it that Negro servants on screen were never allowed to retain the dignity and almost majority rights they were accorded in Mae West movies—or haven't you seen something

like *I'm No Angel* lately?), beyond the fact that the Mammy-Uncle
Tom image is out, or that an occasional nonservant bit part is given
to a Negro, Hollywood has kept a stiff-upper-lipped silence on
an issue that has preoccupied not only the nation but also the
world. It has been truly written, Hollywood is indeed out of this
world. (No, *Lilies of the Field* is not forgotten, but it was not involved with the problems of integration or civil rights or bigotry,
only concerned with the story of a free and independent man who
happened to be a Negro.)

And so, of course, this issue, with its discomforts and contro-
versies, has fallen to the independent producer, the man who has
a dedication or a sense of responsibility and a statement to make
but a man who, above all, can maintain a basic indifference to the
box-office returns from the apathetic North or to no returns at all
from the impassioned South. But the independent whom we
admittedly tend to over-idealize simply because he does not wear
the Hollywood halter—or vicuña coat), despite the best of intentions or integrity, too often dissolves into amateurish error or sudden compromise. And after the first couple of independent forays
into the Deep South, how we longed to have some moviemaking
giant bestir himself and betake himself to the most important social
issue of our time. But then along comes the unexpected.

There were, for instance, three independent movies about the
Negro in this past year of the Hollywood hiatus, and the first
two, albeit on totally different levels, were not good films. *Black
Like Me*, based on a true story of a white journalist's masquerade
as a Negro in the South, was a cliché-laden disaster that literally as
well as critically was beyond belief. Next to it, the second venture,
One Potato, Two Potato, stands as a masterpiece; away from it,
and in the general run, it stands as an adequate little film marked
by two very good performances and integrity as well as by amateurish and arty techniques and, unfortunately, melodramatics
that shift the emphasis of the film. Its story, with some root in some
truth, is of a white divorcée who, because of her marriage to a
Negro, loses custody of her daughter to her former husband, who
objects to the child's growing up in a predominantly Negro household. But after doing the hitherto undone—giving us an interracial

romance and marriage that is believable and touching—the movie's makers begin a slow but savage assault upon our emotions, leaving us finally with heartstrings wrenched and tears flowing for the wrong reason—not because of social injustice to the Negro but because of the heartbreak of a little girl being taken away from her mommy.

When *One Potato, Two Potato*, starting out with so much in its favor, wound up on a siding, we began to long for some of that Hollywood engineering technique. But then along came *Nothing but a Man*, a highlight at the New York Film Festival in September put into commercial release at the end of December. And who needs the old pros when two young moviemakers like Robert Young and Michael Roemer can do the job so well?

Two documentary men, they decided to do a feature in the South and went there to write their story. There they found the truth that is at the root of their film about a young man's coming to terms with himself and with society, a young man whose universal problems are intensified because he is a Negro in today's South. With the clarity and simplicity of near-documentary technique, they let a closeup or a location background tell what other filmmakers attempt with endless verbiage and good intentions. Above all, we see the many facets of a community and a people that happen to be Negro; no one is a hero, a villain or a cause, but everyone is human. Duff Anderson is the young man considering a surrender of his footloose, carefree life on a railroad gang to find in marriage the roots his slum childhood never allowed him. Duff is an independent spirit, quick to rebellion, and his choice is a more difficult one because his wife-to-be, a schoolteacher, is bound to the middle-class get-along-with-the-whites-by-catering society of her preacher-father. They could go north to flee the pressures and the animosities that Duff creates, but after a brief crisis Duff grows to manhood with the realization that dignity and security can come only with the acceptance of responsibility.

Ivan Dixon and singer Abbey Lincoln are excellent as Duff and his girl, and Gloria Foster shines as the woman who cared for Duff's father; all the performers more than know what they are about. More important, Messrs. Young and Roemer know what their movie is about, so that they need resort to neither sensationalism nor melodrama nor schmaltz nor nonsense to explore and expose a human problem—the Negro problem—in universal terms for our understanding. *Nothing but a Man* is a fine film—a first one that sets a towering standard for its makers.

Just a Bookish Sinner
February 11, 1965

Well, here we go again, hitting the old whorehouse trail with Carroll Baker to explore the highs and the lows of depravity and wallow in as much vicarious sin as our stomachs, if not our sensibilities, will allow. And why? You mean why *Sylvia*? To get the message, the uplifting, heartwarming, decent all-American message, baby doll—that so long as a girl keeps her nose in a book, it doesn't matter a bit where the rest of her has been.

Never mind the whore with a heart of gold. This one has a brain of pure plutonium. I mean it's books, books, books and French and real flowers—true culture, you might say—and because she's devoted to them through rape and ruin and all that jazz, she winds up on the verge of marrying a multi-multi-multi millionaire. Who says gentlemen don't prefer blonds?

But let's start from the beginning, or rather the near-end, as this silly saga does. The multi-multi-multi, played in cardigan-and-middle-aged-pot fashion by Peter Lawford, calls in a private eye, played in Bogey-Garfield-middle-brow TV fashion by George Maharis. He wants the lowdown on his fiancée, a gorgeous, wealthy blond horticulturist-poetess named Sylvia. Who can blame him for wanting to know where a combination like that came from? "When will I hear from you?" asks Lawford. "When I have something to say," says Maharis, and off he goes to find his way into the first of the film's innumerable and interminable flashbacks.

In Pittsburgh Maharis meets a librarian who remembers Sylvia as a kid crazy about books (flashback to Miss Baker looking a rather world-weary fourteen saying to the librarian, "I want a book, any book") and crazy about fresh flowers (flashback to Miss Baker saying, "Is them flowers real?"), but alas, "her mother died of tuberculosis and she was raped by her stepfather" (flashback to Miss Baker being raped by her stepfather).

And that's only Pittsburgh. Off we go with Maharis to retrace the Sylvian trail to Mexico with a con-man preacher for fun and games (and presumably lots of reading), in Crib Row, then cross-country with a traveling salesman (nose in book, albeit nude in bed in the motel), a chaste life as cashier in a Broadway penny arcade (nose in two books, since she's now using a dictionary), an unchaste life in the house of a "notorious" madame (nose so deep in book that the madame has to yell at her real loud to alert her to a customer's arrival) and a *real* unchaste life as a call girl for a transvestite. And talk about books!

One of her clients, you see, a real Social Register type called Bruce Stamford III, shows Sylvia a book, and gosh, mums, you can bet they'd ban that one in Boston. Sylvia is, frankly, SHOCKED, and when Bruce wants her to make like in the picture, well, he has to drag her into the bedroom and throw crockery at her (or so it sounds from our side of the door). And when they emerge, with Sylvia clutching a shredded negligee and the audience trying to figure out what delicious perversion it didn't get to see, Sylvia says she's going to the police. He has a wife and kids, Bruce pleads —five hundred dollars? But Sylvia thinks people like Bruce "should be locked up." So she settles for ten thousand. She promptly parlays that into seventy thousand in a year in the stock market "and that money meant travel—Europe—and Culture." See how far books—even picture books—can get you?

And so—the two hours aren't up yet—the private eye now arranges to meet Sylvia himself and—oh, forget it—as if you have to be told.

Miss Baker, as usual, brings a cool prettiness and no sexuality to her role, underlining the inference that Sylvia's professional success is simply a matter of plot mechanics. Maharis manages to suggest that he might be worth watching in a role worth acting in a movie worth making. *Sylvia* wasn't.

Too Great To Be Told?
February 21, 1965

Can it be done? If a man of George Stevens' caliber cannot do it, after devoting more than four years and some twenty million dollars to the project and, far more important than the time or money, maintaining high standards of taste and technique, then, I suspect, the story of Jesus cannot be told, at least not in the flesh-and-blood familiar and literal terms of the spectactular American screen.

Mr. Stevens' film *The Greatest Story Ever Told* is not, of course, a "Hollywood Biblical" as we have come to know and despise the genre, even though it has a cast of more than hundreds sprawling into Cinerama dimensions and a long list of name players in less-than-bit and barely-flash-of-the-pan parts. If anything, credit the producer-director with exercising an almost austere restraint to avoid the milling masses, the orgies vile, the stellar focus and the anachronistic values that have turned Biblical tales into spectaculars and thereby instantly diminished them.

But I wonder whether there is not instant diminution when we put a figure of Christ upon the screen. How to personify the mystery and divinity and, once personified, how to make the figure move among men? These are of the imagination, and our traditional filmmakers leave nothing to the imagination. How, then, are they to "visualize" the vision that has endured for centuries primarily within the human heart?

Mr. Stevens has, in his wisdom, chosen not merely an "unknown" actor but a fine one for the role of Jesus. Max von Sydow, an Ingmar Bergman leading man who impressed us in a variety of roles—the knight in *The Seventh Seal,* the father in *The Virgin Spring* and a very different father in *Through a Glass Darkly*, the suicidal fisherman in *Winter Light*—is virtually unknown to the mass movie audience. He is certainly unfamiliar to us here as the dark-haired, blue-eyed aesthetic Christ, his English speech somehow dignified by the faintest tinge of accent. A tall, slightly remote figure of grace in silhouette or meditative close-up, he satisfies us visually and he speaks the words of the Gospel with authority, and the ear is pleased.

But then—and I believe it inevitable even with this excellent actor, who is undoubtedly the most satisfying Jesus we have had on screen—there emerges an aphorism-spouting Confucius-say edge to his speech, an overtone of pomposity. With the switch from the Scriptures to the script, from the language of the Gospel to the vernacular of the film, illusion is shattered. We cannot swallow "If you're the son of God, turn these stones to bread," answered by Jesus with "It is written man shall not live by bread alone . . ." or the Andy Hardyism of James the Less, "I heard what he said last night, and I liked it. If he's going to say anything else, I'd like to hear it . . . What's your name?" "Jesus." "Ah—that's a good name." "Thank you." Or the even more irritating and oh-so-inevitable-in-Biblicals exchange, "I am Judas—Iscariot." And the reply, "I am Jesus—of Nazareth."

Where the dialogue doesn't shatter the illusion the mute Jesus creates, the familiar faces do. We may not have lay associations with von Sydow, but there's Dorothy McGuire as Mary (a peculiarly unchanging albeit beautiful Madonna) and a rheumy-eyed Claude Rains as Herod to set a Hollywood pattern at the outset; there's Charlton Heston, sans chariot, crying in the wilderness, and Ed Wynn as the sightless Aram, and—hey, there's John Wayne as a centurion and it's Shelley Winters yelling, "I'm cured, I'm cured," and that was Pat Boone in Lazarus' tomb and Van Heflin looking awestruck—and bet you a nickel you don't spot Carroll Baker, black wig and draperies and all, on the road to Calvary. Von Sydow can walk in Galilee with mystic illusion; Jose Ferrer cannot, because his Herod Antipas is Ferrer, and he is familiar. Thus all Stevens has accomplished with his "unknown" is destroyed by the faces required, I suppose, for box-office; what is intended as the grandest illusion degenerates into a game of spot-the-star.

The game is easily hit upon in the deadly pacing of the film.

Stevens has resorted to any number of technical tricks—stereophonic sounds that boom voices from figures near or far, a living-statues effect for some scenes, a newsreel-and-stills mixture for others, endless aerial views, all sorts of color toning, a blue-white-green effect predominating so that we cannot tell whether we are in a land of bluebeards or if the men are walking on sand or salt or snow. But no matter how he colors it, despite the ancient cities or villages painted on the distant backdrop, we are painfully aware (courtesy of John Ford movies, perhaps) that we are in Monument Valley, Utah, a good part of the time and elsewhere in our own Far West and that we are there an awfully long time.

We are free to examine the terrain, because the story is being told with awe and reverence and timing to match. We sit in lethargy because there are no insights, no illuminations, no fresh or even specific points of view to stimulate or satisfy the beliefs or disbeliefs we have brought to the film. And because of the very literal repetition of the familiar Gospels, we are thrown by purposeless deviation. When Pontius Pilate (known gratingly in the dialogue as "Governor Pilate") asks what is truth, we know he will not stay for an answer, and so we are free to keep a critical eye out and wonder why he has to go up a flight of stairs for some unheard chitchat with his wife (hey, there—it's Angela Lansbury!) before returning to his desk to resume his not-staying. And distraction of this sort follows distraction. How long can Van Heflin's look of amazement at Lazarus' rising fill the Cinerama-size screen? Why is Mary Magdalene the only woman to wear a brightly colored dress—a red one, at that—or did the women of the time wear red when they went to commit adultery? Can anyone above the first-year Sunday-school class conceive of Pilate saying to Herod, with a grin, "You know, he's actually telling people to love their enemies!"? And why oh why couldn't Stevens or his coauthor, James Lee Barrett, or Carl Sandburg (credited with "creative association" with the production) have avoided that stale old windup of an official remarking, after the Resurrection, "Anyhow, the whole thing will be forgotten in a week," and a bystander, inevitably a sort of intellectual scribe type, replying, "I wonder"?

No, the great big screen and the great big names are too

much for the survival of matters of the spirit. So many aspects of big-movie-making intervene that the Passion cannot predominate. *The Greatest Story Ever Told* is literal but it is also relatively literate and, above all, relatively inoffensive. The point is, of course, that we must speak in relative terms, for Hollywood has yet to go beyond religiosity when dealing with matters of religion and of the spirit.

The Sound
of Marshmallows
March 3, 1965

Does anyone at this point have to be told that Julie Andrews is the most enchanting and compleat performer to come to the screen in years?

Alas, no. A pity. For I would like to take the coward's (or the critic's) out and go on and on about Miss Andrews, about her youth, her freshness, her joyous way with comedy and her gentle way with sentiment—and go on and on and never have to talk about *The Sound of Music*.

Or perhaps I could go on and on about the Alps, the Austrian Alps, or Salzburg, about all the added grandeur and sweep that TODD-AO can add to their grandeur and sweep and medieval beauty. Alas, no. And yet—a pity. Miss Andrews and the Alps and Salzburg are the new cinematic ingredients in the film version of *The Sound of Music*, and it would be nice to concentrate thereon.

But one star and much scenery do not a two-hour-and-fifty-five-minutes-plus-intermission entertainment make, and the issue itself must be faced. Squarely. That is the way to face *The Sound of Music*. This last, most remunerative and least inspired, let alone sophisticated, of the Rodgers and Hammerstein collaborations is square and solid sugar. Calorie-counters, diabetics and grown-ups from eight to eighty had best beware.

Need one offer reassurance that one is all in favor of God, country and motherhood? And can such a decent red-blooded citizen not then be in favor of a sweet and simple madcap novice who, as governess to the seven children of a stern and sorrowing widower, introduces everyone to music and love and music? You bet your sweet sweet sweet sweet life, especially when all that was a sugar lump on stage has, courtesy of the superspectacular screen, become an Alp.

For let me tell you that there is nothing like a supersized screen to convert seven darling little kids in no time at all into all that W. C. Fields indicated darling little kids are—which is pure loathsome. And great big superscreen nuns singing cutely about their naughty, naughty novice begin to border on the ludicrous, and the naughty naughty novice herself becomes just so cute and athletic and righteous and busting out with such tenderness and *jeunesse* and everything so icky sticky purely ever-lovin' that even Constant Andrews Admirer will get a wittle woozy long before intermission time.

What with Miss Andrews and the Alps, *The Sound of Music* might have withstood the transition to a normal screen, but in supercinematic terms its flaws have been spectacularly inflated. Producer-director Robert Wise, who translated *West Side Story* from stage to screen, apparently did not notice that he had nothing to inflate for screen purposes in this venture. The whole schmear consists of those seven kids, their governess, their papa and, for grinding plot purposes, a baroness who, after putting up a brief struggle, sweetly surrenders daddy to the coach. (Yep, those kids don't want a mama; they want the kind of gal who can win a decathlon in a breeze, be a master puppeteer, a Miss Lonelyhearts and a choreographer to set them up in musical-revue numbers that even Busby Berkeley might have thought a little stagy.)

So what's spectacular? Austrian Alps and Salzburg exteriors and studio-made replicas of Salzburg interiors—and these are Mr. Wise's favorite things. And within the scenery the children haven't anything to do besides arrange and rearrange themselves into singing groups, and their elders haven't anything to do besides arrange and rearrange themselves into the mechanics of the plot. Even a hairbreadth escape from the Nazis is done in slow motion and with barely a hint of a chase.

No screen is too large to contain Miss Andrews racing over a glorious landscape in bursts of song with or without seven children in tow on foot, on bikes, in a boat—the devices are innumerable, the literalness of it all abysmal—or to capture the natural and architectural beauties of Salzburg and its environs. But the panorama soon yields to Gargantuan closeups of Peggy Wood's finely aged features—with a vigorous anachronistic contralto attached to her by sound track; of Christopher Plummer's obviously artificial gray hairs, with his stage-bred baritone diction converted in dubbed song into crooner-type treacle; of those kids grinning, frowning, sobbing, sighing and being such wonderful peachy understanding little clods. Blown up by stereophonic sound, the pedestrian lyrics go clump, the melody pounds away out of all proportion, and a pleasant little family singing group is given all the status of the Sistine Choir.

Not, mind you, that Mr. Wise's sights are set consistently high. Abandoning the Alps or Nonnberg Abbey, he is content to settle for pure and simple Hollywood, whether it's Charmian Carr and her beau flitting around a summerhouse in some ersatz Rogers-Astaire contortions (singing "Sixteen Going on Seventeen" while Miss Carr looks all of twenty-one going on twenty-five) or whether it's Miss Andrews and Mr. Plummer silhouetted nose-to-nose in the same old summerhouse, dueting away on a new and undistinguished Rodgers ballad in a fashion unseen since Jeanette MacDonald and Nelson Eddy set it.

Miss Andrews is a trouper all the way, but Mr. Plummer occasionally looks embarrassed. Eleanor Parker is elegant and teary-eyed as the baroness, and Richard Haydn is completely wasted as a cheapjack impresario. The kids, whose presumed sibling relationship would amaze a geneticist, are simply Central Casting's idea of charming children. I hasten to add that in addition to God, country and mother, I am fond of dogs.

The stage version, a sage said, was "for children of all ages, from six to about eleven and a half." Film, however, is a great leveler. The movie is for the five-to-seven set and their mommies who think their kids aren't up to the stinging sophistication and biting wit of *Mary Poppins*—and who can sit still for hours on end.

Two Big "Little" Films
April 25, 1965

Two films have arrived to cut the seasonal swath of Technicolor, the fading rainbow of sleek, slick hour-after-hour productions that frustrate those among us still stalwart enough to dream of cinematic pots of gold for the audience, let alone for the rainbow-maker. They are "little" films—one in the technical and one in the literal sense; above all, they are un-star-studded films, made by men who seemed to have something they wanted to say about people they and we know, ordinary people, not necessarily admirable or despicable, but people who touch upon our lives. Beyond this, the two movies—*The Pawnbroker* and *Nobody Waved Goodbye*—have little in common.

The Pawnbroker was made in New York under Sidney Lumet's direction at a cost of about $1,250,000. This makes it technically a "little" film these days, as does its star, Rod Steiger, a brilliant and bravura actor whose performances in *On the Waterfront* and *The Big Knife* are unforgettable but who, of course, just doesn't rank at the box office the way a Rock Hudson or a Heston does. Nor would its subject matter bring it into the big-league Happy-Happy-as-in-Entertainment category. It is the story of a man who has survived the death camps of Germany with the loss of family, heart and soul, who has learned that people are scum and thus endures, alienated from humanity and feeding off it, in the East Harlem pawnshop he operates as a front for a local racketeer; finally he realizes that by this very rejection of mankind he has brought his concentration-camp world with him, and the realization, prompted by a young man's sacrifice, restores him to life.

The Pawnbroker might have been a great film had the director been able to restrain his dual tendency toward artiness and toward slickness. A stunning sharp-cut flashback technique that brings us fragments of the pawnbroker's tormented memories is used to eye-jarring underlining excess; subsidiary characters become the stock inhabitants of the Harlem cliché, Geraldine Fitzgerald portrays a neurotic pseudo-social worker to no dramatic purpose, and neat melodrama and embarrassing symbolism are invoked to press home a message. But *The Pawnbroker* is nevertheless a remarkable movie, one that achieves soul-harrowing emotional moments, that creates a duality of worlds with fierce impact (a sequence in which a crowded subway car becomes, for the pawnbroker, a cattle car filled with concentration-camp victims is literally stunning). It is distinguished not only by Mr. Steiger's portrayal of a man encased in the world's anguish but also by several other performers and, above all perhaps, by its dealing with its story on its own terms.

Nobody Waved Goodbye is an even more remarkable film, one of the most distinguished offerings at the 1964 New York Film Festival. It was produced by the Canadian Film Board for less than two hundred thousand dollars, with a young Toronto television performer and an equally youthful beginning actress as its "stars." Written and directed by Don Owen, it is done in near-documentary technique but completely without the "hand-held-camera" amateurisms that blight the work of so many young independent filmmakers.

Its distinction is in its story, that of the middle-class delinquent who is so much with us today, the young rebel without any cause beyond his parents' affluence. Here at last is a recognizable figure for the young people who have reported, at least to me, their revulsion at Hollywood's assumption that they "identify" with the near-morons of beach and surf parties and the leather-jackets of more serious C-epics. And here are the parents so many of us are, the siblings and the girl friend and the social workers and all the adults who are at bay, fazed by the "beat" and the revolt against what once epitomized our youthful aspirations.

Here is a young man caught in the momentum of his rebellion, adults trapped in the dilemma of their helplessness—and none is theatrical, each is an individual that we know, a familiar face in the crowd. It is a pity that Mr. Owen too must resort finally to a bit of a cliché, a touch of melodrama to arrive at his conclusion, but it is a conclusion that has power and lasting meaning. With art, he has made a film of appeal and significance to carry it beyond the limitations of the art houses.

Forgotten Audience: American Children
May 2, 1965

Must it be *Mary Poppins* or nothing, as far as our young ones are concerned, and must our concern with children's films be purely seasonal and holiday-oriented?

The question has been raised in the aftermath of spring-vacation movie fare and in anticipation of the long hot summer to come. And its pertinency has been underlined by the revelation (at least to the layman) that came with the recent first New York International Children's Film Festival, the revelation that when it comes to children's films we are indeed an underdeveloped country, our children underprivileged and our filmmakers, to all appearances, uninterested.

In this era of affluence and of permissiveness, we have, in all but cultural areas, bred a nation of overprivileged youngsters, saturated with vitamins, television and plastic toys. But they are nurtured from infancy on a Dick-and-Jane literary and artistic level; and the cultural drought, as far as entertainment is concerned, sets in when they are between six and eight. At some point in these years they are too sophisticated for the shabbily staged amateurism of so much of children's "theater"; they are too jaded with the endlessly repetitive cartoon anthologies offered them again and again, and they are for the most part too young to enjoy to the full the few Hollywood musicals or adventure movies of high quality that come their way—or ours.

I am speaking, at this point, in terms of the selective parent. The unselective will feel that the venal message of an *Unsinkable Molly Brown* or the sexuality and sadism of a *Goldfinger* do not affect a child and that the raucous and colorful characters and music of one and the derring-do of the other provide sufficient entertainment for the young. The selective parent won't—and, settling for a *My Fair Lady*, will be overly conscious that the Shavianisms are way beyond the youngsters; besides Robert Radnitz' occasional films of such children's literary classics as *Misty* or *Island of the Blue Dolphins*, there is the rarity of a *Mary Poppins*, but the more frequent Disney product, like *Those Calloways*, makes the parent put the emphasis on the scenic and wildlife elements and wonder why a child, via the "family" film, must be subjected to the squareness, the stolid soap-opera plotting and the relative lack of imagination that are the hallmarks of the genre. It has been a long time since Disney hit the romantic heights with his *Treasure Island*; none of today's multicolored wide-screen spectaculars seem to capture the Kiplingesque elements that yesterday's children could revel in with *Lives of a Bengal Lancer* or *Four Feathers* or the swash and buckle of a *Captain Blood*.

It is, in fact, a case of *Mary Poppins* or nothing when it comes to films with the touch of imagination, the injection of magic into everyday life, the element of the fantastic that is an essence of entertainment for children. For them it is no major accomplishment that the ragged flower seller of *My Fair Lady* turns into a princess; they know it can be accomplished with the wave of a wand and that all those speech exercises are strictly figments of a grown-up's imagination. What counts—if you observe the children at *My Fair Lady*—is that Eliza wipes her nose on her sleeve, that she salivates at the dangled chocolate, that she screams at the very notion of taking a bath.

But the Children's Film Festival made it clear that in other countries children do not have to settle for the crumbs that drop from adult fare. Movies are being made for them—not, by the way, down to them—movies of quality in production and performance.

For it is indeed a pity to have to report that the one American entry, a short entitled *King Lavra and the Barber*, was a condescending, amateurish and infantile bit of cavorting by semicostumed semiactors in Central Park, devoid of fun, let alone wit and intelligence.

Wit and intelligence are the hallmarks of the foreign feature films in the Festival, particularly of the Japanese, British and French entries. Japan's 1959 *Skinny and Fatty* is the story of a fat, rich, babyish boy who, through the friendship of a poor, skinny boy in his new school, learns to make his own way in the world. It is perhaps the most realistic of the three, for while it is the most exotic in custom and setting, it deals with the elements of children's life—teasing, popularity, the wish to excel, the basic need for a best friend, the values of friendship and of perseverance.

Britain's *One Wish Too Many* (produced in 1956 by the Children's Film Foundation—and there's a foundation for our film industry to ponder on) and France's 1958 *Kite from the Other Side of the World* also have contemporary schoolboys, aged roughly eight to ten, as their heroes. But both have magic—something neither schoolboys nor, in fact, adults will sneer at.

In *One Wish Too Many* our young hero finds a magic marble. Does he wish for palaces and pleasures, millions of dollars, a jet plane of his own, or, as that dismally cute boy in Hollywood's *Dear Brigitte* did without a magic marble, even la Bardot? Of course not. He wishes himself a toy steamroller and a friend a doll; he rescues a pal from a bully and then punishes—and rescues—the bully; he gets his homework done (only to find he can't do the sums in school the next day when the teacher temporarily confiscates the marble), he refurnishes the family sitting room (only to have an irate mother make him restore it because "your dad was fond of his old things") and, finally, he takes his pals on a near-fatal ride in his toy steamroller. No nonsense—just the wild kind of fun and trouble any boy would have with a magic marble.

The French film, beautifully made in lovely colors, has magic enter the lives of a gang of kids of varied ages in the form of an exquisite kite that lands in a tree. We're in Paris in the spring, and there's a hassle and plot and counterplots to get the kite down, a squabble over possession that nets a renegade the tail, the discovery of a letter secreted in the kite from its maker, a boy in Peking. The address of the Chinese boy is in the tail of the kite, however, and until they get it back from the renegade, the leader of the gang dreams of finding the Chinese kite-pal. There ensues a series of enchanting fantasies of voyages, with kid sister in tow, to ancient and to modern Peking, all stylish and romantic, filled with derring-do and wondrous happenings and the logic that childrer. demand (and even adults rarely get in our adventure films) before the happy ending, at which Paris youngsters send the kite on, with their own message to other children in other lands who dream of voyages and friends in foreign places.

There is style and polish to all three films, a love of subject and respect for the audience, even though the costs are obviously minimal. *Mary Poppins* cost six million dollars; the pride of the Radnitz films is that they are made within a budget of slightly less than one million dollars. But what we wish professional moviemakers would note is that Disney's and Radnitz' movies make money. Where, then, are the moviemakers who could do a labor of love—and make a profit at it? Why must the professionals leave the field almost entirely to the inept and the amateur? Isn't there even the economic motive of getting children into the moviegoing habit, of building tomorrow's audience for adult films? When one considers the level of films to which children are exposed, *faut de mieux*, these days, one shudders at the prospect of what the tastes of that tomorrow's audience will be.

In the meantime, let us hope that the Children's Film Festival will become not merely an annual affair but a continuing one, with wise importers bringing us the excellent fare that is apparently being made abroad. This first sampling whets the appetite. Oliver-like, on behalf of the starving kiddies, we ask for more.

They Almost Got Away
May 23, 1965

It's getting so nowadays that not only can't you tell the A movies from the B movies until after you've seen 'em, but you can't judge a movie by its booking.

Time was when one could dismiss the double feature that opened in the nabes when at least one of the films had not played a first-run house on its own, or when you could write off an "uptown" art house's booking of a name-director's unknown early work as an effort to cash in on his present acclaim. Within one recent week we learned that that time is past. Not only did we find a honey of a film half-buried as part of a quickie double bill but we found a double bill composed of movies that could well have stood on their own in any Broadway or other first-run theater. And then in the relatively off-the-circuit New Yorker Theater we had the privilege of seeing an early Fellini film that ranks with a number of his later works that were given much ritzier showcasing for their American debuts.

When the "Premiere Showcase" bit began more than a year ago we realized that this and similar showcase saturation bookings would change the neighborhood-theater pattern. Its economic motive was not merely the touted goodwill gesture of bringing first-run films to the outlanders who obviously weren't making the Broadway trek anymore but also a method of having a greater number of theaters benefiting from the initial publicity accorded a movie.

The trouble is that some films just aren't accorded any publicity. And while, because of showcasing, entire areas are saturated with overpublicized, overblown bombs (so that the outlander is indeed forced to make that Manhattan trek if only to find a decent picture in a revival house), some fine films go unheralded and unsung into the gaps and holes left by the blanket-booking process. They're discovered sometimes, somehow and by any number of someones, but by the time word-of-mouth begins to build an audience, the film has been whisked away into the no-where.

In the nick of time, we were able to catch *The Rounders*—albeit by then it was in a 42nd Street disinfectant den and a male escort was required for the occasion. And by the time we had done our touting of this fine little film, it had passed on to—well, you tell me.

The Rounders is one of those utterly relaxed comedies that make ideal entertainment because there's tender loving care every step of the way and no sweat. You start out with Henry Fonda and Glenn Ford as a couple of bronco busters—"cowboys with their brains kicked out"—and as cowboys, Ford notes, "You could say we ain't the smartest that ever lived," and Fonda, after a pause for thought, replies, "You could say that." Instead of being miscast as Casanova's legacy to sophisticated romance, Ford portrays Ben, the slightly less dumb member of the team, dreaming of retirement to "one of them sandy places" where there would be no grass and therefore no horses. And Fonda, without the restraints imposed by being Mr. President or at least the man charged with winning the war in the Pacific, returns to the easy, pleasingly boyish charm that was his hallmark. As the agreeable Howdy, he is always ready to concede that "whatever suits you tickles me just plumb to death." Their nemesis of the moment is an ornery roan with a penchant for sour mash, and it's their taming of him (and vice versa) that provides the main line as the boys work their heads off only to be outsmarted by the roan or their employer, encounter a moonshiner with two marriageable daughters, get entangled with a couple of dumb blond strippers and try to make their fortune at a rodeo. Nothing major about it—just a bit of sentiment, a bit of pratfalling, wonderful characters and some pure nuttiness—but *The Rounders*, which almost slipped by, will tickle you plumb to death.

A previewer's whisper got us to *A Boy Ten Feet Tall* and *Crack in the World* on time, a double bill that's a joy for adults and youngsters alike. *Crack in the World* is first-rate science fiction, involving the firing of a nuclear missile into the earth's crust—all

in the name of sound scientific research for the benefit of mankind—
and the ensuing spectacular disasters. There are no mad scientists
or monsters to drive grown-ups equally mad; there's the logic
adults like and the superpyrotechnics we all like, with suspense
and holocaust aplenty.

But it's *A Boy Ten Feet Tall* that is of particular interest,
because it's a Disney-type adventure film done in the sophisticated manner by Alexander Mackendrick. We're introduced to
Sammy, a rather babyish British ten-year-old, suddenly orphaned
in an air raid in Port Said during the 1956 Suez crisis. As he returns to his parents' demolished flat, only to see the police bring
out their bodies, Sammy is taken in hand by the family's native
servant. The Egyptian houseboy leads the child to the rear of the
building and proceeds to scold and beat him, venting both spite
and nationalism upon the boy. It's a stunning moment not only
because of its own realism but because we cannot help but be
aware that in an American-made film of this sort the servant would
more likely wind up as the boy's Gunga Din and hand in hand
they'd show brotherhood in action.

But while there is sentiment, there is no sentimentality in the
film. Sammy, knowing only that he has an Aunt Jane in Dur-
ban, sets out to make the five-thousand-mile trek on his own,
and the film is devoted to his encounters with a Syrian peddler,
an American tourist, a Greek guide and finally the fabulous Cocky
Wainwright, marvelously played by Edward G. Robinson, who gets
all the juice out of his role as a diamond smuggler, spinner of tales
and once-great white hunter. Suspense, humor, adventure and
some home truths are embodied in the film—unheralded, long delayed and hacked to near-bits. For this film, made several years ago
and originally close to two hours in length, has apparently knocked
about a bit before being picked up, trimmed by a half-hour and
sent out in a double package. All for the want of marquee-attrac-
tion names, no doubt—or was it for the want of a critical sense on
the part of distributors who just didn't know what a good movie
they had?

Credit the New Yorker Theater's Dan Talbot at least with
knowing what he had with Fellini's first film, *Variety Lights*, which

Fellini wrote and codirected in 1950 with Alberto Lattuada, another then-neophyte who most recently gave us the superb *Mafioso*. For while this story of a seedy, aging top banana who serves as a stepping-stone for an ambitious young soubrette is old-fashioned and almost naïve, it is told with the humor and compassion, the subtlety and sensitivity, and marked by the satiric eye, the keenness of insight, the appreciation of human frailty, that are Fellini's strong points. The film serves too as almost a dry run for a variety of characters and scenes that were developed to masterly effect in later Fellini films, but *Variety Lights* is more than a milestone in a master's works; it stands as a fine work on its own.

Thus distribution and booking patterns turn, twist and offer surprises. And we realize that much as we are at the mercy of the moviemaker, so too our pleasures depend on the distributor and exhibitor. And for those who break the pattern—much thanks.

The Vampingest Gal
June 5, 1965

They don't hardly make 'em like Joseph Losey's *Eva* anymore, not even in Hollywood, not since Elinor Glyn passed from the script scene and Theda Bara quit as head vamp.

But *plus ça change, mes amis.* And now "It was Venice . . . film-festival time . . ." and Jeanne Moreau is there with a pout on her mouth, stroking a cat and trailing a rose and whipping the fool who is in her thrall. "You fool," she calls him. She says, "I told you not to fall in love with me." "Help me," he moans. "I am a full-time exile in my Babylon."

That Miss Moreau, you see, she's about the vampingest gal ever, in anybody's Babylon, always lying about in bathtubs or on beds with her hair messy and a cigarette drooping from her mouth and playing Billie Holiday records on her record player that she

carries around like a pocketbook almost. And for real vamping—
she's always dropping her clothes on the floor and smashing
crockery when she's finished with it and treating men like they're
dirt, just plain dirt. That's high-style vamping, baby, especially
when she's always not letting men sleep with her, like slamming
doors—apartment doors, bedroom doors, bathroom doors—right in
their hungry old faces and insulting them and—coeeee—laughing at them.

Men, of course, find this irresistible, you fools. But do they
send her flowers? Not on your life, baby, or the Marquis de
Sade's either; they send her whips, baby, as souvenirs of happy
times together.

Anyway, Miss Moreau is a very high-priced prostitute playing
the Jet Set circuit (as in Venice . . . film-festival time), and whose
bathtub does she land in, courtesy of a gondola wreck or something, but Stanley Baker's. He's Jet Set as all get-out, a poetry-
spouting Welshman named Tyvian, whose best-seller about coal
mines has just been turned into a film-festival-winning movie.

Well, one slam of the door in his hungry old face, and Baker
is in thrall, especially when Miss Moreau warns, "Don't fall in love
with me." He's busily two-timing his fiancée, Virna Lisi, that exquisite creature and fine actress to whom the dubbers have
attached an all-American-coed-type voice for this occasion. "You
have been seen with a woman who is well known here," his
fiancée's boss tells him. "As a man, you're a fake, and I think
you're a fake as a writer, and I'm going to prove it."

Before he has a chance to, Baker, the fool, is pouring out the
facts to Miss Moreau, about how his brother really wrote the best-
seller. "I stole my dead brother's soul," he confesses. "Did your
brother need it?" the heartless vamp retorts.

So Baker marries Miss Lisi, but he is still in thrall, spending
time and money on Miss Moreau, and when Miss Lisi finds Miss
Moreau gadding about her bedroom, trailing roses and such, Miss
Lisi goes out and kills herself. Baker tries to kill Miss Moreau, but
he's so in thrall he can't, and she gives him a whipping.

This, of course, gets him hooked for life. He winds up as a Jet
Set bum—i.e., "a journalist and tourist guide"—doing the exile-

in-Babylon bit around Miss Moreau while his dead wife's boss reproaches him with "It's only two years, and there's no wreath from you on Francesca's grave. . . ."

It's only three years since Joseph Losey directed the film, no matter how long you may think it has ripened in the can. Mr. Losey has since said it was cut without his approval—and those fifty minutes reportedly cut must have included everything of quality. What we do see of plot, characterization and dialogue is so quintessentially a midadolescence night's dream of how the arty-smarty set must live and love and suffer that we can't imagine there being more of the same even on the cutting-room floor. And all the rococo ins and out of Venice and Rome and angled glass-and-mirror-reflection shots typical of Mr. Losey help not one whit.

Mr. Losey went on to do *The Servant*, and Miss Moreau and Miss Lisi too have gone on to better things. We suggest that this particular past of theirs labeled *Eva* should indeed be buried.

The Madman Among Us
June 27, 1965

Our cinematic terror symbols, among other things, aren't what they used to be. Give us a Lugosian vampire-in-mufti, a Karloffian monster or a non-Kildarian (and therefore obviously mad) doctor, and we're prepared for guffaws.

These days, as a number of psychological thrillers have demonstrated, we'll settle for nothing less than the madman next door who moves among us as one of us, whose sanity we hesitate to question lest we be called upon to prove our own. For the ultimate thrill—beyond the half-serious derring-do nonsense of a James Bond escapade, beyond even the most challenging puzzlements of a slick whodunit—we want a liberal dose of psychological suspense, the nerve-wracking speculation on sanity; for if a man is mad, he leaves his victim no alternatives, the viewer no anticipatory counter-plotting, but if the madness is in doubt . . .

The burden thus has fallen upon the actor. We can, in the psychological suspense story, have no rug-chewing, superhistrionic madness. We can have eccentricity, we can even have hidden horrors, but the madman must be able to pass for sane before the public eye. Thus we needed the public as well as private Milquetoast figure of Richard Attenborough to counterbalance the "peculiarities" of Kim Stanley in *Seance on a Wet Afternoon*; Robert Montgomery's sweetly smiling hatbox-carrying bellhop in the original *Night Must Fall* is chillingly convincing, while Albert Finney's raving, writhing psychotic in the remake of the film destroys credibility; the power of *Mirage* lies in our sharing Gregory Peck's private nightmare in broad daylight, in sunny Central Park, in a glittering office skyscraper, surrounded by everyday people; the thrill of *Symphony for a Massacre* stems from our slow realization that the man we met as merely a shrewd double-crossing crook is a compulsive and ferocious killer following an inexorable pattern. It is, in each case, the actor who must provide the doubt, who keeps us wary, awaiting his next revealing movement or word.

This is Terence Stamp's triumph in *The Collector*, William Wyler's very high-class horror film based on John Fowles' fascinating novel. I have found, oddly, psychological-suspense-film buffs, including admirers of the book, who balk at the movie. The novel was told chronologically, first by the dull bank clerk who has won a fortune in the pools, then through his victim's diary and then, to the horrifying finale, by the clerk. And there unfolds the story of a dreary paranoid weakling, filled with the erotic dreams of the impotent, a butterfly collector who stalks and captures a lovely girl and attempts to keep her for himself alone, hoping that in her imprisonment she will "get to know" him and love him. Fowles saw his book in more than thriller terms, as an allegory, in which the girl "represents good humanity, hope for the future, intelligence and love," and the young man the opposites, "the affluent society in a world where children eat earth they're so hungry. The generous versus the mean. I'm trying to show that our world is sick."

It is Freddie Clegg who is sick, and in the film we see the sickness slowly emerge. First there is the lyric pursuit of a butterfly across green fields, the discovery of the Tudor house, the realization of the use to which its separate dungeonlike cellar can be put; then we watch as he stalks Miranda through the London streets, preparing the chloroform-soaked wrapping, closing the trap. Of his past we get only a flashback glimpse or two; we explore and discover the girl and the man only as they explore and discover each other in the angry exchanges and desperate attempts at communication between captive and warder.

But we know from the start that he is mad, the carpers protest; the symbolism has been given us, and we know that the captured butterfly will flutter vainly in the poison jar, that death is inevitable. And so for almost two hours we watch a living creature being frustrated to death by the stolid compulsion of a madman; what sort of sadistic offering is this?

Perhaps it is as sadistic as the bare-bone detailing would indicate, this painful exposition of wasteful destruction of beauty by a Caliban, by a sniveling, self-pitying, Neanderthal mentality. But Wyler has manipulated the moments so that there is interruption and accident and irony to divert us from the inevitable—and above all, Stamp never lets us bank on the extent of his madness. I hasten to note that Samantha Eggar, a beautiful young woman, is superb in her portrayal of the temperament, the dignity and decency of a generous and vital girl driven to desperation but never to cruelty, a compassionate and understanding girl at bay before the blank wall of a twisted mind.

But it is Stamp, an extraordinary actor, who provides the uncertainty. The chameleon quality of this performer—the golden-haired embodiment of purity as *Billy Budd* on film, the cheaply near-vicious womanizer *Alfie* on stage—is here apparent within a single role. He is one character as the cheaply dressed bank clerk tormented by his fellows, he is awkwardly boyish one moment, a glowering introvert the next, a prancing fool, a soft-souled lover, a steel-eyed murderer. He defies conclusion; is it mad to kidnap and imprison a young woman for one's own purpose? "There'd be a blooming lot more of this if more people had the time and money" is his retort. After all, he is giving his prisoner all that she demands, except her freedom: "Think a madman would have gone to all this trouble?" Salinger's *Catcher in the Rye* is a worth-less book, its hero a boy who, despite "advantages" is "a mess—he doesn't fit," and a Picasso painting "is just a joke, a bad joke" to Clegg.

Are we up against a madman—or is it the voice of the mob, the know-nothing out to destroy what he does not understand? The Picasso reproduction is ripped, the book torn to shreds with a fury . . . and suddenly we see that Stamp has injected a pathos into the fury, and almost against our will the heart is touched, just as Miranda's is. And we join her in the desperate hope against hope that this is not total madness, that somewhere behind those too-blue eyes there is a vulnerability, the spark of sanity remaining.

It is Stamp who raises *The Collector* to heights of parable, who brings significance to and sustains the suspense. His performance is brilliant in its gauge of the madness of a madman.

Triumph of
Style in Comedy
July 4, 1965

It's the rare mediocre movie that isn't too long, whatever its running time, while a good one will keep us in our seats, hoping for another frame or fifty before the lights go on. But I wonder if this last is true when it comes to comedy, whether laughter isn't the one thing that reaches its pleasure peak and cannot be sustained, let alone revived, thereafter.

The early masters of movie comedy knew exactly what they were doing with those one and two reels of film. And for feature-length comedy, note that the best of Hollywood's past, the ones that made the ribs ache, barely carried their chortles past the hour.

Of our recent comedy fare, it's been the personality and his "bit" that has made the moments merry amid the two-and-more

hours of alleged cinematic fun foisted on us with a plethora of
names, color film, fancy trappings. And the rarity of the deep-
rooted guffaw has been matched by the rarity of our cry for more;
we just got out of the habit of lingering hopefully or—heaven for-
fend—wanting to sit through a second showing.

Thus the jolt—and thus the big bang—when within a few days
of each other *Cat Ballou* and *The Knack* arrive on the scene and
high comedy becomes king again by way of a couple of nonblock-
busters, non-name-ridden superglitter movies. And you can't draw
a single pontification from the pair, for they're as diverse a couple
of charmers as the screen can offer: *Cat* is American, *The Knack*
British; *Cat* is traditional, *The Knack* freeform, and so on. The one
thing they have in common is that they were made by men with a
sense of style—and without it the finest of wits and witticisms get
blown to bits, if only by the inflationary process of moviemaking.

It's that very inflation that makes satiric and far-out comedy
so hard to handle on screen. *What's New, Pussycat?* proves it to a
fare-thee-well. On paper that excellent nightclub veteran Woody
Allen has come up with some very funny and very zany comments
on the neuroses of the chi-chi swingers, their analysts, their
mores and their morals; as a ten-minute monologue with the
movie's title on his latest record, Mr. Allen makes the whole thing
hilarious. But as a 108-minute color movie, with Mr. Allen, Peter
Sellers and Paula Prentiss, the only comedians on hand, wallowing
upstream while such noncomedians as Peter O'Toole, Romy
Schneider, Capucine and Ursula Andress come flooding down-
stream, *Pussycat* becomes a frenetic hodgepodge of smutty remarks, tired routines and unpleasant supercamp. One is left with
the feeling that one has been to the dregs of a post-discothèque
party and watched a lot of sick-sick-sick ones at play, alternating
between telling dirty jokes and doing charades of secret camp
words. The movie—or Clive Donner, its director, who gave us the
very funny British *Nothing but the Best* last year—has fallen into
the trap that has caught more than one off-Broadway play, that
of confusing disorganization, pointlessness and tastelessness with
the absurd or the avant-garde.

It takes style and viewpoint and a very thorough bit of organization to give a movie that freeform look—or is it only us cynical girls who know how many hairdressers it takes to tousle Bardot's hair so it looks so marvelously and carelessly mussed? The director may tell his actors to "improvise" in Stanislavsky's best manner—but oh, what hours he has to spend cutting and pasting thereafter!

What distinguishes *Cat Ballou* is that in this Western to destroy our faith in Westerners, nobody is camping, nobody's tongue-in-cheeking and spitballing around. In the title role Jane Fonda is as sweet and pure and earnest as any schoolmarm turned gang leader and man-killer—and it's not her fault that when she slowly canters away astride her horse the one fleeting rear view director Elliot Silverstein permits us makes Miss Jane in her riding clothes infinitely sexier than Miss Andress in bikini ad infinitum. And Lee Marvin—who runs off with the picture and, if there is justice in the contemporary Far West, an Oscar in his dual role of Tim Straun, the silver-nosed evil gunslinger, and Kid Shelleen, the last alcohol-preserved good gunslinger—doesn't yield by the glitter of an eye as he snarls, as Tim, "If you wasn't a girl I'd split you in two like a chicken," or as Kid, by the blear of a drunkard's eye as he recites a eulogy on the passing of the Day of the Gunfighter. And Stubby Kaye and the late Nat King Cole don't miss a pluck of the banjo or a throb of passion as they appear on screen to punctuate each episode with the ballad to explain what's been happening and why they're hanging Cat Ballou in Wolf City, Wyoming, in 1894.

Producer Harold Hecht, Mr. Silverstein and everyone involved in this enterprise have set out to have a brawl with the mythology of the Western and the Noble Indians, gun-toting preachers, cattle rustlers who won't fire guns in anger, and outlaws and cutthroats who don't want to get the local land-development company mad go through their paces, and lecherous Sir Percy goads a clean-cut American girl to murder, thus delighting the wicked sheriff and the temperance ladies with the prospect of a hanging. It's satire of the keenest kind, deadpan—delicious. And organized.

There's nothing overtly organized about *The Knack*, which is about a quartet of disorganized youngsters. Three housemates—

one with the knack of getting girls, one feeling sorely his lack of the knack and the third an imaginative middle-man with a penchant for painting his room—encounter a girl looking for the YWCA. Despite the aggressions of the knackman, we know from the start, fairytale followers that we are, that the timid but nice one yearning for the knack will wind up with it—or at least with the girl.

But Richard Lester, the director who demonstrated his own knack with *A Hard Day's Night*, knows just how to disorganize a fragile little plot to make it a wonderfully rollicking, go-with-the-breeze film. He has a constantly recurring chorus of the sane folks on hand, spouting aphorisms and truisms and shibboleths and nonsense aimed at the entrancing "mods and rockers" we're concerned with. Colin, the knackless charmer, covets a big bed, bigger than the one Tolen, the ladykiller, has; he and the painter, Tom, and the girl, Nancy, played by that utterly exquisite Plain Jane, Rita Tushingham, get a big brass one in a junkyard, and their getting it home through and over and under the streets, across rivers and over automobiles, up alleys and down staircases, is one of the funniest two-reelers we've encountered. Colin's dreams of Tolen's women inundating the house; Nancy's encounter with a seductive dress salesman; Tom's dissertation on how lion tamers tame lions—all absurd, all comic, all gliding about irrelevantly until they come to rest, down-soft, within a framework of completely charming comedy.

There's nothing superambitious, or even ambitious, about either comedy. Both, in fact, have a sort of coziness, a common understanding of what is funny and can remain so in the larger dimensions of the screen.

Our Favorite
Fornicating Cleric
July 16, 1965

The Sandpiper was made for the voyeurs among us who are willing to pay admission to see Elizabeth Taylor and Richard Burton engage in illicit lovemaking in and out of bed and beach. They do it in Metrocolor and Panavision to boot, with some Big Sur scenery, some prefreshman sociological chatter and some ludicrous artsy-smartsy atmosphere thrown in for the higher thinkers in the crowd.

The prevalence of voyeurism and the cash to be derived therefrom provide the only possible explanation for this two-hour travesty which may not be the most perfectly awful movie ever made but which is right down there fighting for the title. Perhaps it was made for connoisseurs of bad movies who will delight in dialogue that reeks, characters that creak and a plot to make the ghost of Elinor Glyn green with envy. Certainly it was not made for the rest of us, who can just sit back and sigh and watch the money roll in for the various people of previous accomplishment who have joined in this jamboree of tastelessness, pretentiousness and unadulterated idiocy with a cynicism and venality that are indeed something to behold.

But wait—a sudden thought. Perhaps *The Sandpiper* is a belated trailer for *Night of the Iguana*, wherein Mr. Burton was a defrocked cleric. Here, as the becollared head of a posh boys' church school as well as husband and father, he is on his way to defrockment, since his affair with the beatnik Miss Taylor leads him to abandon school, wife and kiddies and go in search of a more "meaningful" ministry, preferably in the slums. Or—wait a minute—perhaps it's a moral for our time, this Martin Ransohoff story converted to screenplay by Dalton Trumbo and Michael Wilson: the moral seems to be that there's nothing like a round of adultery to make a clergyman develop a social conscience.

There's Mr. Burton, who is on his way to becoming the moviegoing masses' favorite fornicating cleric, all staid and proper in dealing with Miss Taylor's wayward out-of-wedlock son. Miss Taylor, presented to us as a free-thinking ungirdled eternal bachelor-girl artist ("I turn out watercolors when I need grocery money"), doesn't want her son conventionalized by way of Burton's school, to which a court has consigned him. So it's hate-at-first-sight for the two—but then, on second, or is it third, sight, Burton stumbles upon Miss Taylor posing in the nude for an artist friend (and covering part of her bosom for the family trade), and before you know it—well. Who among us doesn't know it?

Miss Taylor, lovely of face and quite something of figure (Mr. Burton described her at filmmaking time as "zoftig," and we can but concur), favors plunging sweater necklines and stretch pants that leave no bulge or curve unrevealed while she complains that "all my life men have stared at me and rubbed up against me." Mr. Burton, reverting to soft collars, staring and ultimately rubbing, mutters, "O God, grant me some small remembrance of honor," rambles on about the temptations of Jesus and reaches a soul-searing climax in confessing to his wife that "We made love—even in motels, God help me!"

Not, mind you, that all is sex. Miss Taylor, who inhabits a little Big Sur cliff shack that any decorator could throw together for you for a mere bag of shells, like fifty thousand dollars, and her fellow artists drink cheap wine and talk about life, sex, art and philosophy with an enthusiasm and depth worthy of junior high students feeling their first stirrings of puberty. Mr. Burton, on the other hand, devotes himself to fund-raising for a new chapel until, beatified by his—er—contact with Miss Taylor, he decides that scholarships are better than chapels. He also keeps a straight face while he listens to Miss Taylor say things like "I never knew what love was before" and women should have equal rights.

There are some other quondam performers on hand. Eva Marie Saint, wearing high-necked dresses and gloomy makeup in a vain and insulting attempt to make her look like Burton's "older" wife, does little besides Greek-chorus us along with such sprightly lines as "Good morning—you've slept four nights in the library now—it's time we talked." Robert Webber does his nasty bit as a nasty trustee who, Miss Taylor aptly explains to Burton, knew her "in a Biblical sense—he had carnal knowledge of me." And Charles Bronson and James Edwards are around to show how earthy and democratic the beat art world is.

Miss Taylor and Mr. Burton were paid $1,750,000 for performing in *The Sandpiper*. If I were you, I wouldn't settle for less for watching them.

The Platinum Bomb
July 22, 1965

Well, well, well. Leave it to Joseph E. Levine to turn iconoclast.

I mean, here we were going along, purely on the basis of facts, thinking of Jean Harlow as the Hollywood love goddess supreme, on screen the embodiment of warmhearted wisecracking sexuality and off it an ordinary girl victimized, as so many stars have been, by a voracious public and the greed of her family and her employers. But now we have Levine's *Harlow*—and really, it's all so much simpler.

Jean Harlow, a label applied to Carroll Baker for the two hours of the film, was a skinny blond with an ever-loving mommy, an ever-loving stepdaddy, an ever-loving agent, an ever-loving boyfriend and an ever-loving but-just-materialistic-enough-for-comic-relief producer. She had everything, every ever-loving thing. But this girl was a sick, sick, sick kid, with a type sex fixation it shouldn't happen to your daughter. I mean she was a sort of nut in the middle of this other Eden, this demi-Paradise known as Hollywood.

Worse yet, she was a bore, a whining monotoned bore. "Oh, Mama, all they want is my body. . . . I don't want my career to begin and end on a couch." Ever-loving Mommy says, "I knew you were too young for this business," and her ever-loving agent says, "You have the body of a woman and the emotions of a child." But neither of them has the wit to get her to suck her thumb, because then maybe Jean Harlow could have grown up to be Carroll Baker.

As it is, despite paint, wigs and gowns that along with period automobiles seem to put the film into a sort of never-never-thirties world, Miss Baker never quite grows up to be Harlow. But then, beyond the use of her name and those of her mother, stepfather, first Hollywood husband and press agent, there's little attempt to stick to the Harlow story, with or without the scandalous elements provided by the Irving Shulman book on which the film is officially based. The actual story might have provided a basic amount of drama, drama sadly lacking in the soporific tale John Michael Hayes has offered as a screenplay distinguished only by the studied imbecility of its dialogue.

We're left with the tired and tiresome tale of a sex-shy Actors Studio-type neurotic trying to make it in sex-crazy Hollywood; she graduates from slapstick (Mack Sennett seems to be making comedies in the thirties on sound stages for this one) to sex-symbolism and finally big-studio stardom ("The time has come for us to start making sex films for the family," says her ever-loving producer, a sort of sweet comedy-relief L. B. Mayer stereo). This makes her non-sex-shy: "A bedroom with only one person in it is the loneliest room in the world," she phrase-coins.

Given a choice between a sexy hard-drinking star (he takes her to prizefights) and a non-sexy sober studio executive (he takes her to concerts), she marries the executive for no apparent reason and then gets hysterical when he proves to be impotent. When he then kills himself, she goes into a sex-and-alcohol frenzy, even trying to seduce Mommy's husband, who thereupon reveals that he isn't the lecherous leech she (and we) thought he was but simply an ever-loving stepdaddy. "I am not unprincipled," he says firmly.

Obviously this Jean is a sick kid, even though all kinds of girls and department-store dummies are wearing platinum-blond wigs just like Miss Baker's and people are lined up in front of her movies—not one of which bears the name of any that Jean Harlow ever appeared in. But she solves everybody's problems by racing out to the beach to wallow in the sand in her nightie and contract pneumonia as a prelude to one of those under-the-oxygen-tent-without-makeup death scenes with that inevitable bystander to flatly contradict the doctor's diagnosis with a bit of sententious slop. "She didn't die of pneumonia—she died of life," is the kiss-off here.

And thus Hollywood has again succeeded in reducing one of its few fascinating realities to the sleazy, turgid level of its more sordid fictions. Nowhere in story or setting does the film capture the atmosphere or even the prosaic details of the Harlow era of moviemaking, nowhere is there a suggestion of the personal Harlow mystique.

The last is, of course, attributable to Miss Baker, who, despite a two-year sex-goddess build-up, still is more bomb than bombshell, and *Harlow* as a whole becomes a giant dud.

And so endeth—we hope—the great Harlow hysteria.

Less Showmanship
and More Taste
July 25, 1965

What we need, a seasoned movieman was telling us the other day, is less quotation of the critics to plug a movie. We need a return to showmanship, to the big promotion, to the gimmickry and gaggery that made like all the time was circus time. That's the way, he insisted, to get the mobs back into the moviehouses.

This spring the Screen Publicists Guild named Joseph E. Levine showman of the year, crediting him with reviving the glamour mythology of Hollywood, bringing back the mood (if not the day) of the moguls. I dare say they had in mind the foreign blockbusters, the Sophia Loren and Marcello Mastroianni costarrers, the record-grossing *The Carpetbaggers* and the long-touted *Harlow*. But I think my movieman's notion of showmanship would, in Mr. Levine's case, be in terms of his precultural pre-Carroll Baker enterprises, when he scattered in his lavish wake solid-chocolate Hercules dolls graven in Steve Reeves' image, pocketwatch wall clocks inscribed "Watch Out for Jack the Ripper" and little kiddie-sized medical satchels pierced through with a bloody rubber dagger and a note also advising us to watch out for guess-who. That was Levine showmanship of a sort unmatched until quite recently. Under the auspices of other film men, girls in bikini-and-net outfits with long swinging tails and feline masks to hide their identity (and/or blushes) went around town proclaiming themselves "Pussycats" for the benefit of guess-what, and the opening of *The Hallelujah Trail* was celebrated by the classiest and most lavish barbecue ever thrown in a parking lot on West 51st Street.

If this is a resurgence of showmanship—ah, yes, there were popguns as invitations for *A Shot in the Dark* and sweatshirts bearing a legend about John Goldfarb and the seal of Fawz U. (which made nasty-minded mothers hesitant about letting the young wear them) and lip-shaped celluloid pins urging the world at large to kiss-me-stupid in eleven languages—if this is showmanship, let's beware. Greeks and press agents bearing gifts usually have a dubious movie in the can behind their backs.

It has, in fact, become almost a truism among movie-anticipators, professional and amateur alike, that the more boola-boola, the more personal plugging and junketry and the bigger the prerelease build-up of a movie, the likelier the letdown. I often wonder if *Cleopatra*'s thud would have been as resonant if the film had arrived much in the manner of a *Genghis Khan* or even *Fall of the Roman Empire*. It's a rare show indeed that can survive showmanship *in extremis*.

But paradoxically, we resent the showman's letting a movie of value sneak up on us. We love, of course, to pat our own shoulders and crow with the delight of discovering a "sleeper," but when all is said and done, it's the industry man—producer, distributor or exhibitor—who's been doing the sleeping. *The Rounders* and *A Boy Ten Feet Tall* came upon us totally unheralded through major studios. So did an exquisite independent production like *The Winner*, Reichenbach's lovely, glowing, lyric story of a young Senegalese boxer's discovery of himself and of Paris, perfectly arranged

for American audiences by Noelle Gillmor's excellent English
soundtrack (not dubbing, mind you, but the first successful breakthrough of the film language barrier). Scorned last year by the
New York Film Festival authorities on the technical excuse of its
not having its "original" soundtrack, this beautiful film was on the
market for almost a year before it was finally booked by an art
house and, unheralded and unsung, lingered all too briefly.

Well, money, money, money. No trouble booking a Taylor-
Burton sextravaganza, a too-tired-even-to-suds-up big-name World
War II soap opera or a near-nudie foreign mediocrity. Let the other
items kick around until there's an emergency, and then—maybe.
That's showmanship, man.

In 1961 Joseph Losey made a movie called *These Are the
Damned*. It was released in England two years later, shown at the
Trieste Festival last year. It's a mixture of sociology and science
fiction, a melodrama spiced with undertones of incest and over-
tones of sadism, a passionate statement against the dehumanization
of man in any acceptance of the inevitability of nuclear annihilation and, strangely, a forceful suggestion by way of the plot that
those who do not accept it are damned, or at very least doomed.

It bears, as do *The Servant* and *King and Country*, Mr. Losey's
hallmark, and by that I do not mean, as so many of his devotees
do, his penchant for mirror-photography or for symbolism that a
cultist can run into grounds I am sure the director never explored.
To me this expatriate American's hallmark is his ability to tell an
engrossing story in such powerful cinematic terms, to fascinate us
so visually that we can forgive even major lapses—not such super-
major and prolonged ones as in his *Eva*, of course, but his occasional touch of the artsy-smartsy or the banal.

Just as *The Servant* can, as I noted on its release, stand as a
story of two men in a house and let the viewer do all his fantasizing
and symbol-finding and moral-gleaning, so *These Are the Damned*
offers a fascinating story that despite its various imperfections
holds your interest every step of the way—and packs a final wallop
that will stay with you.

You're hooked at the outset with the rock-and-twist chant—
"Black leather, black leather, crash crash crash crash—black leather,

black leather, smash smash smash"—fronted with a juvenile and menacing motorcycle group of Teddy boys; their leader's sister serves as decoy to land an American tourist, and they smash smash smash orgiastically, taking his wallet.

Passersby bring the battered victim to a café, where a detached, somehow official older man and a beautiful worldly-wise sculptress have been talking about her again using a studio on his property. He had not expected this kind of attack in England, the American notes. "The age of senseless violence has caught up with us, too," the older man replies. The American leaves them and conversation resumes; we gather that the sculptress and older man have been lovers but that his present "secret" work has alienated them. She seeks a hint; to know his work, the man replies, would be to condemn herself to death.

The American, the Teddy boys and the girl meet again in nerve-tingling circumstance; always with the threat of present violence we are given hints of the terrible work the older man is conducting and, suddenly, again with terror and accident and the constant immediate threat to life, everyone is involved in the secret, with nine innocent children at the heart of the horror. The ruthlessness of the fanatic older man is counterpointed to the weary humanism of the American; the devotion to creative life on the part of the sophisticated sculptress is juxtaposed to the nihilism of the leather-jackets, and the children talk of "the black death," the rabbit that died, the warm-bloodedness they yearn for. Are they and their master the damned—or are those who must die for trying to save them?

Lack of big names? Macdonald Carey, Shirley Anne Field, Viveca Lindfors, Alexander Knox—we've had lots less on marquees. And yet the film has lingered in a major studio's hands, a remarkable movie unsold and, when finally sold, unsung, to be discovered in a 42nd Street grind house or on the bottom of a light-topped double bill at a neighborhood house.

Is it lack of showmanship? Or is it, perhaps, a lack of interest or a lack of courage in coping with a film that sticks to the ribs, that bothers you in its implication, that makes you do some of the work of interpreting what you have watched? Put any name on it. Showmanship, sensitivity, guts—certainly something is needed if a film like *These Are the Damned* can slip in and out of storage without anyone hearing a single feeble sound of trumpets, while Pussycats roam the town.

Grand Hotel at Sea
August 8, 1965

Somebody out there is remaking *Stagecoach* with ads in the trade papers about how even the greatest of classics can use updating. This apparently means wide screen and color and the casting of Ann-Margret as a latter-day Claire Trevor, Alex Cord as a neo-John Wayne and Bing Crosby as a sub for Thomas Mitchell, with Gordon Douglas, whose most recent work is *Harlow*, replacing John Ford at the directorial helm.

So if you can redo *Stagecoach*, why not *Grand Hotel*? They have, of course, been redoing *Grand Hotel* every year on the half-year ever since that first blueprint for centrally housed and very high class soap opera appeared in 1932. But certainly the classiest remake of them all is Stanley Kramer's *Ship of Fools*.

The initial mark of "class" is, of course, that the Abby Mann screenplay is based on Katherine Anne Porter's novel, one of the most highly acclaimed and, according to its latter-day derogators, least read best-sellers of 1962. Whatever the novel is or isn't, its bones are visible in the screenplay. Bones are, after all, what you have left when you take away a writer's writing—a privilege for which Mr. Kramer paid some five hundred thousand dollars. And did he finally face the frequent Hollywood dilemma, finding himself with a title—and little else of the stuff to make movies on? If so, he half-solved the problem by casting, by evoking several performances of such quality that from time to time we forget the inertia, the banal dialogue, the clichés of script and character. It is, after all, performances that immortalized *Grand Hotel*.

What we have to animate *Ship*'s bones is Mr. Mann's writing and Mr. Kramer's direction and a handful of brilliant performances, and we hasten to agree that no screenwriter can cram a fifty-character five-hundred-page novel, distinguished for its writing rather than its plot or drama, into a two-and-a-half-hour movie without taking certain liberties. But the transformation of Miss Porter's perceptive and pessimistic examination of the failure of Western man into a plotless *Grand Hotel* on the high seas is less than we expected from either writer or director, less than the author deserves.

This is, let's note, old hat decorated with social significance, the latter something we have come to expect from Mr. Kramer, who has established himself as that rarity, a moviemaker willing to comment on the state of society. But it is, after all, a little late in the day for those too tidy ironies about how no one really took the Nazis seriously or expected Germany's Jews to be exterminated, least of all the Jews themselves. We're right back with "The Archduke has just gone to Sarajevo, so, of course, there will be no war this year" or "Oh, what a peaceful Sunday—there's nothing like Pearl Harbor in December!" Neither topicality nor logic affects the Kramer-Mann polemic: on his German ship in 1933, when Jew and dwarf are segregated in the dining room and even a German found to have a Jewish wife at home is banished from the all-German captain's table, the Jew and the most vocal Nazi aboard get along just fine as cabinmates—except, ha ha, for the Jew's snoring. And when a crude Texas ballplayer (a non-Porter creation) says to his tablemate, a self-centered Virginia divorcée, that the Jews were not bothered "back home," Kramer's Southern lady retorts, "Maybe you were too busy lynching Negroes to take time out for the Jews," a remark one would scarcely attribute to even the more enlightened Southern ladies of the time and one Miss Porter attributed to a young socially conscious artist.

But the ballplayer is played by Lee Marvin and the Southern lady is played by Vivien Leigh—and Simone Signoret and Oskar Werner are aboard—and before you know it, polemics to the side, we're elevated to the *Grand Hotel* level. As a matter of fact, we were placed there at the start by Michael Dunn, a shrewd-eyed

antic dwarf telling us with significant mien that we are aboard
"a ship of fools" and might find ourselves among them, and acting
as a Greek chorus and man-about-the-deck thereafter. And in no
time at all we are given the Garbo-John Barrymore mystique,
with the world-weary ballerina and the declassé nobleman trans-
muted into Simone Signoret's drug-addicted revolutionary contessa
and Oskar Werner's cynical ship's doctor suffering a fatal heart ail-
ment. "Are you happy?" Signoret asks. "Who's happy?" Werner
replies. "You're strange—sometimes you're so bitter—yet you're
so soft and warm, like a child," Werner says. "I'm just a woman,"
Signoret replies, and by George, the two of them can go through
this and any number of banalities and break your heart every step
of the way, right through Werner's, "She's the only real thing that
has happened to me" and Signoret's bravado as she disembarks
for exile in Tenerife and he stays on board to die quite literally of a
broken heart.

Their performances—let us say "as always," even though we
know Werner only through *Jules and Jim, Decision Before Dawn* and
Lola Montez—are impeccable, a triumph of casting. There is perfection in Vivien Leigh's "forty-six-year-old woman with a six-
teen-year-old heart" terrified at the loveless aging that is driving
her toward degradation, in Marvin's bumbling lecherous ballplayer
writhing over his inability to "hit a curve ball on the outside
corner," in Dunn's puckish aplomb, in Heinz Ruehmann's opti-
mistic and superpatriotic German Jew. These players put some
flesh upon the bone. All else seems to rattle—a pair of screechy
young lovers (let the actors be nameless), the Spanish dancers
(a terrifying troupe in the original) apparently on hand only to
provide some nonverbal activity, as well as a heart-of-gold prostitute who initiates the fumbling schoolboy with "Tell me, am I
your first girl? The first time is very important. . . ." And there's
even a plump, plain schoolgirl to be converted into a charmer by a
borrowed evening gown. And incident after incident, significant in
the character delineation emphasized in the book, becomes a matter of contrivance, of over emphasis—of shouting a truism where the
novelist whispered a truth.

There are those who contend that movies, by their very tech-

nique of magnification, vulgarize and broaden, and that we cannot
condemn the moviemaker, who must simplify his material so
that the enlargement will be clear. Even if we grant this, we cannot excuse the oversimplification, the soapiness, the sheer boredom
of so much of this latest Kramer production. Despite the aspirations
of his title, Mr. Kramer has done little beyond floating *Grand Hotel*
out to sea, with a handful of brilliant performances to keep it
above water.

Giulietta of
the Rare Spirit
November 7, 1965

There are the boys and the girls and the sexpots and the men,
but there's been a recurrent dearth of women in our screen fare.
By women I mean very specifically female adults and would, in
fact, be willing to settle for adult females.

The dearth—and I suspect it is of actresses as well as of material—is reflected in the fact that more and more serious movies
are skimping on the female role or skipping it entirely: consider
the all-male (except for a glimpse of the commandant's bedmate)
cast of *The Hill* and of *King Rat*, in which writer-director Bryan
Forbes resisted the book-given opportunity to oil up the box office
with even one Malaysian beauty. Even bleak war dramas have in the
past boasted a chesty cabaret bit or a camp-follower scene or two.

Directors of taste seem to be deciding to bypass the obvious.
But let's consider *The Cincinnati Kid*, which is *The Hustler* in
spades, poker replacing pool as the showdown game. Again the
match is between an aspiring youth and an established champ, with
a gambler providing the suspenseful triangle. In the card melodrama they've substituted Steve McQueen, Edward G. Robinson
and Rip Torn for the Paul Newman, Jackie Gleason, George C.
Scott poolroom trio. *The Hustler*, made a mere four years ago,

also boasted a major female figure, the crippled girl so sensitively portrayed by Piper Laurie. *The Cincinnati Kid*, however, which offers one of the best poker games on film, eliminates women as anything but box-office attractions—goodness knows, nothing but a box office would be attracted by the short-lipped poutings of Tuesday Weld, the almost antisexual cardboard-and-suet-meringue posturing of Ann-Margret. And, as if to underline the clawless felinity of these two sex kittens, there is Joan Blondell as Ladyfinger, an overripe poker dealer who's played the circuits and the boys thereon and whose every gesture in this minor role exudes the mystique of the grown-up woman.

It is, perhaps, Simone Signoret who has become the embodiment of female maturity on screen, the eternal Eve wearied by her own eternities, a modern Minerva sated with the disillusion of her wisdom. Miss Signoret conveys all this by her very presence and with Oskar Werner as her counterpart in weltschmerz brought whatever little quality there was to *Ship of Fools*. (And I wonder whether it is not too late to suggest that we tend to overrate both their performances because of the kvatch that surrounded them in that pretentious and pointless film?) Here we have the actress—but where is the material?

Certainly *Darling* has dealt with a woman of our times, but primarily as a girl becoming a woman, a creature of human potential caught into the attitude and the ego of a shiny society and ending up more creature than human. We had our own *All About Eve*; there has been the superb Sophia Loren of *Two Women* and the superb Sophia Loren of *Marriage Italian Style*.

And now there is the Giulietta Masina of *Juliet of the Spirits*, Federico Fellini's new film. At first glance it could be described as a female version of *8½* in Technicolor; here we explore the psyche of a woman, shattered by the loss of her husband's love, in search of survival. And at first glance—and the eyes and mind cannot leave the screen for the film's two and a half hours—it is indeed the most beautiful color film we have seen, a proliferation of the mood imagery and startling symbolism that distinguished *8½*. Progressively—as she tastes her husband's indifference, suspects and then confirms his infidelity and finally realizes that she has lost—

Giulietta retreats into a daydream world and seeks comfort and advice in seances, from fantastic gurus, from vicarious participation in a hedonistic paradise next door and in memories. Anyone familiar with Fellini's work can almost, but not quite, imagine the range this provides his wit, his wisdom and his creative talents. For cinematic brilliance *Juliet of the Spirits* is at very least the equal of *8½*.

But this new film surpasses its black-and-white predecessor in one important aspect. It has warmth and compassion, and these are provided by Miss Masina. The one flaw in *8½* always seemed to me to be its dispassionate intelligence, its cool emphasis on the appeal to the eye and the mind; splendid as Marcello Mastroianni's director was, he was a man who held our interest only on the surface; his problems appealed to the mind, but neither they nor his fate touched the heart.

Here Miss Masina is transcendent. The battered, wise wife of *Variety Lights*, the pathetic prostitute of *Nights of Cabiria* and the heartbreaking clown of *La Strada* has come of age. Familiarly, the lips purse and the soft rounded chin still rises with the appealing child's strength that is uniquely hers, the smile is still joyously vulnerable, the eyes wide with poignancy. But they are a woman's eyes, those of a little girl grown up to the dependency that is the motif of so many lives—a dependency on a love that has become a habit, on the saints and sins established in childhood, on the domination of family, on the social circle that encloses nothing.

Fellini, through Miss Masina, explores the universals of frustration and desire, of the concrete symbols of the public life one leads and the fantasies of private existence. The two are beautifully blended: one early sequence, for example, as Giulietta daydreams on the beach, discloses that a surreal, phantasmagoric Freudian caravan is but a household outing.

But most important, through the fantastic we get to know a flesh-and-blood woman, glowing with affection, quick to anger, unashamed of her pruderies, finally willing to fight her own devils and discover her own strengths. There is, innately, a gentleness, a childlike wonder about Miss Masina; no matter how high the fashion that clothes her, she manages to look a tiny bit blowsy, to retain a simplicity amid the cynical complexities in which Fellini wraps his tale. She is a woman who is among us—a rarity on screen, a rare and wonderful creature in *Juliet of the Spirits.*

The Eleanor
Roosevelt Story
November 9, 1965

"There are fairy tales in all the tongues of the world about children who live under the spell of sleep in a magic prison surrounded by thickets and thorns: a prison from which they are one day awakened by a touch, to turn into shining figures of life. No one knows how they become what they are at the end—only that they are."

Thus Archibald MacLeish begins his chronology of Sidney Glazier's documentary film, *The Eleanor Roosevelt Story.* It is, appropriately, a poet's tale, this biography of "an unhappy little girl in a lost family in a vanished world" who became the universally beloved First Lady of our century. It is equally, however, a historian's tale, for Eleanor Roosevelt's story is in large part that of modern America, spanning the transition from that vanished Victorian world into the turbulence and complexities of our time.

The triumph of this feature-length documentary, culled from still photographs and newsreel footage gathered from all parts of the world, is its application, through Mr. MacLeish's script, of the poetic eye to the historic fact. The result is a compassionate but unsentimental portrait worthy of his subject, a vivid reconstruction of a fascinating and inspiring life.

The hallmark of the film is, for me at least, a photograph of that "unhappy little girl" Mrs. Roosevelt herself recalled, the bruised-looking mouth and pudgy nose justifying the label (if not its application) of ugly duckling in a family of beautiful women; but the eyes, the loneliness-haunted eyes, already have the searching and unflinching honesty that was to distinguish a lifetime. It is among the first of countless family-album photographs with which the film re-creates the wealthy nineteenth-century society milieu into which Eleanor Roosevelt was born and lived a childhood and girlhood of lovelessness and social deprivation more befitting a Dickensian waif than an offspring of one of New York's Four Hundred.

Throughout the film the narration is shared by Mr. MacLeish and Eric Sevareid, with frequent recorded comments by Mrs. Roosevelt, but in the early segments there are recollections by Mrs. Francis Cole, Mrs. Roosevelt's first cousin and childhood friend. It is Mrs. Cole's genteel voice that brings so much of the early years to life as she recalls: "They were a pretty lot—her aunts and her mother, above all, her mother, whose clothes she loved to stroke. But her mother preferred her little brothers and showed it and called her 'Granny' because Eleanor was so old-fashioned," or remembers the house the orphaned Eleanor later lived in with her grandmother as "the darkest, most desolate house I have ever seen," or that the wedding of Eleanor to Franklin Delano Roosevelt, on March 17, 1905, "was a most exciting affair, with the bridesmaids—I was one—in cream taffeta."

With marriage Eleanor Roosevelt became what she herself described as "a fairly conventional, quiet young society matron." But with World War I, with her husband's service as Assistant Secretary of the Navy, the world into which she was born vanished, and Mrs. Roosevelt became a participant in the one that emerged.

The rest is history, seen through the activities and words of a woman whose new awareness of social ills and social action led to a guiding thesis that "What one has to do usually can be done." There was the campaign with Wilson for the League of Nations, a defeat for Roosevelt as the Democratic vice-presidential candidate in 1920 and a return to "domesticity" until the personal tragedy of her husband's paralysis. Her fight to restore him to a socially and politically active life, his governorship of New York, his first presidential campaign, follow.

We see Mrs. Roosevelt as the peripatetic First Lady, fighting the fears and problems of the Depression, entering the field of controversy in her fight for racial equality. We see Marian Anderson singing at the Lincoln Memorial as a guest of the United States, we see Mrs. Roosevelt speaking plainly of the growing dictatorships, facing the American Youth Congress with candor and courtesy, covering the war fronts with unflagging energy, fighting for the peace as a private citizen, a United Nations delegate and a world figure.

"She was a 'great lady,' as everyone kept saying over and over—'the first lady of the world,'" the narrative concludes, "but what the world found in her was a woman—a warm, completely honest, fearless woman who lived a woman's life, accepted a woman's responsibilities and changed the history of her time."

The Eleanor Roosevelt Story presents us with this woman.

Hildur's Wedding
Day and Night
November 15, 1965

Small wonder that the Swedes are notorious for their extramarital affairs if *Swedish Wedding Night* is a sample of what the formalities engender. Or, speaking cinematically, rather than sociologically, do the film's sponsors feel that after all those simpleminded little Ingmar Bergman fun films we are ready for some really serious down-to-earth Scandinavian cinema?

"Earthy" is, in fact, the sponsors' term for this chronicle of a rural wedding celebration, and earthy apparently means some quick flashes of flesh, lots of nuzzlings and clutchings, a couple of seductions, a suicide and an overall atmosphere of such gloomy frustration as to make Strindberg at his starkest read like a Marx Brothers scenario. And all of this earthiness is shoveled at us at so monotonous and tedious a pace, with such incoherence of plot and befuddlement of character, that one can barely stay awake to see the nudes flash by.

Gloomy dawns Hildur's wedding day, with a mysterious stranger prowling around the barnyard. A teary-eyed Hildur, who is to marry a butcher named Hilmer, explains to her glum-faced mother, yclept Hilma, that she is pregnant by Martin, their erstwhile farmhand. Hilma tells Hildur not to mind Hilmer's drinking and to be kind to Hilmer's daughter, Siri. Hildur's sister, Irma, then makes it clear via quick puffs on a cigarette and hollow eyes that she is jealous of Hildur because she had no one to marry when she was pregnant and because she had a yen for Martin herself. Hildur's father stays up in the attic; it turns out later that he is in love with a dead cow.

Meanwhile, at the bridegroom's happy homestead, Hilmer tells his housemaid that she sure can't prove that he got her pregnant (neither can we, since we've watched her rouse herself from the bed she enthusiastically shares with a farmhand), while daughter Siri lounges around naked (quick angled shots here, boys) holding monologues about what a nubile virgin she is.

And so the stage is set for high drama, with Hildur marking time until the nuptials, trying to lure Papa out of the attic, Hilmer getting himself plastered and Hilma luring an aged and apparently demented opera singer out of the local sanatorium to sing at the wedding.

Then things really get going after the ceremony, what with the liquor flowing and passions unleashed in yard and loft. By the time Hildur is ready to climb into the marriage bed, Martin (yes, for the mysterious prowler proved indeed to be he, dear reader) has hanged himself in the loft, Papa is asleep in the stall of his dear departed cow, Siri has been seduced by a hobo who confides that he is a murderer on the lam and that it wasn't much fun devirginizing her, the opera star is back at the sanatorium having a fatal hemorrhage under the ebullient ministering of a fellow inmate known as Loony-Anders, and Hilmer has passed out cold on his way to bed. So naturally the best man does his (or Hilmer's) duty, and that, a poetic-type voice tells us in a series of poetic-type subtitles superimposed on poetic-type scenery, is how the kneck brod crumbles.

If you can bear to think back on all of this, you realize that there have been flashes of perceptive performance from several players, a number of interesting faces and some moments of impressive photography along the way. But why bother?

Don't Just Twinkle, Rise and Shine
December 5, 1965

And where did *you* come from, movie star dear, out of the nowhere into the here? All of a sudden it's George Segal and Ann-Margret, and why doesn't anybody tell us about Harry Andrews, and where was everybody when Lee Marvin was putting it right on the line for all to see?

The query is perennial in these latter days of starmaking, when there are no longer paternalistic studios to nurture and train the talented and keep on hand a reliable company of character actors to provide the background. Instead we have the instant-star system, whereby we have a ready-made "personality" foisted upon us; beyond the instant stars, there are the reliables or, we more often suspect, the relatives, for yeoman service. What the teen-agers like, the grown-ups get, and the common denominator is more often than not the lowest.

These ponderings have been prompted by a series of recent experiences and the looming consideration of the best performers, let alone the best films, of the past year. The New Yorker Theater's recent Marlon Brando cycle, for example, steered our thoughts into that question not simply of star presence but of the performer who transcends his material. Beyond his early vehicles— *On the Waterfront, A Streetcar Named Desire, Viva Zapata!*— and with the later exceptions of *The Fugitive Kind* and *One-Eyed Jacks*, Brando has invariably stood apart from the quality of the film, our attention riveted on him, our expectation high and almost invariably rewarded. That semantically obnoxious "almost invariably" is prompted by foul memories of *Bedtime Story*, wherein Brando's venture into fey comedy, involving primarily an apelike impersonation of a mentally retarded nobleman, was, to say the least and even avoid noting his unfortunate juxtaposition to David Niven, disastrous. No matter what muck surrounds him, however, whether it is the vapidities of *The Young Lions* or the inanities of *Morituri: Codeword Saboteur* (or whatever name that movie was ultimately stuck with), Brando retains his stature, enhanced by our conviction that here is one of the fine actors of our time. (Is it heresy to suggest that eventually our loyalties will falter? How long can a conviction endure without being put to the test—or, perhaps, how long can an actor refuse the challenge of finding a vehicle worthy of his demonstrated abilities?)

Brando came in at the top and stayed there, and yet it is not the star mystique alone; the excitement is there, the potential apparent in every minor move and gesture. It's there and always has been, really, with a number of nonstars. Where did Lee Marvin come from before his burst of comedic glory in *Cat Ballou* and a repeat thereof in *Ship of Fools*? A year earlier he'd been on screen in *The Killers*, as a good gray gunman looking for the big haul as a prelude to retirement, and a year before that as a brawling sidekick for John Wayne and *objet d'amour* for Dorothy Lamour in *Donovan's Reef*, and all along, we're told, he'd been great guns (badman guns) on television. But ten years earlier there was *Violent Saturday*, and if you just ignored Victor Mature, the nominal star thereof and surprisingly easy to ignore, you could concentrate on Marvin as a benzedrine-sniffing hood, catch his every nuance, watch his perfect pace, revel in a superb monologue on the skinny broad he married whose perpetual contagious colds gave him the benzedrine habit. And you realize, watching this performance, that Marvin stood distinct and apart from the maudlin melodrama swirling around him. A pity we had to waste ten years watching any number of "stars" do ineptly what he had clearly mastered long ago.

Can you keep your attention from Rod Steiger, whatever the scene? There is a sense of completeness in each of his portraits, major or minor, from his cringing triumph as the producer in *The Big Knife* to the groping, untidy psychiatrist in *The Mark* to the

searing excesses of *The Pawnbroker* and the very high camp of
The Loved One. We can trace the origins of Anthony Quinn's final
strength from his first tango with Rita Hayworth in *Blood and Sand*
and all the minor gangster roles that come before and after.

Now our eye is fixed on Harry Andrews, given his top role to
date as the brutal sergeant major in *The Hill.* On another screen
down the street he was doing the fancy-dress as Bramante, the
anti-Michelangelo chap in *The Agony and the Ecstasy,* and he
stood apart with authority amid the vacuities. At the moment he's
in a thoroughgoing piece of foolishness, *Sands of the Kalahari,* a
man-meets-baboon sort of epic, with the baboons coming out on
top even, with few exceptions, when it comes to acting. But watch
Mr. Andrews, as an old German hunter wise to the ways of flora,
fauna and human fools; he holds your eye in his every scene and
demonstrates, moreover, that he is one of the most versatile newcomers to the screen.

Andrews, Marvin, add Richard Attenborough and Dirk Bogarde—all men who have invariably provided excellence in their
varied screen roles, with the flicker of stardom only at the end of the
long haul. Add James Fox and Tom Courtenay. And by their pro-
pinquity, how they make the instant stars diminish. Certainly by
the presence of the last two in *King Rat* the inadequacies of George
Segal were underscored; again, Segal could only suffer in the glare
of finished performances provided by Marvin and Oskar Werner in
Ship of Fools. And where have the starmakers been in the years between *Decision Before Dawn* and *Jules and Jim,* with Werner's potential made plain?

1965:
The Top Ten
December 26, 1965

1. *Darling*
2. *Juliet of the Spirits*
3. *Mickey One*
4. *To Die in Madrid*
5. *Those Magnificent Men in Their Flying Machines*
6. *Cat Ballou*
7. *The Ipcress File*
8. *A Thousand Clowns*
9. *Nobody Waved Goodbye*
10. *The Eleanor Roosevelt Story*

'Tis the season, and everyone's been rushing it, and a tradition is a tradition. The tradition is that on the last Sunday of the year the movie critic comes up with a list of the year's Top Ten, in the last analysis, making an arbitrary and personal choice. The word "choice" is peculiarly appropriate this year, because while there have been a number of very good films, there is none that stands far out beyond its contemporaries with the stature, say, of a *Dr. Strangelove* or a *Tom Jones*, as in 1964 and 1963. Further, this has been a year of remarkable performances, wherein Rod Steiger, Terence Stamp, Sidney Poitier, Richard Widmark, Tom Courtenay, Edward G. Robinson, Shelley Winters, Viveca Lindfors, and Rita Tushingham have lent not merely distinction but an aura of brilliance to sometimes basically ordinary and even unsatisfying films.

A British film, *Darling*, a cool, clear and devastating look at the glossy success set, securely heads the list. Exploring, through Frederic Raphael's original screenplay, the career of the girl who makes it from "professional bosom" to cover girl to real-life princess, it offers an audacious yet stringently realistic and carefully understated portrait of the jet-set happiness seekers, the bored, fashionably amoral empty-headed despoilers. The film glitters, under John Schlesinger's fluid direction, with the brilliant performances of Julie Christie, Laurence Harvey and Dirk Bogarde.

With Schlesinger holding the honors for ruthless contemporary comment that have been Federico Fellini's in other years, the Italian director has turned from the pure intellectual brilliance of

8½ to bring a humanity and compassion to *Juliet of the Spirits*. As a result, his first work in color, an introspective and deeply humanistic exploration of the psyche of a woman jolted by her husband's infidelity into a search for her identity and independence, emerges as an unforgettably beautiful film, crowded with the fantastic imagery, the satiric view and prodding wit that distinguish Fellini's work. Both the exotic and the erotic are brought to everyday significance through the irresistible performance of Giulietta Masina; emotion and imagination transcend the purely intellectual for a poetic blend of form and content.

An American work is our third choice, Arthur Penn's *Mickey One*, a film throbbing to the tempo of our times and thoroughly refreshing in style. It deals with the theme of flight from unidentifiable fears, on the concrete level, through the story of an entertainer on the lam from the syndicate, and, on the philosophic level, through the consideration of the grotesqueries of contemporary life. Mr. Penn probes past and present with his own rhythm and chronology. The result is an unorthodox and deeply exciting allegory—complex, demanding and rewarding.

The French documentary *To Die in Madrid* stands fourth, a historic record and a human document of the Spanish Civil War that can be termed a masterpiece. From newsreels and still photographs Frederic Rossif has recreated a time and a tragedy and the passion of a nation in both terrifying and lyric terms.

Those Magnificent Men in Their Flying Machines, in fifth place, is a spectacular worthy of the name, an uproarious and beautiful tale of the crazy crates of early aviation and the equally crazy cranks at their controls, jam-packed with top-notch comedians, superslapstick and all the never-never-land trimmings of the Edwardian age—and this is packaged in melody and affection. A movie like this more than justifies the widest and tallest of screens, overflowing, as it is, with varied delights.

Cat Ballou, our sixth choice, is the ultimate American spoof of the American Western, done with a judicious restraint and sly satire and, above all, a consistency all too rarely found in Hollywood. The film boasts the brilliance of Lee Marvin, just plain wonderful as both the meanest and the drunkest gun in the West.

Seventh is Britain's *The Ipcress File*, an antidote to Bondage and our introduction to the Canadian director Sidney J. Furie, responsible, too, for this year's very good *The Leather Boys*. *Ipcress* is the deglamorized espionage story, but with plenty of tingle and zest, both in plot and camerawork; and bespectacled and disillusioned Harry Palmer, the reluctant spy, is beautifully portrayed by Michael Caine.

A Thousand Clowns is eighth, as that rare film that surpasses the Broadway play on which it is based, not only in physical dimension but also in character and significance. With Jason Robards and young Barry Gordon repeating their stage roles as uncle and nephew and Barbara Harris making a most auspicious screen debut as the inept social worker, the film becomes a broad and joyous comment on the rebellions and concessions of our daily life, a mature comedy that mixes its compassion with hilarity, and a film that does lyric justice to its New York locale.

Next comes *Nobody Waved Goodbye*, a "small" movie and a universal one. Done in quasi-documentary style, with improvised dialogue, it is a story of the affluent delinquent, his girl, his parents, all decent, well-intentioned people unable to understand or cope with the teen-age malaise of our time. The triumph of the film, beyond its far-reaching truth, is the performance of Peter Kastner, who makes of the restless, amoral, uncertain hero a strangely appealing and certainly familiar boy.

And finally, an American documentary, *The Eleanor Roosevelt Story*, completes the list. Much in the *To Die in Madrid* manner, this biography is a compilation of still photographs, brought to remarkable life by the probing motion-picture camera, and of newsreel clips. But its primary distinction is the screenplay by Archibald MacLeish, narrated by him, Eric Sevareid and an elderly cousin of Mrs. Roosevelt. It is through this commentary, which casts the poet's eye upon history and an understanding and affectionate but unsentimental insight into a great lady, that there emerges a portrait worthy of its subject.

(And were we not chronology bound, we would have included high on this list Fellini's 1950 *Variety Lights*, shown here for the first time this year.)

Well, eleventh on our list—yes, here comes the eleventh on a

Ten Best list, and it's *The Knack, Help!*, *Life Upside Down*, *The Overcoat*, *The Spy Who Came in from the Cold*, *The Pawnbroker*, *A Boy Ten Feet Tall*, *Symphony for a Massacre*, *The Leather Boys*, *Sallah*, *The Rounders*, *The Collector*, *The Winner*, *Kwaidan*, and *Moment of Truth*. Then *Viva Maria*, *The Love Goddesses*, *A High Wind in Jamaica*, *Life at the Top*, *That Darn Cat*, *These Are the Damned*, *Hush . . . Hush, Sweet Charlotte*, *Thunderball*. And come to think of it, we had a pretty good time at *Banana Peel*, *How To Murder Your Wife*, *Mirage*, *Male Hunt*, *Masquerade*, *Il Successo*, *The Cincinnati Kid*, *Laurel and Hardy's Laughing Twenties*—and here we are hitting a total of forty films in 1965 that wouldn't make you want to kick the nearest usher on the way out.

Not that there weren't other films that would have prompted you to more exquisite mayhem. I am not talking about the run-of-the-mill unpretentious B, C and D movies, nor am I talking about the sincere films that despite various virtues fail to satisfy—*King Rat*, *The Hill*, *The Loved One*, etc. And I am not including *The Agony and the Ecstasy*, *The Greatest Story Ever Told* or *The Sound of Music* because you know what you're in for beforehand, and it's not cricket to kick ushers thereafter.

No, I am talking about the pretentious films that have swept in on a flood of great expectations and/or great drumbeats, that have offended the sensibilities and destroyed the cachet of directors or performers or producers who helped create the flood.

But picking the ten worst films of the year is no simple chore. Right off the bat or scoop, the list comes easy—*The Sandpiper*; *In Harm's Way*; *John Goldfarb, Please Come Home*; *What's New, Pussycat?*; *Red Line 7000*; *Harlow* (either one or both); *Eva*; *Rapture*; *Baby, the Rain Must Fall*; *Sylvia*—gosh, do we have to stop before we get into *The Hallelujah Trail* or *Joy House* or *None but the Brave* or *A Rage to Live* or *Swedish Wedding Night* or— No. I'm not going to list *Love Has Many Faces*. That's the one where Lana Turner says to Cliff Robertson, "Please don't hate me, Pete," and Cliff says, "I could never hate you," and Lana says, "Please don't hate yourself," and Cliff pauses and says, "It might take a long time." And come to think of it, wasn't it in *Joy House* that Jane Fonda or somebody says, "I broke the Ming—do we glue it to-

gether?" With lines like those lying around loose, can any movie
really be bad? After all, isn't it a function of film, to borrow a lyric
phrase from the dubbed narrator in *Buddha*, to "blighten the rives"
of the oppressed?

☆
☆ **Part IV** ☆
.....**From Darling**
.........**to Georgy**

A Balalaika
Named Rosebud
January 2, 1966

We're standing pat and looking onward and upward and straight ahead at what the new year will bring. And at this point we're not even thinking about what the year promises; promises are for press agents.

If that's a bitter note for the season, it comes in retrospective contemplation of promises unfulfilled and prospective undertaking of at least one resolution. No more chatter about "art" form, medium or what have you when it comes to movies. Let's go right along with the big boys of the business and say we're dealing with an industry and that when anything resembling art is produced thereby, it be regarded as the unexpected, the exceptional and the extraordinary fringe benefit.

The resolution is prompted by the advent of *Doctor Zhivago*, David Lean's eleven-million-dollar version of the Boris Pasternak novel that was more than a year in preparation, a year in production and in final editing stages right up to its premiere ten days ago. When artists finish a monumental work (more than thirty hours of film were cut into this three-hour-and-seventeen-minute epic), they can contemplate it at leisure, brood over its totality, gain perspective from the whole. But when one is concerned with a multimillion-dollar enterprise, in which corporate interests and careers are involved—well, this is an industry, and you get your blockbuster out and shown before the end of the year so that it is right there in line to get not only the big holiday business but also possible Oscar nominations and, hopefully, Oscars that give the box office a jolt come spring.

In anticipation, testimony to the monumental-type work *Zhivago* was expected to be lay in the hardcover publication of Robert Bolt's screenplay (which, now that the film has been cut, has added interest in providing not only a great deal of background for the film but also clues to Mr. Lean's editorial judgments) and in the great number of glowing advance tributes to the film in various periodicals not usually given to blurbery. (Although none of their glowing reporters had seen the finished film, a few had been allowed to see unfinished excerpts in the cutting room.) But of course when you're dealing with eleven million dollars' worth of product, you don't stint in the build-up. Indeed, there was no need to stint.

David Lean is one of those rare directors who has proved himself not once but twice master of the spectacular, with *The Bridge on the River Kwai* and *Lawrence of Arabia* (both, it is worth noting, with Sam Spiegel as producer; Carlo Ponti, a spectacular-maker of a rather different batting average, let alone stripe, took over *Zhivago* production chores); but obviously Mr. Lean is not a man to be fazed by millions or by bevies of stars or thousands of miles of location or film footage galore—as the seven Oscars apiece garnered for his previous blockbusters prove. No, indeed—with Mr. Lean, Mr. Bolt, such rocketing stars as Julie Christie, Omar Sharif, Rita Tushingham, Tom Courtenay, and Geraldine Chaplin and such established stars as Rod Steiger, Alec Guinness, Siobhan McKenna and Ralph Richardson—there was much for the moviegoer to anticipate. Those among us who had faced the past year's movies with relatively jaundiced eyes chose to look to *Zhivago* as the film that would make the movie year.

Alas, *Zhivago*, in many respects, could be termed just another mammoth spectacular in that it is much too long, much too padded, over-elliptical in some spots, over-inflated in others, with the occasional babel of dialect and accent common to international casts and the reduction of historic events into oversimplifications or banalities. But in many other respects this film has distinctions that, despite his overall failure with it, fully justify Mr. Lean's artistic cachet. There are performances that are remarkable indeed; there are incidents of high drama and there are moments of exquisite beauty—whether they come in the panoramic sweep of snowbound horizons, a microscopic examination of the stellar wonderland of a frosted windowpane, an intimate gesture between two aged travelers, the quivering of a wind-wracked aspen or a young woman's sudden laughter. In Mr. Lean's huge forest of a spectacular there are any number of lovely and memorable trees, but we are left with the unfortunate impression that the director never took a good look at the forest he had created, a spectacular one that could be subtitled *A Balalaika Named Rosebud*.

There were few pretensions. From the start, Messrs. Bolt and Lean emphasized that Pasternak's vast multicharactered canvas could not be transferred or even compressed with complete fidelity for the screen. Their plan, they said, was to bring the personal story—of the doctor-poet's agonized love for both his wife and another woman—forward and use the Russian Revolution and Zhivago's disillusionment with it as background for the thirty-year chronology. This they have placed in flashback form, arranged as part of a search for Zhivago's lovechild.

The premise, since there was no pretense, was, alas, wrong. So vast a canvas does not let the Revolution take on mere backdrop proportions, and even as a background it dwarfs the love triangle, which is relatively amicable, ordinary and undramatic despite the personal agonies involved. Neither love story nor Revolution attains stature. Above all, what could be described as Dickensian coincidences in the novel's plot and dismissed as secondary to Pasternak's poetic values and human insights emerge on screen as soap-opera mechanics that compromise the authenticity given the characters and their background.

Plot, easily overlooked amid major values in Pasternak's work, becomes vital to the three-hours-plus film and cannot be dismissed in favor of stunning landscapes that bring memories of *Lawrence of Arabia*, of eerie graveyard scenes and icy decaying mansions that

remind one of Lean's *Great Expectations*, of character bits and
pieces and of the workers' marches and carloads of refugees with
which we are too familiar. And for a plot that centers on domestic
and extramarital love we must have intimate knowledge of and
involvement with the central characters; their motivations—many,
incidentally, apparent in the Bolt screenplay—are missing from the
final film version. We watch men and women perform, and they fade
into the panoramic canvas, which is all too often all too obviously
filled for effect rather than meaning. And not all the cinematography, not all the swelling music and surging mobs, not all the
snowfall and fields of daffodils and talk of The Party and The Workers is going to cover up the contrivance involved in our lovers'
meetings and partings, the confusion in the secondary characters'
comings and goings, the use of symbols in the absence of substance.

Scene after scene is beautiful per se; we catch the breath
at the camera's searching eye from horizon to snowflake—and find
ourselves unenlightened by foreground or background beyond shiny
handsome surface. Neither love nor revolution is done justice.
We're down to a search for Daddy, who, through thick and thin,
managed to carry along the beautiful balalaika which was his sole
inheritance as a beautiful boy orphan, even though he couldn't
play a note. And what do you know, the girl who might be his long-
lost daughter, even though she's a humble laborer, carries along a
balalaika—and she plays it just the way Daddy's mommy did, because "it's a gift."

And thus we have a high-class industrial rather than a work of
art, a spectacular soap opera.

That Was the War
That Wasn't
January 30, 1966

Screenwriter, with a revolutionary glint in his eye, was telling me
the other day he's going all-the-way original: he's writing a World
War II movie with bad Nazis.

I know I shouldn't throw it out cold at you that way; I myself
haven't yet readjusted to so avant-garde a script idea. But at
least I didn't give you both barrels the way they were blasted at
me. Take a minute to recover and prepare for the second blast.
The bad Nazis, see, they're going to be all-the-way-bad, not merely
bad-for-a-start, but bad-for-the-end and ever after.

By this my friend means that right from the start these Nazis
know all about the concentration camps and the blasting of hospital ships and sites and all and they love every minute of it because they hate the Americans like mad. They keep on hating them
like madder after a couple of them are captured by those stupid
bumbling Americans and they let their stupid bumbling American
captors stupefy and bumble their way to victory all by themselves,
without a helping hand and sacrificial soul from the Nazis, who—
and how revolutionary can you get?—lose the war convinced that
Hitler was the best thing that ever happened and all set to keep his
spirit going in the best of all possible postwar worlds.

It is, of course, a long time twixt inspiration and screenplay
and movie. There's no doubt that my friend was inspired by the spate
of World War II movies in which, sure as shootin' (and what a
boom-boom-boom these big war retrospectives make!) and sure as
you'll find stupid American brass for the drama and venal American
noncoms for the laughs, you'll find a Nazi who, just before his capture and especially thereafter, makes it clear to us that he was
against Hitler all along and then proceeds to save the day for the
Americans by Nazi know-how or, at very least, returns to his homeland a confirmed democrat who'd put Tom Paine to shame in any

contest of conscience. Scratch—or corner—a bad guy and you find
a good guy.

Thank heaven for the Nazis, or we'd never have won the war
against Hitler! This is not, of course, the way we movie veterans
watched World War II being fought on film during and after the
fact, courtesy of Bogey and Errol and Dana and Mitchum and, *uber
alles*, Warner Brothers' morale-building schedule. Catch the irony,
since the latest contribution to the good-Nazi bit is in Warners'
Battle of the Bulge (with Robert Shaw as the shrewd panzer commander who doesn't quite have faith in the Nazi regime, and Hans
Christian Blech as his faithful batman who turns humanistic anti-
Nazi along with the tide of war); but other companies have done
their bit with *36 Hours, The Train* (albeit here Paul Scofield's Nazi
was a lover of Art, if not of mere humanity), *Up from the Beach,
Morituri, The Bedford Incident* (a postwar good Nazi helps against
the Russkies), *Situation Hopeless . . .*—and we're not counting
good Japanese (like in *None but the Brave*) or good Fascisti (*Von
Ryan's Express*) or good Nazis in foreign films (*Taxi from Tobruk*).

Non-avid moviegoers are, apparently, unaware of the good-
Nazi trend. *Herald Tribune* columnist Art Buchwald, for instance,
recently speculated on the response American moviemakers might
make to German restiveness at being portrayed as the "heavies" of
World War II. Casting, he suggests, is a primary factor, and he envisions Pat Boone, Pat O'Brien or Jimmy Stewart as the SS men,
Otto Preminger, Helmut Dantine and Paul Lukas as the American
GI's. In what he terms "the Nouveau Vague World War II film," he
sees Pat Boone as a U-boat commander who refuses to fire on a
passenger ship, noting, "I'd rather risk getting sunk than torpedo a
ship with civilians aboard. Hitler would want it that way"; Bing
Crosby as a Gestapo chief and Fred MacMurray as his assistant,
who remarks, during the questioning of a tight-lipped Resistance
fighter, "There's nothing we can do about it. If we lay a finger on
him we'll have to answer to Himmler for police brutality"; and
finally Buchwald comes up with the new POW drama, *Stalag
Hilton*, which "would star Henry Fonda as the camp commandant.
Doris Day would play his wife, who rolls bandages for the Jewish
prisoners in the hospital," and when SS Sergeant Glenn Ford

rushes in with the announcement that the prisoners are escaping, Fonda says, "Don't talk to me. I'm in on the July '44 plot to kill Hitler," and Ford says, "Aren't we all?"

Well, what with Yul Brynner having a sudden change-of-Aryan-heart and helping Marlon Brando, a relatively uncommitted German type, save a cargo of rubber for us stupid Allies and being kind to a nice Jewish girl being mistreated by the Gestapo and raped by Americans, all in *Morituri*, and Marius Goring, as a Nazi occupation officer, saving some nice French civilians not only from air raids but also from idiot Americans like Cliff Robertson and Red Buttons in *Up from the Beach*, I'm afraid Mr. Buchwald is getting a lot closer to the things-that-are than to the things-to-come realm of satire.

Without resorting to superchauvinism, flag-waving or "the only dead Nazis are good Nazis" school of thought, conceding that there were changes of heart and regenerations galore, we can still object to this good-for-foreign-exhibition view of history. Let me note that I am not concerned with serious wartime dramas that explore the humanistic elements, the clouded loyalties of "little" people and the borderlines of nationalism. But in slambang adventure stories this nagging and subtle perversion of history—brought to a cynical overtness in a film like *The Americanization of Emily*—is no longer, I feel, to be dismissed as just another war-movie cliché.

Once we survive the war that wasn't, we come to the tragedies that were.

The tragedies that were, of course, include above all the extermination of six million Jews; the glories that came after are highlighted finally by the establishment of the state of Israel, and a reference to either, in serious context, cannot, I think, fail to stir the heart and quicken the pulse.

Beyond *The Pawnbroker* and *Judgment at Nuremberg*, beyond the indirection of *The Condemned of Altona*, the post-facto stereotyped allusions of *Ship of Fools*, the occasional concentration-camp reference in war movies and Otto Preminger's *Exodus*, American moviemakers have had little serious concern with either concentration-camp tragedy or Israeli achievement. This is not, of course, surprising in view of their general lack of concern with—nay, aversion to—domestic social issues. And certainly Europeans have a closer concern, both physically and morally, with the crime of our century.

Genocide is a concept of such enormity, its twentieth-century manifestation so bestial in its details, that the imagination shrinks from its depiction. But in *The Shop on Main Street* we are able to see it at last in comprehensive and comprehensible terms, with a simplicity and humanism that are soul-searing, an honesty and integrity that are unforgettable. A company of Czech filmmakers has omitted the beasts with the whips and the barbed wire, the emaciated corpses and the fragmented survivors. They have presented to us the tragedy not only of the millions who died but of the millions who stood witness to their murder in terms of a handful and epitomized it in a couple—a doltish, dim-witted carpenter and an elderly, doddering shopkeeper—a foolish, well-intentioned young man and a sweet, harmless old lady.

The triumph is that the tragic emphasis is not on the elderly Jewish widow, carrying on the ritual of business in her bankrupt little button shop with failing eyesight, near-deafness and a purity of spirit, living in lonely memories with deep religious faith. It is rather on the carpenter in this village in Slovakia during World War II, on the good-natured man whose reaction against fascism is as much due to his personal antipathy to his brother-in-law, the local fuehrer, as to his basic sense of decency. Fascism is, in fact, presented to us most directly in the fatuous, vulgar greed of the brother-in-law and the nagging, blowsy earthiness and avarice of the carpenter's wife; in contrast, the carpenter's ordinary average humanism becomes almost—but never quite—heroic.

The carpenter is appointed Aryan controller of the widow's shop, only to discover that there is no profit there beyond the salary the Jewish community will pay him to let Mrs. Lautman live in peace, nor is there pride, for the near-senile little lady, insulated by deafness, is under the delusion that he has been brought in to assist her, and she is kindly, patronizingly tolerant of him.

A warm relationship develops, as does the crisis—the deportation of the town's Jews—and Tono, the carpenter, is suddenly confronted with the dilemma of protecting the widow or of saving his own skin. Dreams and drunkenness provide no solution, for the nightmare is reality, and there is no slick escape, no easy out for the ordinary man. And thus—through the brilliant perceptiveness of Ladislav Grossman's screenplay, the expert, sensitive direction of Jan Kadar and Elmar Klos, the overwhelming performances of Josef Kroner and Ida Kaminska, and, indeed, the contribution of everyone involved—we come to know and understand, through laughter, through tears, through the ordinary actions of ordinary people, just what the tragedy of millions, of both victims and survivors, has meant in our century.

But that, assuredly, is not Hollywood's way of presenting tragedy. In a cinema industry that sees Doris Day as the average American housewife, Carroll Baker as the girl to have sex dreams about and Rock Hudson as the man we should want to marry, it follows that Sophia Loren should be a concentration-camp survivor—in Technicolor, of course—with all her hourglass endowments intact after years of Dachau and even a session in a Nazi officers' brothel.

Thus, within a week when *The Shop on Main Street* comes upon us in all its simple truth and beauty, we have *Judith* to give us the American view of tragedy and glory in one mouthful. The mouthful, in Hollywood's nothing-but-the-best tradition, is provided by Lawrence Durrell, who, in Hollywood handout terms, is "the one author who has stamped his name across the concept of drama in the Middle East." Handed the "idea" of *Judith* by producer Kurt Unger, Mr. Durrell "came to Israel to see the country about which he was to write."

That's half the battle, since the author's plot was to involve Sophia, the survivor; she is smuggled into Palestine on the eve of Israeli independence to identify for the underground Israeli army her ex-husband, a Nazi tank general, who is advising six Arab nations on how to invade the new state. The movie was, in fact, made in Israel. As the handout puts it, "For more than three months the weather held, until it was long past the season of the rains. All that time cameras ground out their footage on the bleak hill near Israel's northern border. When the filmmakers moved to the sea, the waves quieted. When they needed clear skies, they came. And on the day that they finished, when they were preparing to move away, the heavens opened up. Winds came out of the sea and smote the land, and rain cut deep channels into the dry sandy soil. Thus, in harmony with the elements, did the motion picture *Judith* come to completion in the Holy Land."

And on the fourth month, of course, the cameras rested.

The film, directed by Daniel Mann, who has done excellent stage and screen work in the past, is, unfortunately, as tasteless and pretentious as the handouts that accompany it. To plunk Miss Loren down on the shores of Galilee in all her unhidden Hertha-like glory and pretend that she has survived a decade of horror, living only for personal vengeance, is insulting enough to those who survived the holocaust. But to dress her in slightly anachronistic (the year is 1948) short shorts, tapered slacks and huge-lensed sunglasses and have her wander among real-life Israelis in a kibbutz as part of the independence effort goes even beyond the ludicrous to border on the obscene. And even those lovely tawny Loren eyes brimming with tears or the equally lovely Loren lip trembling with secret sorrow cannot distract from the even lovelier and lush Loren bosom and hipline with their swell and sway.

To pad out the script (and not, of course, Miss Loren), we are given folk dances in the kibbutz, an *Exodus*-like debarkation of a shipload of illegal immigrants, the work and sweat of pioneers and the gallantry of the Haganah soldiers. The heart quickens at such scenes—and then the mind revolts, for here is tragedy and glory being used as window dressing for some cheap little undercover-agent episodes and fleshly exploitation.

And we are left to remember how a battered and ragged Miss Loren, under Vittorio De Sica's direction, managed, without black-lace underwear and personally designed beehive coiffure, to embody in *Two Women* the tragedy of war's civilian survivors, and to ponder the effects of stardom and the concepts of American directors.

But we have also had with the Czech film the exhilaration of seeing that there are moviemakers who can translate apocalyptic tragedy into human terms and tell of it with the beauty of truth.

This Is Where
We Came In—But
February 6, 1966

Miss Miriam Dressen of Los Angeles, now renowned, courtesy of a press release that describes her as a "fifty-eight-year-old domestic worker" and with masterly understatement as an "ardent" moviegoer, has seen *The Greatest Story Ever Told* sixty-three times, "often," we are told, "at the rate of twice a day."

Well, the lady has us beat. We have frequently felt that we have seen the same movie sixty-three times but are the first to admit that it's just a feeling generated by genre. There were four *different* James Bond movies, and there have been five or six different takeoffs thereon. There were seventy-six *different* versions of *Grand Hotel* and there have been ninety-two variations on— Shucks, which *was* the original of the crash-in-the-desert-and-who-survives movies?

Small though the differences may have been, we will concede that the names and faces and even the places have varied. But the conditioning remains. Give us a young man on the make, out to match himself against the champ, whether in the ring or the poolroom or Madison Avenue or at the card table, and we can pretty well carry the ball, right along with our young man, to the moment of triumph and to the bitter discovery that certain triumphs are in the gall-and-wormwood department. Give us that plane's worth of characters, that world in microcosm, and we can almost predict who's going to get his before the doughty aerodynamicist aboard (captain or hidden genius) finally gets the plane airborne again or rescue arrives over the horizon.

The thrill—and moviemaking—lies, of course, in what does not happen, in the twist, in the change, in the variation on the theme and in the new dimension of character. In retrospect, for example, one appreciates the particular triumph of *The Cincinnati Kid* over, say, *The Hustler*. In the first film, which had relatively little distinction before the climactic poker game, we arrived at a brilliant finale: the ambitious flashy kid is finally up against the old champ; a hard, brainy Steve McQueen confronts the seasoned and civilized Edward G. Robinson—and loses. And he loses, under that magnificent Tiffany-glass lampshade, not because we've been handed lots of shibboleths about "character" and born losers and born winners but because the old pro is pro enough to know when to do the wrong thing. The build-up is artier and a lot more psychological, let alone complex, in *The Hustler*—but all the shadowy atmosphere and painfully elaborate insights and really fine performances are shot to pieces when the climactic scene arrives and a hard and bitter Paul Newman confronts the cold-eyed and imperturbable Jackie Gleason at the pool table—and wins. The only conclusion we can come to is that there's nothing that improves your pool game like having your girl commit suicide, and that's hardly why we have arrived at the expected gall-and-wormwood triumph.

The true moviemaker takes us up the familiar path and makes us love every minute of it, recovering the initial excitement that is, in fact, enhanced by the recurrent flashes of recognition—a feeling that it's the same, only different in a better way. Earlier this season on Broadway there was, for example, a fine old-fashioned melodrama, *The Right Honourable Gentleman*; it even, one critic noted, had French doors at stage left, all ready for some unexpected visitor's entrance. Indeed it did—and, by George, we just couldn't wait to see who it would be. Style, performance, the perfection of the expected "unexpected"—these constitute the craft that carries the day, and us along with it.

This is what Robert Aldrich achieves in *The Flight of the Phoenix*. There comes the slightly shabby plane skimming over the desert with motley and slightly raunchy characters aboard. Good heavens—not another *Sands of the Kalahari* so soon—well, at least there's no woman aboard, although there is one listed at the very end of the credits, and at least there aren't any apes skittering on the outskirts, although—oh, dear, one of the men is clutching a little monkey. And wait—no, not a storm of locusts—it's a sandstorm—sputter—spew—clack clack clack—and down we go.

Yes, down we go and up we come, thanks to Mr. Aldrich, Lukas

Heller's intelligent screenplay and an excellent cast. The framework is there, ready for all the clichés of the desert-survival story,
but somehow each expected cliché never quite develops as one.
(Even the girl remains only a transparency—literally, as a miragelike
daydream of one of the least appetizing characters—and though she
is totally extraneous, even from a box-office point of view, she is at
least forgivable.)

We have, for example, James Stewart as the aging all-American
pilot—all-American because he is guilt-ridden and compassionate;
but he blasts the cliché by not being very efficient or bright and by
having a nasty streak. There's Dan Duryea, the stodgy bookkeeper,
who doesn't go berserk. There's Peter Finch, surface British brass,
below the surface surprisingly decent and dutiful; Hardy Kruger,
surface "good-Nazi"-brain type, stickler for authority, below the
surface a childish enthusiast, a sulky man capable of a decent gesture; Ronald Fraser, surface thirty-year Army man, below the surface a man who explodes into stubbornness. And above all there's
Richard Attenborough, so beautifully the mediator-conciliator, the
average man made up of so many weaknesses he can supply
strength to others.

Mr. Aldrich's camera eye probes their very pores, and instead
of the bare-chested sweat and primitive-emotions hoopla of *Kalahari* we see the heat blisters, the swollen lips and festering sores
of dehydration and controlled reactions of men who are living and
thinking beings and not contrivances paying script service to a survival story. And yet, as plot develops and the big push is on,
we're with them, muscles tense for the big haul, rooting for the good
guys, and understanding why the bad guy can ride with them.

Performance is triumphant here, as it is in *King and Country*,
Joseph Losey's film that through a World War I incident offers a
bitter and grim comment on the "facts" of that war, the futility of
any war. Again we have the clichés of the lowly soldier as victim of
the machine, the "volunteer" who discovers the horror of battle and
cannot face it and thereby becomes the necessary sacrifice to the
ritual of building morale. Stanley Kubrick explored the theme brilliantly to its ultimate effectiveness in *Paths of Glory*; Mr. Losey's
attempt to cope with it on a smaller scale gleans its glory chiefly

from Tom Courtenay's haunting portrait of an inarticulate clod, scarcely human save for his overwhelming humility; from Dirk Bogarde's masterful playing of the officer who is not quite as inured or as cynical as he would choose to be, but who is duty bound, and from the director's unrelenting and unrelieved concentration on the entrapment of men in subhuman affairs.

We have been there before, but all credit to the craftsmen on hand, it isn't the same.

The Role
or the Star?
February 13, 1966

We want, it appears, even Othello to be Laurence Olivier, so strong is the star cult among moviegoers. What, Olivier a black-face tragedian in this film version of Britain's National Theater's triumphant stage production? Heavens no. The star-worshipers among us cannot concede that a great actor may choose to lose his identity in a revolutionary concept of the body and soul of the Moor; they want some nice nut-brown makeup, transparent enough to disclose the non-African features and familiar face—let's have the marvelous romantic matinee idol of stage and screen go through the baritone agonies the way we learned Othello should from the secondary-school experts.

What is so stunning about the Olivier Othello is that the artist has seen him physically as the Negro in an all-white society to which he is indeed almost a minstrel-show stereotype; thus the shiny ebony makeup, the white flash of eyeball and teeth, the crimson slash of a mouth made meatier in the pitch-black face. More important—and here is the brilliance of the Olivier concept of the soul of this suddenly contemporary character—his Othello brims with neuroses as he skims the surface of paranoia, a man who walks among strangers with supersensitivities: superhumility before his superiors, superpride in his accomplishments, supercamaraderie and trust toward his fellows, supersexuality and superpossessiveness toward his wife. He is a taut man on an emotional tightrope, his nerves rubbed raw by the exigencies of his profession and his involvements with a society from which he stands apart in that most terrible apartheid of the skin.

And on film, as it certainly could not have been to such powerful effect on stage, his makeup changes as his emotions do and as his very soul is hammered at and distorted; the shining ebony turns, or perhaps only appears to turn, to the dull grays of anguish, the greenish tones of raging hatreds and diabolic suspicion, the taupes of self-realization and deadly resolution. Here is something so revolutionary, so hypertheatrical and cinematic that the traditionalists cannot cope with it; they retreat muttering that this kind of caricature is irreverent, not quite nice, just as many of them insisted *Strangelove* wasn't quite nice.

No, as the partisans want us all to agree, Othello has to be the familiar Olivier. He is our star. We'll accept the unfamiliar only on foreign terms—and, in fact, one suspects that so long as the foreign element is there, we're supposed to accept just about anything—and glorify it because of its foreign setting.

A major example is *Italiano Brava Gente*, which I hasten to note means "Italians Are Good People," and this film sets out to demonstrate it ad absurdum in the context of World War II's Eastern Front, much in the Germans-are-good-people manner of some American producers. The Italians, we are fascinated to learn, in this black-and-white spectacular filmed in Russia, never fired a shot in anger, unless it was at their allies, the beastly Nazis, who snubbed 'em and treated 'em real mean, or at the nasty Fascists in their own army. For sheer lovable antiwar spirit, they were, in fact, matched only by the Russians. The film manages to encompass every peace-loving cliché of every film that offers its antiwar preachment in terms of the foot soldier and vainly attempts to capture the exquisite essence of Lewis Milestone's *All Quiet on the Western Front* of thirty-six years ago.

The mark of that final scene, of Lew Ayres reaching for the butterfly, is endlessly upon this movie: Russians and Italians, stale-

mated on opposite banks of a frozen river, take potshots at a hare;
one man from each side emerges from the trenches for a friendly
foot race to the wounded quarry, and everyone is laughing and
cheering until a dastardly Italian sergeant (Fascist, of course)
shoots the Russian, and the Russians shoot the Italian, and the
corpses artistically flank the still-quivering hare. Then there's the
simple Italian farmboy, a fair-haired type played by a Russian—
but what with Arthur Kennedy and Peter Falk making the American
contribution to this three-nation venture by playing a vile Mussolini-
type major and an effete Neapolitan playboy-doctor, all dubbed into
Italian by Italians, let's not quibble. The quibble is that naturally
the farmboy is shot down amid the eye-high sunflowers as he is
making loving overtures to a lovely Russian girl partisan.

War, we are told for two hours and thirty-six minutes, is hell—
hell frozen over, when it comes to Russia in forty-three—and soldiers
of all nations are human beings who do not find war a ball, but
Italian soldiers are more so. They are good people. They tear that
vile Mussolini-type major to shreds when he tries to beat a faster
retreat to the rear than they.

Well, you can hardly recognize Arthur Kennedy all made up
with that billiard-ball bald head, so it's all right. They're strangers
and we don't recognize a soul, and therefore it's real. The movie
does at the very least say Nazis and Fascists are bad people. And
that's one point on the side of history—or moviemaking.

Only in Hollywood—
The Oscar
March 13, 1966

Moviemaking, we are told, is a cooperative activity; hardy and
rare and usually nonexistent is the individual who can take full
credit for much more than a moment, and superperceptive and
equally rare is the critic who can tell at a glance just where the
credit lies.

It's really no easier in the blame department, and after the recent weeks' series of goodies—*The Chase, Inside Daisy Clover, Moment to Moment, Promise Her Anything, The Oscar*—the instinct is, I'm afraid, to start looking for fall guys. But no, positive thinking . . . eye of the beholder and all that . . . and before you know it, you're giving credit all over the place.

Not that you can be positive in this business, not for long. There I was absolutely positive that the best bed-line of the season had to be credited to *Doctor Zhivago*, to Robert Bolt for writing it, to director David Lean for letting them say it and, above all, leaving it in the film despite all the other goodies that toppled to the cutting-room floor. It's a great moment on the cyclorama-size Metrocolor-Panavision screen, with boy and girl bare-shouldered and nuzzling around in bed. Says Miss Christie: "What are we going to do?" Says Sharif: "I don't know." But then along comes another bit of cinematic grandiosity, and we get another bed-line to top all, with Shirley Knight and Hal Holbrook doing the bare-shouldered bit this time in *The Group*. The just deflowered lady assures her swain that he is so right for her, so wonderful. "Do you think I should join the Abraham Lincoln Brigade?" he asks fondly.

So certainties, as I say, are fleeting in this business, but I am tempted to go all-out so far as one aspect of *The Oscar* is concerned. Nowhere, on stage or screen or even in a revue skit, has there been so complete a cliché of the Hollywood-heel-on-the-rise-and-fall theme to the tune of such ripe dialogue. "Ripe"? The word is all too feeble, and "dialogue" itself inadequate to describe the verbiage that pours from the people involved. Only from Hollywood, as we say. . . .

Only from Hollywood could one expect, too, so total an abortion in the course of transferring a novel to the screen. Richard Sale's *The Oscar* was a creditable work, a stringent insider's story of the five actors nominated for the best-performance Oscar, with four of them cheating, blackmailing and conniving for the prize, only to have the fifth, passive by virtue of his alcoholic disinterest, walk off with it. It was, of course, an anti-Hollywood novel (refreshingly enough, by a Hollywood writer-producer-director). Could one expect perhaps an anti-Hollywood movie? There have been such. One could have expected. But a cynic would have thought: *The Oscar*—this is a name for an anti-Hollywood movie? Oscars, baby, you don't kid about. As a fellow in the abortion that is the movie labeled *The Oscar* says, "The Oscars are a symbol, and we don't like them tarnished."

So we telescope the five heelish nominees of the novel into one heel, see, and we have him competing for that Oscar against Richard Burton and Burt Lancaster, and then the voice fades so we don't know who the two other jokers are, so that—hey, Charlie, guess who the sleeper is in this one, because he's not even listed in the cast credits that have Edith Head, Hedda Hopper, Merle Oberon and Nancy Sinatra all appearing as themselves. And I'll play dirty pool with the plotters and just ask you to wonder why Nancy Sinatra gets a show-in in the cast.

The plotters are Clarence Greene, Russell Rouse and Harlan Ellison. The last is coauthor. Messrs. Greene and Rouse are, besides coauthors, producer and director, with Joseph E. Levine as executive producer; the three are teamed with *A House Is Not a Home*, and that ought to give you some standard to work down from. Then repeat to yourself *Darling, Marriage Italian Style, 8½* and so on in Mr. Levine's behalf; mumble *Pillow Talk* for Messrs. Greene and Rouse if you wish.

So Messrs. Greene and Rouse and Ellison have concocted this classic about Frankie Fane, sweating out the Oscar ceremony, sitting on top of "the glass mountain of success," while his erstwhile buddy, labeled Hymie Kelly ("My mother was Sadie Rabinowitz, my father Michael Kelly"), remembers 'way back when ...

There's the Good Woman ("I'm not the kind of woman who uses sex as a release or a weapon," she says; "You free thinkers confuse me," Frankie says). There's the Psychological Motivation for Heelsmanship: Frankie brought his father to see his mother carrying on, but to his dismay, his father blew his own brains out, right in front of Frankie, and ever since, Hymie explains, "No woman's ever any better than his mother." There is Frankie's Discoverer: "He's very important to me," she tells the Big Agent, who replies, "Is it possible he's *too* important to you?" The Big Agent helps make Frankie a Star: "Success, the wildest narcotic known to man," hits Frankie, Hymie tells us.

But Frankie meets the Good Woman again: "It's that seed of rot that makes you what you are," she says. "You represent everything I loathe." "You mean everything you love," he says, and so they get married. But Frankie is still a Womanizer: "He used them like Kleenex—once—and threw them away," Hymie reports. He has Betrayed his First Girl (pregnant, yet, and though good old Hymie married her, she still died in childbirth), his Discoverer ("The sadness is, Sophie," the Big Agent tells her, "that you couldn't possibly do the hurt to him he has done to you"), his Good Woman-Wife ("My head's splitting," he tells her; "And so's our marriage," she ripostes), his First Producer, his Big Agent—and even Hymie. "Go on—run—who the hell needs you?" Frankie howls after them all, having already declared that "It's a spiked boot on anybody who gets in my way" and figured out a fiendish plot for winning the Oscar. He has, of course (the antitarnish influence here), carefully informed us that "I can't rig the votes—but I can rig the emotions of the voters."

. Not really. And the fact that all the people involved in *The Oscar* think they can rig ours completes the totality of the cliché. But credit them with still thinking so in this day and age. As we noted, it's not nice you should call it blame.

Too Many Girls
To Worry About
March 20, 1966

High on our list of movies-to-suspend-your-critical-faculties-during is the perennial one about The Girls. Not Les Girls, not girls-girls-girls. The Girls.

We've been encountering them through all the Hollywood years, usually as roommates and more often in trio, as Ziegfeld girls, jills in jeeps, tossers of coins in fountains, nurses, business girls, career girls, airline stewardesses, marked women, actresses, gold diggers. Invariably there was the nice, usually blond, clean-cut,

honest, talented one who won either the star role and/or Mr.
Right; the unscrupulous, usually brunette, overambitious or over-
sexy or (recent development) overneurotic one who came to a bad
end (frequently imprisoned in walls of gold, but preferably a
suicide) all because of Mr. Wrong; and, of course, the comic-relief
Plain Jane one, the good sport who got both the spot in the chorus
and Mr. Mediocre.

I can see Loretta Young now—and it is Lynn Bari, isn't it, vamping away Mr. Right—and Patsy Kelly gets to be bridesmaid at the
wedding, which in retrospect seems always to have included Don
Ameche.

And if the references seem a bit antediluvian, kiddies—go
ahead, you tell me the names of the actresses in *The Best of Everything.*

The newest version of the old familiar the-girls-and-how-they-
make-out theme is, of course, *The Group*, which involves, reflect-
ing our age of affluence or else-misguided fidelity to the Mary Mc-
Carthy best-seller, eight girls. And I have the suspicion that we are
all going to be able to remember a number of their names eventually, perhaps after their second or third film. For seldom have so
many gifted and relatively unknown actresses displayed such promise and achievement in the creation of so many unmemorable screen
characters. Some have hitherto earned distinction in the theater,
only two or three in films, but I urge you to keep your eye on Joan
Hackett, Candice Bergen and Joanna Pettet in particular and gaze
with renewed interest on Shirley Knight in her best film performance to date.

But who, basically, despite all the nuances and intensity of individual performance and all the phony cachet of the novel, are they
on screen? Who is Miss Knight among The Girls? She is the Good
Girl, Polly Andrews (pipe the good-girl name, yet!), blond and
steadfast and true, bearing financial and romantic losses and
family burdens and friendship with courage and winding up with
Mr. Right. Who is Miss Pettet? She is the Bad Girl, Kay, who
weekended with Harald before marriage and therefore, by Hollywood standards, let alone those of the author, must come to a Bad
End; her marriage is a fraud, she is overneurotic, she is a status-

seeking snob, she falls out of a window. Who is Miss Hackett? She
is a Half-Bad Girl: her night of sinful sex and excursion to get a
birth-control device are half-forgiven by Hollywood (and the ex-
Legion of Decency, which required only partial snipping of the
birth-control sequence to leave the film uncondemned) because
she believes herself in love with her seducer and throws away her
birth-control device; so she only half-suffers, marrying a loving
millionaire and having uncontrolled birth but hitting the bottle and
getting assigned the least becoming of the 1930's wardrobe of the
film. And Miss Bergen, the loveliest of all the ladies—well, she's
an anachronism for the Hollywood cliché. The Girls used to have
a sort of neuter dedicated-career type around; *The Group* has that
too, in fact, doubled, but in the 1960's fashion it has the exquisite
Miss Bergen as a lesbian ("a Sapphic—a lesbo," the script says with
a vulgarity that even Miss McCarthy eschewed, despite her book's
earning its reputation for the clinical details of intercourse, pessary
fittings and breast-feeding, only the last of which, with tedious
tastelessness, is transferred to the screen). Other actresses, all of
them very good, portray The Neuter, The Sexy-Talking Frigid
Virgin, The Dominated Wife and The Comic-Relief Plumpish
Stupid. They were suitemates at Vassar, now grads of the class of
thirty-three making their way in New York.

And so we are back with Hollywood girls-and-how-they-grew
nonsense, in all its slickly photographed, carefully detailed, very
well acted banality. Made entirely in New York, directed by Sidney Lumet, it's Hollywood-on-the-Hudson, glossily designed for
the buck, with the name of the McCarthy book to supply the box-
office draw that its very good but unstellar cast lacks.

But there is more than merely the name of the McCarthy book
here, and *The Group* comes a particular cropper because of it.
Here is a case of overfidelity to a source proving disastrous. A
novelist, particularly of Miss McCarthy's skill, can keep eight major
characters in focus with ease; neither the author nor viewer of this
movie can. Motivations and dimensions go by the board as we whirl
from girl to girl, with alumnae-newsletter snippets giving us details we couldn't care less about, with an interesting personality like
Kay dropped time and again for iteration of the dull frigidities of

one character or the pediatric quandaries of another. The merry-go-round technique producer-writer Sidney Buchman has undertaken skimps quality for quantity, and we whirl about to an ultimate blur. For contrast, think back to *The Women*, on stage or screen, where the focus was on one woman's domestic crisis and all other characters were positioned along its path. There was a resultant perspective, depth and developing interest. And think back too on the wit.

Miss McCarthy is a woman of wit, without, I suspect, any delusion about the skeleton of her novel; she did, however, manage to disguise it (for some) with the Vassar mystique and her recreation of the intellectual and political attitudes of the thirties. Typical was her scathing portrait of Gus Leroy, the radical book editor who brings his political, domestic and psychoanalytical problems into Polly's bed. But when, in the inflated superficial way of the slick moviemaker, this is transferred to the screen, it becomes ludicrous and witless. A typical moment: as Polly sighs with the ecstasy of their lovemaking, Gus murmurs, "Does it make any sense, Polly—my wanting to join up and go to Spain?" All the references to the era—its politics, its passions, its crises—become as artificial and unnecessary as the period sets and costuming.

Trotsky-shmotsky, lesbian or adultery-wise—any way you slice *The Group*, on screen it's the same old baloney about The Girls. The only question is how you like to slice your life. I just happen to think that eight heroines in two and a half hours is too big a slice, and much too long for the suspension of critical faculties. Let's bring back the traditional trio; our diet permits us just enough candy bars to get through their crisis.

Return of
the Pre-Bond Man
April 3, 1966

Saw *Frankenstein* the other day, not the most recent *Frankenstein Meets the Space Monster*, or the previous batch of *Frankenstein Meets the Wolf Man, Abbott and Costello Meet Frankenstein, House of Frankenstein, Bride of Frankenstein, Ghost of Frankenstein, Evil of Frankenstein, Son of Frankenstein, Frankenstein's Daughters* or *I Was a Teenage Frankenstein*—and not the aborted ersatz Frankenstein spawn of *The Munsters* or *The Addams Family.* THE *Frankenstein,* vintage 1931.

It's refreshing to return to the source of it all, depressing to realize the degeneration of a genre. All the distinctions of the original manufactured-monster film, particularly the agony of the creator and the pathos of his creature, have been lost, and the essence of each has been perverted for ensuing generations. The rivet-necked Karloffian hulk, now labeled "Frankenstein," epitomizes mindless savagery and strength; there is no trace of the childlike grotesque who was delighted by a child's game and charmed by music and could only lash out, without gauge of his own power, at his frustraters and tormentors. But now the monster is for burning; it is ironic to recall that Colin Clive's Frankenstein and his doctor friend were primarily concerned with putting the creature out of the way painlessly, humanely.

Much of the same dehumanization has taken place with the private eye, now more fashionably the semiprivate spy. (The analogy between monsters and Bonds is not really far-out; both are Hollywood automatons.) Returns to the eye-spy beginnings, via revival houses and television, have not only reminded us of the perfections of the root source 1941 *The Maltese Falcon* but of the original private operator created therein by Bogart as Sam Spade. He existed relatively intact throughout the forties, most often as Philip Marlowe, created by Bogart for *The Big Sleep* and re-created by

Dick Powell, Robert Montgomery and George Montgomery for such films as *Murder, My Sweet, Lady in the Lake* and *The Brasher Doubloon*. Then, during the fifties and on into the sixties, with the global and sexual and sensational reorientation of movies, he underwent steady transformation, until he was lost completely to the Bonds and the Matt Helms, the Dragnet robots and the agents from U.N.C.L.E., the paperback-boned and television-bred men—and I use the last word ill-advisedly.

Men they are not. Symbols, yes—men, no. The psychiatrically oriented critic can find the latter-day Bond and his imitators symbolic of latent homosexuality in all the excessive surface virility and the denigration and maltreatment of women. The sociologists among us can attribute the harem motifs, the luxurious appointments and the sci-fi excesses to our own affluent space age. But the moralists are left open-mouthed and empty-handed when they look behind the womanizing and the whiskeying to the agent's worktime proper. At best they may find a lip-service kind of job loyalty that permits the symbol to deal out death at worst with indifference and at most times with pleasure and to undergo assaults and torture as if he had been a favorite tutelee of Von Sacher-Masoch. But most often we find the agent doing a job against his will, yanked from the easy (and more often lecherous) life by Duty, stern (and more often bosomy) daughter of the voice of M. Much like a dog-face who signed up for service by mistake, much like a button-down-collar type who is on the treadmill because of the mortgage and the new T-Bird and the private-school fees, even more like the blue-collar drudge in servitude for the rent and three squares a day for too many kids—our glamorous male symbol is stuck with his job, which just happens to be making the world safe for the right team to rule it. (Everybody wants to rule the world nowadays; petty crime like a multimillion-dollar jewel robbery or a venal kidnapping or a simple international-currency racket is out.)

And we think back to Spade and Marlowe and their contemporaries, guys who were private investigators because they chose to be, who knew there was nothing pretty or glamorous or even slightly thrilling about work that involved the criminal, the abnormal, the abused and their abusers. They were men who saw

women as people rather than as receptacles for sex or sadism, who
gave of themselves in adult fashion, and, more important, behaved
in adult fashion. They weren't from comic strips, with a pow-zowie-
zam pleasure in combat and a resiliency comparable only to
Marlon Brando's in *The Chase*, when, bloody and bleeding to hemorrhage point, double-visioned by blows that mincemeated the flesh
and scrunched the bones, he buckles on his belt and sets out to take
on a whole town. When they got hit, they hurt, and they needed
time to recover; when they killed, they flinched and were gnawed
by regret. Above all, they did what they had to do because they
were men, in the head and the heart and not exclusively the groin.

This used, somehow, to be an American symbol or ideal of
manhood. I think it is as much a nostalgia for this as a faddishness
over mannerisms that has led young people to their Bogey mania,
because they are the first to know the fraudulence into which these
un-Stetsoned big-city sheriffs have degenerated. The beau ideal
was long ago—and lost.

Or was it? Let me tell you about *Harper*—Lew Harper, private
investigator, who sleeps in his underwear and his socks on his
office studio bed and wakes to find the TV still on and his head big
and has to use yesterday's coffee grounds to make a brew to get him
in shape for the day's work. And all of this we learn wordlessly,
along with the good-bye kiss to a woman's photograph as he
leaves the office, as the titles and cast and credits go by and we
start out on a case.

All the old-time trappings are in this new Warner Brothers
movie, provided by Ross Macdonald's novel *The Moving Target*,
on which William Goldman has based his first-rate screenplay. The
pros are here too under Jack Smight's intelligent and tight direction,
with Paul Newman, at his best since *Hud*, going 'way past the
inhibiting nouveau-Brando mystique to show his real range as
Harper.

The plot has an honest complexity, with a missing husband—
"He's worth twenty million on the hoof, and he's an alcoholic—and
that's just for openers"; an unloving and rapacious wife in search of
him: "I'll never divorce him—I just want to see him in his grave";
an exquisite unbright and oversexed stepdaughter; the family's pilot,

beloved by the daughter; and the family's lawyer, who loves the daughter; a nightclub singer given to dope; an over-age starlet given to drink; and religious fanatics and gangsters, petty crooks and big operators—and half a million dollars in cash at stake and a couple of corpses. The complexity is honest because you follow the trail with Harper and get the clues as he sees them.

But what is more important is the man on the trail, a gum-chewing guy who's a self-described "new-type" private eye because he doesn't drink before lunch. Harper hurts when he's hit; he needs time to catch his breath. Harper tries not to kill; he is sickened when he is forced to. He has compassion and he has righteous wrath and he knows the stupids and the phonies and the rats. He knows that the job began as a matter of "a bitch sending you in search of scum," but even though he'd rather have been sent after Cinderella by Prince Charming, he hasn't lost his awareness of what is right and what is wrong. And he happens to like his work and love his wife—and he knows that nothing, not even right and wrong, is quite that simple.

Harper can be dismissed as just another private-eye story, beautifully performed and even more beautifully directed. But we'd rather hold on to it as a return to a classic—a triumphant return to something that's been missing from the screen, something for grown-ups by grown-ups. And the rest of you can go watch Frankenstein meeting that old space monster and getting his mechanical brains blown up.

The Seal That Came
Out of the Code
October 9, 1966

The other shoe has dropped. The long-awaited revised Code of Self-Regulation of the Motion Picture Association is now with us, designed, it says there, "to keep in closer harmony with the mores, the culture, the moral sense and the expectations of our society."

It is designed to give MPA authorities a lot more leeway, since its taboos are stated in generalities rather than the specifics of the old multirevisioned 1930 code; it also authorizes the administrators to label certain approved films "recommended for mature audiences." The latter, it has been explained, is primarily a warning device for parents. And once again the rest of us can cuddle in the comfort of being considered "mature."

The "maturity" factor is difficult to determine in this year of *Who's Afraid of Virginia Woolf?*, for which the old code had to be suspended, as it was for *Alfie*. (There will be no exemptions under the new code, Jack Valenti, president of the MPA, has stated.) The gratifying assumption that anyone over the age of eighteen is mature (that's the official age limit for seeing *Virginia Woolf* without parental escort) would soon be put to rest by a simple scanning of the mail that this critic alone has received about the film. But it isn't the maturity of audiences that should concern us; it's the maturity of the moviemaker.

"Self-discipline," the MPA code preamble notes philosophically, is the ideal, but its results "are always imperfect because that is the nature of all things mortal." But this code and its administration will make clear that freedom of expression does not mean toleration of license. The test of self-restraint, the rule of reason, lies in the treatment of a subject for the screen. The SEAL of the Motion Picture Association on a film means that the picture has met the test of self-regulation.

There's a film going the rounds that has a SEAL, under the old code, yet, under that antique that didn't have such liberal views as the new one. The new one speaks in generalizations about "evil, sin, crime and wrongdoing shall not be justified," that "the basic dignity and value of human life shall be respected and upheld," and that "detailed and protracted acts of brutality, cruelty, physical violence, torture and abuse shall not be presented."

The movie-cum-seal is *An American Dream*, in which a successful television commentator and his multimillionaire, alcoholic, nymphomaniac wife beat each other up smash-bash-crash from room to room while shouting crudities at each other. ("Obscene speech, gestures or movements shall not be presented. Undue profanity should not be permitted," says the code—and where would old "hump-the-hostess" *Woolf* go for a seal in these days of "no exemptions"?) Then, as she's about to brain him with a rock, he shoves her slowly but surely over the edge of their thirty-stories-up penthouse. It certainly makes you appreciate the basic dignity and value of human life.

We can suppose that this film would, under the new rules, be earmarked for the "mature." After all, consider the plotting: the wayward wife falls squish thirty stories down to land under the wheels of a car containing a Mafia leader the commentator has been after and a Mafia moll the commentator seduced and abandoned some years before. It is, obviously, a small world, further depleted by finale time, when the Mafia mows down the commentator. And the moll, who loved and fingered him, contemplates the corpse and asks it, "Well, what did you expect from a whore?" The flaw is that she doesn't turn, Alfie-like, and direct the question to the audience. After all, we're the mature ones—and, hopefully, alive enough to answer back, even if *An American Dream* comes complete with seal.

Alfie had to have code suspension to get its seal, because it involved abortion, almost incidentally. (The new code doesn't specifically bar the subject; it simply says "illicit sex relations shall not be justified. Intimate sex scenes violating common standards of decency shall not be portrayed. Restraint and care shall be exercised in presentations dealing with sex aberrations.")

Alfie takes flight on film, the loose series of vignettes strung together in the stage play by the charming monologue of Terence Stamp given cohesion and cumulative power by both the camera and the subtleties of character revealed by Michael Caine in the film's title role. Stamp's performance was a very good one, but through the camera's magnifying eye we now see the boyish charm as veneer, the equally thin layer of callous cruelty beneath it and, at the bottom, the ego and ignorance and lovelessness that made *Alfie* the frightening hollow man of our time, the taker whose groping awareness of his futility and his unhappiness does not impair his glibness or his reach. *Alfie* emerges as a stingingly funny and perceptive comedy, with a thoroughly discomforting and discomfiting moral and very little to offer the sensation seeker.

Mr. Huston declared that the movie he would like to be "remembered by" is *The Bible*. Before it, he noted, he would have cited *Sierra Madre*, but now it is *The Bible* on which he would stake his stature, because it is the "one" movie on which "no compromises" were made.

Well, certainly there is no compromise with the fundamentalism of the text of the first twenty-two chapters of Genesis (don't let the title or the film's three hours fool you; even the subtitle, ". . . In the beginning" applies to only the beginning of the beginning); and expurgation—of Noah's drunkenness, of Lot's daughters' incest, of Sarah's concubinage while passing as Abraham's "sister" —does not necessarily mean compromise. But one wonders what compromise does mean when an artist of Huston's stature can reduce the power and glory of an Old Testament God to thunder, lightning and an offstage voice (incidentally, Huston's own—and he serves also as narrator and as Noah, as well as director), the giants on the earth to the dimensions of Sunday-school study cards, and the wondrous legendry to a series of elliptical pantomimes and attenuated, dreary dramas. The initial sequence of the Creation—near-impressionistic, sweeping, surging natural scenes—surpasses mere spectacle and offers hope that Mr. Huston will bring inspiration and imagination to his obvious mastery of moviemaking. But here is an all-American Adam rising right out of a little puddle of dust much like Frankenstein's monster emerging from sedation, but with far less charm, and here is a Swedish Eve surprisingly *not* popping out of rib chop, and off they scoot through a decor-type Garden of Eden to the fig-leaf stage wiggling their bare behinds. (Bare behinds, you see, are acceptable; rigid drapery of Eve's golden tresses, some contorted knee flexes by Adam and camera cutoffs shield us from a shocking encounter with the rest of the human body.)

The Hollywood stage is set (yes, we know the film was made in Italy—how else would Stephen Boyd be on hand as Nimrod?). We're not surprised thereafter by a Noah who starts out as a canny man of faith but winds up, after what literally seems to be forty days and nights, as a sort of low-comedy Dr. Dolittle (some real crowd-serving slapstick there when he gets his foot stuck in a pitch bucket and tussles with an elephant; no wonder, as Huston told

Miss Walters, he had wanted Chaplin for the role!); a Cain given
to fist-shaking angry-young-man melodramatics; messengers of the
Lord who are simply blue-eyed Peter O'Toole in triplicate and a
Katherine Dunham-choreographed Sodom that sticks to the ballet
school of sin, with the emphasis on gold-painted eyelids and lots of
writhing on the floor and hardly merits destruction by a mushroom
cloud that marshmallow-roasts Mrs. Lot into salt. What is surprising
is that finally, after all the dull dull Illustrated Highlights, we are
touched and roused by Abraham—or more specifically, George C.
Scott (for it is indeed he behind that Hugh Griffith makeup). Here
is a glimmer of passionate faith of Old Testament stature, but only
a glimmer, for the finale fizzles to a ring-around-the-rosy by Abraham
and Isaac in silhouette and long-shot, on top of Old Smoky.

We are left with clichés rather than truths, with tedium rather
than spiritual gleanings. A wit close to the production of *The Bible*
had predicted that I would start my review of the film with "Is
God dead? He wasn't until John Huston killed him." On the con-
trary, I rather suspect that the eighteen million dollars killed John
Huston. In succumbing to the eternal temptation of the artist to
translate the greatest stories ever told, he has attained neither the
humbly passionate humanism of Pasolini's *The Gospel According to
St. Matthew* nor the vulgar excitement or sheer entertainment of
the De Mille school of Biblicals.

Because there is little vulgarity (in the vulgar sense), and no
breaches of taste (in the blue-nose sense), the notion may get
abroad that this is a fine film for the kiddies. Harvey Cox, of the
Harvard Divinity School, suggests ironically in *Look* that *The Bible*
is a film "for which we need a new pastoral classification: corrupt
for adults, fine for children." How sad, really, to put this prosaic
brake upon the imagination of the young, even though the brake
is in 70mm Deluxe Color; how wrong to convince them that The
Book is a bore.

No, come to think of it, I'd almost prefer to expose them to the
Hollywood Biblical in its purest form. Consider how my colleague,
dance critic Walter Terry, recalls the original *Ten Commandments*
of his childhood: "Part I was in Biblical times—Robert Edeson was
Moses and Estelle Taylor, later Mrs. Jack Dempsey, was Miriam,
who writhed before the Golden Calf.

"Part II was set in modern times. Rod La Rocque was a clean, upstanding young builder, happily married to Leatrice Joy. Well, Rod, as he climbs the ladder of success, falls into the arms of Nita Naldi, a vamp. To get more money to lavish on her, Rod cheats on the great new church he's building. There's too much sand in the cement. And at dedication time the church crumbles, collapses and kills all Rod's loved ones and the only part of the wall left standing is the one with the tablets of the Ten Commandments.

"Meanwhile, back at the nest, Nita is lying on a couch in seductive pose. Rod leaps on her and covers her with kisses. She looks at him with those teasing evil eyes and then throws back her head and laughs. 'I've got leprosy!' she chortles."

Now there's something for Cecil B. De Mille to be remembered by.

"Money's Worth"— A Long Story
November 6, 1966

The vicious producer-consumer cost circle is closing in on movie-goers, and we face a future of continual endurance contests. Costs are rising, admissions are rising and, alas, we're being given our "money's worth."

Just what our "money's worth" is was stated succinctly by an unusual man involved with *Hawaii*, the most recent of our spectaculars. The man's unusual in that he's quite rational about the movies for which he has to thump the tub. Would not *Hawaii*, of which he was sincerely fond, be—er—better (the hesitation was ours in editorializing) if it had been cut to two hours instead of three— Indeed it would, he agreed, "but when you charge four bucks a seat, people want their money's worth."

Let's concede that *Hawaii*'s multimillion-dollar production cost calls for the admission price. Must we, in ever-rocketing cycles, face the prospect of longer and longer movies manufactured on the basis of quantity rather than quality? Let's suppose that there are those among us who wouldn't pay a high reserved-seat price for two hours of top-notch entertainment (which is exactly what Broadway at its occasional best offers at twice the price, albeit padded out with intermissions) and that we prorate movie entertainment at $1.25 an hour. Certainly, from the vast and wonderful array of short films displayed at film festivals but rarely on theatrical display, in this country, at least, another hour's worth of fine cinema could be culled.

Audiences can be conditioned. Time was when we were more than willing to disappear into moviehouses for nigh on to four hours (and even sit through that twice) for a main feature, a second feature, a long short and a short short, a newsreel and a fine orgy of coming attractions. There are times when we'd be willing to sit forever; times when half a film is more than enough. The money's worth is the quality and not the quantity.

There is something "old-fashioned" about *Hawaii* in its attempting to be one of those generation-type sagas, starting out with Abner Hale's ordination and missionary call, etching in his family background, proceeding to his search for a wife, his courtship, the couple's setting out to cross the world of the 1820's, the careful detailing of the voyage, the initial impact of the missionaries on the natives and vice versa.

But we still have at midpoint twenty years to go; we get crisis strung on crisis with the spectacles-of-nature-and-people that the wide screen demands. The decades are dealt with in elliptic confusion, and we wind up with a muddle of plot and theme, with justice done to neither characters nor history nor sociology. We have retrospectively only the impression of an arrogant Bible-thumping, fire-eating preacher endlessly undergoing the agonies of fundamentalism until suddenly he goes soft-headed (or -hearted), of a sort of Yiddishe-mama-type Hawaiian queen providing moments of fat-lady humor and chicken-soup sentiment and of the missionary's lovely wife wasting away because she didn't have the gumption to go off with her sea captain in midfilm. And all of this does total injustice to Max von Sydow's portrait of a rigid Calvinist tortured by love of God and woman, Julie Andrews' of a woman growing into an understanding love of an unlovable man or Jocelyn La Garde's of primitive regal dignity; they are buried in the bog of multiplotting and multidetailing that pads out and overloads the three hours.

It's the quality and not the quantity that clocks out the hours. *Gone with the Wind*, that greatest of spectacles, runs three hours and forty minutes, plus intermission. We last had a chance to re-view it six years ago—happily, we will again next October, on its next release. We know that at fadeout time we will linger, wishing for "and then what happened." It holds us with classic force, the sweeping background of the ante- and post-bellum South, the war spectacle itself, the power of four movie stars involved in triangles epitomizing eternal romance. And there is not—I say this retrospectively, with a promise to recheck in eleven months—a frame of film I would surrender.

There are few films of any length for which this holds true, that could not be trimmed for quality. *A Funny Thing Happened on the Way to the Forum*, only ninety-nine minutes long, would be even better with some snippets out of its chariot-race sequence; *The Fortune Cookie*, running two hours and five minutes, would attain the perfection it misses if about eight minutes were chopped right off the end, leaving us high on Billy Wilder's cynical pinnacle of fun and saving us from the obvious sentimentality of its fashionable-social-comment happy ending.

What of major surgery? Certainly until one has seen the uncut version of Max Ophuls' *Lola Montez* one cannot even suspect the artistry, let alone the thematic basis, of this work. On the other hand, there is currently an interesting case in point in a Japanese film, Hiroshi Inagaki's *Chushingura*. It was shown here first at the Toho Cinema (and how we miss that showcase!) three years ago. It ran one hour and forty-eight minutes. At that time we described this classic and beautifully performed tale of forty-seven eighteenth-century samurai who are loyal until death as "the slow-paced stuff of legendry told with the passing of the seasons, as cherry blossoms flutter and as the snow falls. It is leisurely, but excellent narration and succinct subtitles sustain the interest even for impatient youngsters while the eye feasts on loveliness."

We did not know at that time (and its producer and the theater operator, the Toho Company, was apparently not about to tell us) that the film had been cut virtually in half. About a year after the eight-week New York showing, Edward Landberg, owner of the Berkeley Cinema, in Berkeley, California, acquired distribution rights to the film—and in its total form—running three and a half hours; it lasted for forty-one weeks at his theater.

Now *Chushingura* is here in its entirety for us to see. Certainly for those who missed this color film originally it is a must, for rarely have we seen a chivalric romance told so befittingly, the heroic blended with the humanistic, the poetic with the derring-do. But actually, half a movie was as good as the whole. If anything, the uncut version demands a much more special interest and, while it does provide an enhanced canvas of the period and further detailing and probing of motive and manner, the profusion in the subplots and additional minor characters can well be confusing to the non-Oriental-oriented eye.

It is, of course, the classicism of the tale of knighthood, of beautiful men and women sacrificing all for love and for principle, of vows fulfilled and tragedy larger than its participants, that sustains the hours of film. Its enactment by superb players and exquisite camera work sustain the viewer. The money's worth is there in a quality that justifies the quantity. But the *Chushingura* quality, exceptional as it undoubtedly is, also proves that very good things can be encompassed in smaller packages as well.

Tongue in Cheek
or Foot in Mouth?
October 23, 1966

There's such a rush of entries in the funny-oops department these days that one begins to suspect that all is not straight in the face and square in the intention in the cinema factories. I offer the suspicion that the tongue is in the cheek somewhere because it's getting pretty hard to imagine that they're doing what they're doing in earnest.

The funny-oops department includes all those characters, lines, scenes, sequences and even whole movies that are very, very cogent and serious and poetic and only make you giggle nervously, titter hysterically or simply explode in a whoop of laughter that makes you very, very unpopular in the more formal moviehouses. The familiar funny-funny and funny-peculiar departments are still getting their screen credits, but the rush of items in the funny-by-mistake area is such that there's a new cult coming up that's accusing The Hollywood Establishment of camp, of doing it all on purpose, yet.

The cultists, for instance, latched on to John Ford's *Seven Women* as an *auteur* triumph, while the rest of us just relegated it to the status of funniest-by-mistake of the season. And the little-magazine cineastes are extolling *Time of Indifference*, in the words of one, as "the first camp movie the Italians have made."

I cite *Time of Indifference* because not all cinema-factory sins should be laid at Hollywood's door. But it's the Hollywood build-up on which the Italians are resting in this one, since it would not have come to our attention were Paulette Goddard, Rod Steiger, Shelley Winters and Claudia Cardinale not its stars and/or victims. Along with a native named Tomas Milian, this quartet portrays a group of decadent Italians decaying some more, and the whole thing sounds like an Upstairs at the Downstairs cabaret sketch, except that the lighting and the audio would be better in that tiny bistro. In bare outline, Miss Goddard, a decaying socialite, is the mistress of

Steiger, a decaying profiteer, who goes on to make Miss Cardinale, Miss Goddard's far-from-decaying daughter, his new mistress, while Miss Winters, a decaying friend of the family and ex-mistress of Steiger, works away at seducing Milian, Miss Goddard's almost-decaying son. And all of this goes on to the tune of dialogue that, alas, is not decaying—it's as ripe as it's ever been—and "ever" is a long, long time. "Michele," Miss Winter coos at the lad, "you're always so strange." "What do you mean so strange?" "I don't know" . . . "I like the rain, don't you? I feel much better when it rains" . . . "I want it to be different for us . . . I want it to be beautiful. . . ."

Cut. Next movie: "What's that?" asks the girl as the boy whistles a tune. "It's the slow movement from my jazz quartet," he replies— and yes, folks, we're back in Hollywood's domain. Boy has "been" with girl. "I feel like praying." "Go ahead—pray." "I don't know how," he says, lapsing into a twenty-minute harangue to the tune of "All you gods, nod your big shaggy heads and shower us with blessings." But them gods don't, and before long there's the abortion bit, and selling out that jazz quartet that somehow has turned into an octet ("What's that? It's lovely," another girl says, and he replies, "It's my jazz octet") for success in the record business. "I got news for you—it's a lousy world out there" . . . "Life's the biggest crap game going" . . . "There's a name for women like you" . . . "Somewhere down the years we lost the only thing that mattered" . . . "We're dead, we're dead . . ." And finally, "Dear God, let her live . . ."

And there you have, as any moviegoer can tell without any more detailing, the entire plot, mystique and philosophical content of *Mister Buddwing*, with James Garner as the suffering amnesiac (Mr. Garner suffers by way of brow wrinkles—two for anguish, three for agony) enmeshed in flashbacks; Katharine Ross, Suzanne Pleshette and Jean Simmons, as the composite of the girl-woman he's looking for, and Angela Lansbury the only nonlaughable in the proceedings. But it's put forth as serious melodrama, straight from the pen of Dale Wasserman by way of an Evan Hunter novel, with Delbert Mann supplying further incoherence by way of direction. They've not only established *Buddwing* as best bet so far for funniest-by-mistake of this year, but have provided us with as good a glossary of hambone lines as we've come across in a decade.

The funny-oops, admittedly, provides some of the lighter moments in the life of the Constant Moviegoers—and, alas, the angrier ones. These occur when the filmmaker and the viewer are in rapport, when a mood has been established and atmosphere created and an involving story begun. Then, suddenly—*kaboom*. The wrong note, character, moment—and we part company, however briefly; but more often than not, the unity of feeling can never be recaptured.

The current regrettable example thereof is *Seconds*, which hooks you for exactly half of its one hundred and ten minutes in true thriller fashion with its latter-day Faustian tale of a middle-aged and frustrated Scarsdale banker who makes a deal with the "organization" to give him a second chance at life. Grim humor is not missing from the initial incidents, properly meshed with the eerie science-fiction and terror-in-the-sunshine atmosphere John Frankenheimer creates for the matter-of-fact efficiency with which identities are switched, corpses are substituted, bodies rejuvenated, faces rebuilt. With that fine actor John Randolph as the client, and Will Geer and Jeff Corey leading organization men, with the tone set by Saul Bass's ghoulish titles and James Wong Howe's macabre camerawork, we are in the midst of a thinking man's horror movie. And then . . . the transmutation has been finished with supernatural superscience; Will Geer, the Devil in Midwestern twangy disguise, peers at the product with a "Well, I never—how you boys do it, I'll never know!" and the bandages are withdrawn for our benefit. And out pops—Rock Hudson.

From then on things get even funnier-by-mistake. Hudson, who suffers by watering his eyes, encounters Salome Jens as the Lilith of his life, and they not only go to a Santa Barbara grape fiesta (Mr. Frankenheimer's notion of an orgy, involving beatniks tromping grapes in the buff, is not quite as exciting as family night in a Turkish bath, but six times funnier), but they talk. "You're beautiful," she says. "You're an ocean," he says. It's enough to make you start listening to the rest of the dialogue and start questioning the logic of the rest of the plot—and all that, alas, proves fatal.

It's mad-making that a filmmaker can't leave a good thing alone

—or keep it going. But the disturbing thing is that he was in dead earnest all the way.

Idle Dreams
About Idols
November 20, 1966

Let a Dwight Macdonald take a cool look at the cinema scene from the relative calm of his monthly stint and retreat from the shadow-land to politics. As for us, so long as we got our 20–20s (and not many in the movie-reviewing game can make this contact-lensless boast) we'll stick to the screen and dreams thereof. And anybody who can survive these noisy days of falling idols, crashing hopes and shattering dreams will probably wind up still lensless but soundly ear-plugged.

Let's differentiate from the start twixt hopes and dreams about idols. One would hope, for example, for cinematic appreciation of such fine performers as George C. Scott and Dick Shawn; after all, this is the year full justice was done Alan Arkin in *The Russians Are Coming* and Walter Matthau in *The Fortune Cookie*. But when one sees Scott struggling through to some semblance of dignity in the morass of *The Bible* or just plain struggling amid the tired idio-cies of *Not With My Wife, You Don't*, or Shawn frenetically follow-ing frenetic direction in *Way . . . Way Out* or just lethargizing through the lethargy in *Penelope*—well, we hoped. The idol remains upright, on the shelf; our hopes are dispassionate and frail when it comes to Hollywood happenings.

But the realm of dream and idolatry has a firmer base in re-spect to certain directors who have turned our immediate hopes into a sort of survival-schmerz. On the foreign scene alone, let's say, if we cannot await with great expectations that next Fellini or Malle or Schlesinger or Resnais or Truffaut or Polanski film—then, hell, let's turn to a political scene fraught with situations either Sennettesque or Strangelovian.

Well, two down and four to go, *mes amis*. We've had the Truffaut and the Polanski, and we use "had" almost advisedly. Some idols fall to rise—or be raised—again. But it will be a while before we have the heart to pick up the pieces.

First came Roman Polanski's *Cul-de-sac*, loaded down with awards from Berlin and Venice festivals. Our hopes had been soaring as we awaited a maturation of the very great talent this young Polish director exhibited to varying effect in *Knife in the Water* and *Repulsion*. Both were marked by the pure cinematic eye with which he explores the surface of atmosphere and relationships, the probing suggestions of subsurface malaise and complexities. *Repulsion* was the lesser work in content, a voyeur's wallow in schizophrenia and murder to no point beyond sensation—but no one could deny the creative talent at work.

Why not, then, expect a great deal of his next film, a "bizarre comedy" about "an off-beat couple who are kept prisoner in their own castle by a pair of colorful gangsters"? The "bizarre" part of the label is a masterpiece of understatement for the sadistic perversions expounded, and "comedy" is apparently the word for the exposition of necrophilia, nymphomania, murder, homosexuality and sheer and pointless depradation of everything animate and otherwise. Weird grotesqueries right out of Genet at his most outrageous are proposed as comic. At least it's not labeled "black" comedy. I hesitate to tell you its true color. To think that we thought *Morgan!* on the sick side; golly, it only proposed that there's nothing funnier than a madman who winds up in an asylum. Elementary. Split your sides in *Cul-de-sac* at the slow death of a pop-eyed gangster with a belly full of bullets, at an aging paunchy Lionel Stander whipping a nymphomaniac Françoise Dorléac or tossing a trembling transvestite Donald Pleasence into a grave and tumbling a corpse on top of him. (Stander, graying and gravel-voiced as ever, is a nostalgic sight, but as a colleague remarked, we are paying the price for McCarthyism, which banished this actor at his prime and therefore allows his "rediscovery" in a vehicle of this sort.) Polanski's singleminded macabre mood, admirable in

Repulsion, is shattered here by dreary by-play and pointless characterization; suspense deteriorates into attenuation and bad jokes. Once again you watch—to no purpose or point. The talent is there— wasted on tripe. And we are nagged by the suspicion that, laurel-laden, Polanski is now off into that chic world of sick jokes that are even passé with teen-agers. Let's just say that the English atmosphere (this is his second English film in the making and the language) is not one in which his gifts are ripening.

Nor, alas, is England—or English, perhaps—the milieu for François Truffaut, whose *Fahrenheit 451* is neither science nor fiction nor good old moviemaking. The Ray Bradbury book took us to a never world where the printed word is illegal (books burn at 451 degrees Fahrenheit), television absorbs the mind and unthinking obedience makes for happiness. But Truffaut's land is English to the core, with some sort of Council houses, furnished in three little Sachs modern, prewar dial telephones and contemporary clothing, accent on short skirts, to set the period and render ludicrous the monorail and Buck Rogers-type flying policemen we're given glimpses of and dialogue like "Is it true that a long time ago firemen used to put out fires and not burn books?" or "What's that?" "A rocking chair." And everyone talks English English—except for our hero, Oskar Werner, whose German accent is totally inexplicable in the context of the film.

It's all cleanly detailed and very pretty in color, but where is Truffaut in this tedious tale of the book-burning fireman who, urged on by a pretty girl (Julie Christie in miniskirt and cropped hair), reads a book, *David Copperfield,* yet, and gets so hooked on reading that before you know it he's plodding through *Webster's Unabridged* and hoarding books like mad, until he's reported by his wife (Julie Christie in negligee and long hair, and don't ask why the dual role, except that either part in itself—or both, for that matter— scarcely merits the attention of an Oscar-winning actress). But our fireman escapes, to the "book people," each of whom has memorized a book for posterity. A pretty thought—how darling, those identical twins memorizing *Pride and Prejudice,* the ardent girl who says, "I'm *The Jewish Question,* by Sartre," the youngster who says, "I'm *The Martian Chronicles,* by Ray Bradbury."

Aha—you spotted it, eh, in that last little "in" joke, Truffaut's *hommage à* Bradbury. There's Truffaut, fans, in the books being burned—*Cahiers du Cinema, Zazie de le Métro, Mad* magazine, Genet and Genet and Genet and Behan, lots of Henry Miller—oh, the books they read in Merrie England—and most of them, of course, in paperback, which keeps production costs down.

But beyond the little jokes, where is the Truffaut of the fey plot, the probing characterization, the pertinent comment, the imagination and the unforgettable image? We are left only with a beautiful and slightly hysterical Julie Christie, a deadpan Oskar Werner, and an obvious language difficulty between an American science-fictioneer, a French-speaking director and a made-in-England movie.

Two, as noted, down. And we're reaching for the earplugs and pondering politics.

Hey There, Quasimodo!
November 27, 1966

Everybody was there except Quasimodo. It was one of those "Hey there!" occasions—hey there, it's Kirk Douglas—and, hey there, it's Glenn Ford and Jean-Paul (Belmondo, you shnook—you were expecting maybe Sartre? And come to think of it, why not?) and Simone and Yves and, hey there, Tony Perkins and, cheri, Charles Boyer and Alain of the pouty mouth Delon and your favorite Untouchable and Deanna Durbin's, Robert Stack—and dahling chubby Orson Welles. What an occasion—and Quasimodo, poor *petit* hunchback, he miss it all—*quel dommage!*

Because by the time the huge old bell of Notre Dame, cobwebbed after its four years of disuse, starts being pushed into a sway, slowly, slowly, gathering momentum—of course we all know that somehow it will be Lon Chaney swinging on the rope or pushing the slide trestle for the bong-bong-bong. Because that's the way it is in *Is Paris Burning?* By the time finale-time comes around, all we haven't had is Quasimodo.

Which brings us smack up to the total misuse of that "cameo" bit that Mike Todd created to such superb advantage in *Around the World in Eighty Days* and that has been so dishonored in the imitation. And this brings us to the use of the familiar face in contemporary factual events, to the strange mixture of truth and fiction that it results in, and to the ultimate effect of the star on his story situation.

I don't think any spectacular in the making had had more non-fan-mag interest in advance than *Is Paris Burning?*, not only because of our interest in the fascinating factual yet scenario-like story of the city's nick-of-time liberation in the best-seller by Larry Collins and Dominique Lapierre. The auguries and auspices seemed auspicious: the French, right up to De Gaulle, were all-out cooperative, and René Clement, the French director, was to be at the helm. He not only had such films as *Forbidden Games, Gervaise, Purple Noon* and *Walls of Malapaga* to his credit, but had actually lived through the occupation and liberation of Paris in August of 1944 and had already come up with *Bataille du Rail*, a film of the wartime Resistance activities of France's railroad men. He knew whereof he filmed.

Or did he? The director was French, but the money for the film American. And for American money you got to have box-office appeal, *nicht wahr*? And if you make a film in three languages (even though you dub it into a fourth—vaudeville-dialect—for presumably idiotic American audiences), there are three nations you must please. For the Germans you must show that there were good as well as bad Nazis, and the good Nazis triumph even though the bad Nazis lose the war; for the French, you must show that there were superb French and good French and no bad French at all— no definable strife within the Resistance movement and no personal ambitions or power politics anywhere on the part of anybody, no collaboration, no relations with the Germans except pure hate; for the Americans, you must show those wonderful GI Joes who talk about life and death and their dreams of Paree while they smoke Camels and kiss the pretty girls and get shot through the head the minute they utter one of their just-folks phrases.

And once you satisfy national prides—oh yes, there is box office. So how does the Resistance get word to the Allies that the hour has arrived, that they must strike before the Germans fire the city? Tinkers to Evers to Chance—Delon to Douglas to Ford (the last two as Generals Patton and Bradley, no less). And how do the Free French and the GI's come upon Paris? The common soldiers of each are represented, respectively, by Yves Montand as a French tankman and Anthony Perkins as a golly-gee-it's-Paree doughboy, with Simone Signoret as a barmaid, yet, to cheer them on their way.

And as each of these familiar faces appears, all that the film has created, all that it has attempted in the way of authenticity, by location filming or by snippets of newsreels, is completely un-done. We just know, with no room for quibble, that none of these movie stars was involved in this particular way—if perchance he happened to be out of swaddling clothes at the time. The major cheat and idiocy is, of course, the assumption that anyone is going to plunk down several bucks to see any of these celebrities for their three or four minutes in the film. I can hardly picture a Signoret or Boyer or Belmondo fan making the pilgrimage without suing. Do the tub-thumpers actually appreciate their misrepresenta-tion in touting that "stunning international cast" (which includes such stunners as Robert Stack, who has a stunning two minutes im-personating General Sibert, contact man for Glenn Ford-oops, Gen-eral Bradley, and Skip Ward, renowned, of course, as the bus driver in *Night of the Iguana*, if not as one of the stunning drivers in *Red Line 7000*)?

But let's consider the filmmaker's viewpoint, rather than the thump of tub or cash of box office. Is there no awareness of the vitiation of truth by the splash of star faces in bit roles? Contem-porary events cannot withstand the assault. It's different with the past. Disraeli becomes George Arliss; Elizabeth is, as any movie-goer knows, Bette Davis; Pasteur and Juarez are Paul Muni; and Rembrandt and Henry VIII, Charles Laughton. (As for Napoleon— well, Boyer or Brando—you choose.) The more contemporary an im-personation is—just about anything post-Sergeant York—the more it is strictly for the kiddies. We grown-ups know our famous men, and we know our movie stars. You can't fool us, and neither can they.

That is why, of course, children of a star system that we are, the first samples of Italian neorealism had such impact upon us. Everyone, even the leading characters, was unrecognizable and therefore very real. The illusions were enhanced by the grubbiness, the unchic, the smell of poverty and humanity that seldom penetrates the Hollywood screen; but it was an *unknown* De Sica, Magnani, Gassman and Loren who gripped us then, as they seldom have since.

The Spy Who Came in from the Cold is more noticeable than he should be—simply because Richard Burton is a noticeable man, no matter how he blanks himself into a role; the physicist in *The Defector* takes on the ravaged tremors of Montgomery Clift because Clift in his last days was a ravaged man; *The Professionals* fulfill themselves because Burt Lancaster and Lee Marvin and Woody Strode and Robert Ryan are pros in the fullest sense. Stars are stars, and they cannot be converted to faces in a crowd. And when somebody starts ringing that old bell at Notre Dame, by George, I want Quasimodo at the end of the rope—or at very least Lon Chaney, Jr.

Drunks and Lechers
and Good Guys All
December 4, 1966

Gone are the wine and the song. It's whiskey, women and gold for our heroes today, at least the home-grown Hollywood ones. And it's reached the point where, once a man is described, in effect, as a venal, hard-drinking lecher, or a lecherous, drunken mercenary, we know he's going to prove himself decent, human, red-blooded and capable of giving old Lancelot a run for his money in the pure-of-heart sweepstakes.

We used to be able to blame it on the British via Bond, but it's a characteristic we currently claim for our own. Take but two recent examples, high and low. No sooner is Burt Lancaster, one of

The Professionals, in what is about the best movie-type movie of recent months, described as dedicated to "one-hundred-proof whiskey, ninety-proof women and fourteen-carat gold" than we know he will prove to be the highest-principled man on the scene. Let William Holden, alias *Alvarez Kelly*, in one of the soppiest and sloppiest of Civil War cow-operas to have come our way in years, be similarly accused, and we anticipate his ultimate ultranobility—though few of us would indeed anticipate it to reach quite the mawkish heights the screenplay achieves.

The acceptance of this sort of thing is quite general, even though it prompts the National Catholic Office for Motion Pictures to award the films an A-III rating as "morally unobjectionable for adults," and, in fact, to criticize the Motion Picture Association's failing, under its new code, to label *The Professionals* "suggested for mature audiences." (*Alvarez Kelly* had been rated during the old non-label-suggesting Code, even though it just went into release here recently.) Even for adults, or mature audiences, of course, a combination of alcohol, ladies and loot isn't allowed to make for happiness in any film dedicated, as *Alvarez Kelly* is, to the total cliché. "Money, whiskey and women—your three deities," the virtuous Union major sneers at Kelly, the "eye-eye-eye-Irish señor," as the title ballad has it, who's bringing Mexican cattle to feed the Grand Army of the Republic. "Has this made you a happy man?" "No," Kelly replies, "but not as miserable a one as you." And in no time at all Kelly's virtues start to seep through, and he's telling the snobbishly wisecracking major, "Make jokes about the war, about God, about me—but don't makes jokes about my father." Complete with his trilogy of vices, he's one of nature's noblemen, let alone Hollywood's—a status, by the way, that apparently doesn't entitle Mr. Holden to the luxury of proper process shots (he looks as if he's pasted onto a movie screen of another color to make him seem surrounded by stampeding cattle or hard-riding Rough Riders or cavalrymen).

What we must do, however, is simply chalk up another cliché for the moviegoer to cope with. (Even clichés change with the times, and try dragging even the immature away from Bond to a soft-drinking, horse-loving, woman-venerating type!) What would be nice, of course, is to have an occasional reminder that a drunken, money-grubbing womanizer might be just that and nothing more or, even better, utterly unheroic and unprincipled and perfectly happy. (Lancaster is *almost* perfectly happy, but he does have a conscience and he is a whale of an explosives expert and just fine for the derring-do schmaltzerie of his film.) Any break in the mold, any departure from the truism, and you can thrill us movie-goers to our very marrow.

Two recent and dissimilar films make a move in the right direction; one succeeds in breaking the mold, the other in merely cracking the shell before quitting. The mold-smasher is Woody Allen's *What's Up, Tiger Lily?*, a total takeoff on the Bondian frenzy, in a fresh and double-joke fashion. Mr. Allen has simply taken a typical Japanese spy-and-intrigue movie, typically photographed in beautiful color, replete with all sorts of characters guaranteed to provide incoherence for the non-Oriental mind, and deadpan-in-earnest in direction, and dubbed in English dialogue that is right out of his own stand-up-comedian mind and madness. It's not an original technique, Mr. Allen modestly explains in the prologue: "*Gone With The Wind* was a Japanese movie; they just dubbed in Southern voices." But the result is a mad incongruity between hilarious lines and serious-faced performers playing it straight, sight and sound gags galore in and out of the film's framework, a slapdashery of wit and nonsense—and, above all, despite the occasional bog-down and the basic overworking of a single gag, a refreshment for the viewer. For above all, we have in Mr. Allen someone who has taken a fresh look at film and decided to have some silly fun with a number of its clichés. And his fun is ours.

On a completely different tack, Raoul Levy suggests that he is taking a fresh look at the serious-spy cliché and coming up with an intriguingly new viewpoint in *The Defector*. He starts out with Montgomery Clift, who gives an excellent performance in what turned out to be his last film, as a reluctant spy, a physicist virtually forced by the CIA to undertake an espionage assignment in Leipzig. (And beautiful color photography, albeit in Munich, lends authenticity to the tale.) We're on a trite though undoubtedly true path as the Russians and East German security men go the brainwashing and won't-you-defect route, but suddenly there is novelty in the air. Hardy Kruger, as an East German scientist reluctantly in espionage at the behest of his government, is ordered, when he fails to get Clift to defect, to pose as a defector, go west and worm out the secrets of science from Clift on his home grounds. There's fascination in the confrontation of two reluctant spies, two men who would by instinct and intellect be friends in other circumstances— and what a fine twist, to see where they will wind up in the West. But no sooner does Kruger cross over than he's killed by a truck—by accident or CIA is never quite made clear—and all that we're finally left with is the cliché, a relatively new one, along with the triple-viced hero, that spying is not a nice profession but the good guys have to go in and win for our team.

Well, East, West or Western, what this country needs, moviewise, is a good cliché-breaker—and hang the expense.

A Film
for All Time
December 13, 1966

A Man for All Seasons is a beautiful and satisfying film, the ultimate demonstration, perhaps, of how a fine stage play can be transcended and, with integrity and inspiration, turned into a great motion picture.

It is, above all, a masterpiece of restraint on the part of all, a thinking man's spectacular in the best sense. Here is history with the pomp and circumstance understated, a gripping human drama in which the passions and turbulence are underplayed, a probing study of conscience whose complexities and subtleties are indicated with brilliant clarity and whose contemporary significance is forcefully presented by implication alone.

The temptations facing the creators are all too obvious in this story of the sixteenth-century conflict between Sir Thomas More, the reluctant martyr, and Henry VIII, the pragmatic tyrant. But in adapting his stage play to the screen, Robert Bolt—that rare writer who can make Tudors talk without recourse to ersatz Shakespeare—has eschewed expansion for its own sake or the slightest vulgarization for the benefit of the box office. And director-producer Fred Zinnemann once again demonstrates his own particular genius for discipline in letting cast and camera tell all, concisely and precisely.

The two-hour film traces the last seven years in More's life, from refusal to support Cardinal Wolsey in seeking Papal approval for Henry's divorce from Catherine of Aragon and marriage to Anne Boleyn, through his imprisonment for the silence that implied disapproval of the *fait accompli*, to the execution for refusing to betray himself by voicing approval.

What makes More fascinating—and on screen, in close-up, Paul Scofield is, if possible, more brilliant even than on stage in the role—is that he is no martyr by intent; here is a man of learning, of wit, of sophistication, a wordly but devout man who finds that ultimately, in a corrupt world, "to be human at all—perhaps we must stand fast a little, even at the risk of being heroes." In Scofield's craggy face and slightly stooping figure, in every gesture and word, there is heroism and saintliness without a hint of heroics or sanctimoniousness.

There is fascination too in Robert Shaw's Henry, a golden young king whose respect, nay, affection, for his scholarly antagonist is as evident as his vanity, whose self-knowledge is as apparent as his despotic inclinations. It is the aura of intelligence Scofield creates that encompasses his opponents, whether it is Wolsey, a crude behemoth created by Orson Welles; his pursuer and prosecutor, Cromwell, a shrewd scoundrel shrewdly portrayed by Leo McKern, or the young toady, Rich, who ultimately sells his soul not for the world but Wales, a Judas played with sharp insight by John Hurt. Each encounter is a duel of wit and wisdom, each foeman worthy of More's moral steel.

In much the same way, Scofield's humanity brings vitality to his family circle, with Wendy Hiller giving the performance of her career as More's unsubtle, brusque and deeply devoted wife; Susannah York as the daughter who is as intelligent as she is beautiful; Corin Redgrave as the son-in-law who is more principled than practical, and Nigel Davenport as the Duke of Norfolk, simple in mind and in affection.

The role of the Common Man, who served as general factotum and commentator in the play, has been assigned to the camera. Mr. Zinnemann gives us a complete picture of the age in a snatch of dialogue with a boatman, a trailing sound of Parliamentary debate, a glimpse of dockside crowds; the mood is in the calm of the river, the blustering breeze in the woods, a servant's moment of shame; time is glimpsed through a dungeon window noted in a neglected garden; a wife's heart is in her stumbling footstep on prison stairs and a king's decision is set by the erotic pursing of his bride's lips.

The bridal scene typifies Mr. Zinnemann's genius for precise detail and concise narrative where others would resort to panoply and spectacle. In this very brief scene of the festivities, we see the sensual relationship between Henry and Anne, the romanticism of the King, the custom of the time; yet all these are subsidiary to its purpose—to show Henry's disappointment at More's absence and make us sense that it will not be forgiven. It is brief, almost fleeting; Anne says not a word and is not even identified in the cast. But you will not forget her; it is, you see, Vanessa Redgrave.

Whether minor or major, each figure is perfectly drawn, an essential to the rich and glowing tapestry on which the leading characters emerge. This is the film that blazes forth with something to say and says it perfectly. *A Man for All Seasons* is a film for all time.

Antonioni in London
December 19, 1966

Blow-Up is a beautiful and startling film, startling because if the credits didn't say it was coauthored and directed by Michelangelo Antonioni, you'd never believe it on the basis of the movie itself, and beautiful because in his first made-in-England English-language film the Italian director proves himself a master of the use of color, both literally and figuratively.

The startlement of authorship stems from the relative absence of what we have previously recognized as the maestro's staples— Monica Vitti, cinema for its own sweet sake, Alienation in excelsis and inertia in excess. The Mod and Carnaby Street aspects of London life have obviously altered Antonioni's ambience, and he captures the mood and the style, the tempo and the temperature— and even verges on presenting us with an engrossing thriller based on photography itself.

But the breakthrough, alas, is not clean-cut. Atmosphere and a self-indulgent cinematic exploration thereof are still the director's primary concern; plot and character and, above all, human emotion go by the board, and we are left with a heavy-handed dose of symbolism and a rather obvious message instead of the absorbing and satisfying film that we are led to expect and almost get.

With what, in comparison with the torpor of his previous works (*L'Avventura, La Notte, Eclipse,* and *Red Desert*), is lightning speed, Antonioni sets his scene and central character. We follow a jeepload of careening clowns, pre-dawn revelers, through the early-morning streets, then latch on to our hero, a very fashionable photographer, a blond, blue-eyed, Edwardian-beatnik type. We follow him from a night in a flophouse, where he's been photographing the inmates for a book, to his multilevel studio dwelling, where he works at breathless speed with shifts of hideously high-fashion models in outrageous *haute couture.* Time out for brief relaxation with a low-fashion but lovely "bird" seemingly attached to an artist friend, then off to negotiate the purchase of a fusty antique shop (bound to be a money-maker, because he's already spotted "fags and poodles" in the neighborhood).

It is while waiting for the shop owner to return that the photographer wanders into a nearby park and almost idly begins photographing a distant couple that seems involved in bucolic courtship. The girl spots him and her frantic efforts to get the film from him arouse his curiosity. After he puts her off with a fake roll of film—and she him with a fake phone number—he gets to work.

The photographer develops the film, blowing up the distant figures. Suddenly the expression on the girl's face strikes him; he follows her glance, blows up another section of the print, blows up still another and another—and in a magnificently tense sequence between darkroom, developer and studio wall on which he is tacking prints in story-board fashion, we see the picture-story of a murder emerge.

Antonioni has brought us to a fascinating point of excitement. David Hemmings has made the photographer a world-weary, physically exhausted, cynical but oddly vulnerable young man; Vanessa Redgrave has given the mysterious girl a claim upon our feelings as well as our curiosity; Sarah Miles, in a cameo role as the "bird," has suggested poignancy. There is a flesh-and-blood puzzle at hand, demanding solution. We have seen the corpse and the principals and await the unraveling.

But Antonioni couldn't care less. There are phone calls, deliveries, a roll-in-the-buff with two aspiring models, a visit to a rock-'n'-roll session that ends in a riot, a night to be dawdled away at a marijuana party. What might have been suspense devices have become attenuated digressions. By dawn the photographs and the corpse have disappeared, and all the photographer finds in the park are the clowns, de-jeeped, pantomiming a tennis game with invisible balls and racquets. No solution, no Vanessa, no Sarah. Just a message belted at us with a twang of invisible catgut.

You get the message, of course—life (presumably even beyond the Carnaby Street confines) is not an honest-to-God bowl of cherries. And *Blow-Up* is a cheat. But a beautiful one. Antonioni more than justifies his own infatuation with the minutiae of the

social segment he has chosen; even without the obvious clown symbolism, the artifice of the op-and-pop life and the basic ugliness
of its creatures and rituals are explored and expounded brilliantly.
To appreciate the unhuman, however, there must be human involvement, and Antonioni gives us only disengagement and symbols.

Blow-Up must, therefore, be taken on its own purely visual
terms and our frustration at the simplistic content be soothed by an
appreciation of Antonioni's artistry. I suggest you try it.

1966 at Its Worst:
The Dishonor Roll
January 1, 1967

1. *Is Paris Burning?*	6. *An American Dream*
2. *Fahrenheit 451*	7. *The Silencers*
3. *Follow Me, Boys*	8. *Mademoiselle*
4. *Cul-de-sac*	9. *Seven Women*
5. *The Appaloosa*	10. *Mister Buddwing*

Happiness is too many things these days for anyone to wish it on
anyone lightly. So let's just wish each other a bileless New Year
and leave it at that or, better still, start off on a nasty note to be
silenced hereafter—hopefully. Let's get rid of all the nasty notions
that beset us last year and make sweetness and light the leitmotif
of sixty-seven—if only they will let us.

The "they" are the unforgivables, the moviemakers of experience and high repute who promised us everything and delivered
bombs. Thus, in compiling our list of the Ten Worst movies of 1966,
we're cutting a careful path between the "what-would-you-really-
expect" and "this-is-incredible" categories.

What would you really expect from *The Singing Nun*, starring
Debbie Reynolds as a guitar-thumping Dominican adept at playing soccer, riding a motorscooter and lousing up the lives of those
around her? Or from Sophia Loren kibbutzing around Israel in a

little item called *Judith,* or Natalie Wood being a tomboy-type sweet
kid converted into neurotic movie star via *Inside Daisy Clover,* a
Tennessee Williams-type, Southern-Chekhov heroine (she vants to
get to N'Awlins instead of Moscow) in *This Property Is Condemned*
and a Greenwich Village kook turned frustrated respectable in
Penelope? (You would expect maybe that the much-employed Miss
Wood would hit one uncondemnable property, but at least she's
right up there trying for the Worst Actor Award, in the face of some
pretty stiff competition from Ann-Margret, Michael Parks, James
Garner and the rest of the gang.)

You know you're in for less than perfection with Claudia
Cardinale all mixed up with incest and hereditary hysteria, instead
of good old un-neurotic lust and lechery, in *Sandra*; with the spy-
spoof being dragged on and on in items like *A Man Could Get
Killed* or *That Man from Istanbul*; with Doris Day losing the bottom
of her mermaid costume right at the start of *The Glass Bottom
Boat* (helas, Miss Day reduced to the baggy-pants comedian last-
gasp of dropping his trousers for a laugh!); with Sammy Davis,
Jr., who can do just about everything in the entertainment dodge
except play a trumpet or Hamlet, playing a Hamletesque trumpeter
in *A Man Called Adam.*

These are all imperfectly awful movies from which one expects little; title and star give most of it away. And of course, to
those for whom happiness is a perfectly awful movie (count me
in; I'm among those who bless television for each of its revivals of
Autumn Leaves or *Love Has Many Faces*), there've been a number to delight the soul, so thoroughly did the perfection of their
awfulness exceed even our cynical expectations: *Time of Indifference*, with Rod Steiger, Shelley Winters, Claudia Cardinale and
Paulette Goddard splashing around in the same bowl of warmed-
over-in-weltschmerz minestrone to prove that when all roads lead
actors to Rome they don't give a damn what they do once they get
there; *The Oscar*, which proved that Hollywood pros cannot only
parody their own worst works with straight faces but serve as their
own cliché experts and anthologizers; *Madame X*, which showed
that dead dogs and dated melodramas can still be beaten by cinematic sadists; *Modesty Blaise*, which demonstrated that Joseph

Losey is completely without a sense of humor when dealing with comedy (he's shown before, as in *Eva*, that he can be unconsciously funny when dealing with melodrama); *What Did You Do in the War, Daddy?*, which showed what happens when a man as gifted in comic devices as Blake Edwards gets just too funny for polite words; *Gertrud*, which indicated that the genius of young manhood cannot endure, even in the case of Carl Dreyer, on static technique and philosophy. The remake of *Stagecoach; The Idol; Assault on a Queen; Not With My Wife, You Don't; Moment to Moment; Promise Her Anything; Italiano Brava Gente;* and *Way . . . Way Out* are all awful—but I hate to attribute perfection of any kind to them.

In the second category—in contrast to the "what did you really expect"—there is, as noted, the "this-is-incredible" film, for the most part made by the unforgivables, men whose cachet raises our expectations, the high and the presumably mighty upon whom our hope of heavenly moviegoing rests. And this has been a come-a-cropper year, with the toppling of idols and fall of heroes rampant here and abroad.

Above all stands *Is Paris Burning?*, a major international effort under René Clement's direction, an incoherent, ponderous and shallow tribute to one of the great experiences of our time, an insult to those with intimate knowledge of or experience with the liberation of Paris, an embarrassment for those interested in spectacular moviemaking.

François Truffaut's *Fahrenheit 451* is an inexcusable bore, a tedious, pedestrian *reductio ad nihil* foray into Ray Bradbury's realm that presents two stars, Julie Christie and Oskar Werner, as dreary automatons involved in the obvious. It is distinguished by a heavy hand, a dull mind and a humorless technique, above all by a shocking lack of imagination.

Follow Me, Boys, on another level, is one of the worst films to emanate from the Disney studios, a near-parody of all the lowbrow small-townery that has given Disney's features a bad name among intellectuals who never go to Disney movies. It is unworthy of the Disney trademark.

Roman Polanski's *Cul-de-sac* is sheer waste of a talent shown to us in *Knife in the Water* and employed, albeit to small purpose, in *Repulsion*. Here it is not even employed; it is thrown away on tripe labeled "bizarre comedy," a catch-all name for depictions of perversion, mayhem, necrophilia, nymphomania, homosexuality, sadism, murder and a variety of mental disorders. Like Truffaut, whose fiasco was made in England, as this one was, Poland's young Mr. Polanski does not thrive on foreign soil.

The Appaloosa is in the pop-art category as the ultimate artsy-smartsy just-plain-silly version of the south-of-the-border good-gringo bad-Meheecan mythology that makes you remember Wallace Beery's Pancho Villa as sociological realism on the rampage. Director Sidney J. Furie reduces the camerawork that was artistry in *The Ipcress File* to a frenzy of beady eyes, sweaty foreheads, spurred boots and anonymous midriffs being studied in pointless detail through tequila bottles, cook-fires, fingers, feet, grillework and the rear end of horses. He also postpones the hoped-for happy meeting of Marlon Brando and a director who will use the actor to proper purpose.

An American Dream is a Hollywood nightmare. Norman Mailer's novel has been stripped of whatever passion and contemporary coherence it might have had and been converted into an idiotic melodrama laced with the salacious syndromes and little-boy nastiness that are the hallmark of today's "mature" film. No actor—not even the perpetually numb Stuart Whitman—can survive the hysterical nonsense of sight and sound.

The Silencers holds honors as the dullest, dirtiest thud excreted by the sex-and-sadism spoofs of Bondism, and not even adding Ann-Margret and assorted pseudoadolescent fun and games has enabled its current sequel, *Murderers' Row*, to reach the low standard set by this first in the Dean Martin-alias-Matt Helm series. The prurience of its ads were more than matched by the cavortings of Martin as a drunken, sun-tanned satyr, the floppings of flesh of assorted females and the moron level of its plot and humor.

Mademoiselle, with Jeanne Moreau providing from the start a bad imitation of Bette Davis, winds up as the giggliest horror movie of the year. Tony Richardson's handling of Genet's screenplay is perhaps comparable to Rebecca of Sunnybrook Farm taking over as one of Dracula's daughters. Let's simply hope that the English director has had his fling into degeneracy, fetishism and dubbing for the nonce.

John Ford's *Seven Women* is the nervous-giggle movie of the year; the kindest reaction is to decide it's a put-on, but then one giggles nervously at the horrible realization that they're not kidding. In a cramped Hollywood studio set pretending to be a mission in China in 1935 beset by bandits, we have Margaret Leighton as the rigid mission head with an eye for young blonds like Sue Lyon, portraying a sweet young thing; Mildred Dunnock and Flora Robson, portraying Mildred Dunnock and Flora Robson as mission types; Betty Field as an overage pregnant type; Anna Lee for ballast and Anne Bancroft as a tough cynical lady doctor who's come to the Orient with a broken heart, Bronx accent and unlimited supply of cigarettes. Miss Bancroft pulls a Sidney Carton, giving herself to the bandit chief (portrayed by that good old sergeant Mike Mazurki of the Ford Western Repertory Company) in return for his letting the ladies go. Though it is a far-far-from-better bit, she shares a poisoned brew with the non-English-speaking brute, tossing it off with a gallant "So long, you bastard," as she keels over dead. A sad farewell to greatness all around.

Delbert Mann's *Mister Buddwing* does for the New York success story what *The Oscar* does for Hollywood's—collects all its clichés, presents them in and for every possible situation and lines up performances to match. Its distinction is its pretension, its banality and its complete success in making all the authentic New York backgrounds look like the studio's cheaper backdrops. It gets on this list by the skin of its flashbacks. After all, no movie with straight-faced dialogue like "There's a name for women like you" or "Life's the biggest crap game going" or "I got news for you—it's a lousy world out there" or "Somewhere down the years we lost the only thing that mattered" falls too far short of the "incredible" category.

So here we are, all meanness vented on the unforgivables, ranging from René Clement through Truffaut to Ford to Richardson on up and down. But it's a new year and we're all set to put the idols back on the shelf. For sixty-seven, then, nothing but the best—huh, please, maybe—above all, hopefully.

1966 at Its Best:
The Top Ten
January 8, 1967

1. *A Man for All Seasons*	6. *Dear John*
2. *The Shop on Main Street*	7. *Harper*
3. *Georgy Girl*	8. *Shakespeare Wallah*
4. *Loves of a Blonde*	9. *Our Man Flint*
5. *The Wrong Box*	10. *Crazy Quilt*

It's moment-of-truth time, when one must stop talking about shoes and ships and sealing wax individually and start comparing them to find a "best" list. Should it be sealing wax first, then shoes and ships— or do ships edge out shoes, or shoes just top sealing wax?

Every year we precede that moment of truth with one of self-pity. And every year we go right ahead comparing the noncomparable, after, of couse, some sort of decrying. For years we decried the dearth of American films to match the foreign offerings; last year seven of our ten choices were home-grown or home-financed. For years we decried the dearth of quality films from any source; last year we found ourselves virtually flipping coins to determine precedence and presence on the Top Ten list and then listing some thirty more films that were well worth sitting through.

Well—chalk sixty-five down or up as a vintage year. For sixty-six we arrived at the brink of the December deadline without a clear-cut best-of-the-year favorite, although we had a candidate or two but nothing to be all that passionate about.

And then came *A Man for All Seasons,* and what more could we ask? For here was that once-in-a-long-time film that rises far above all others, a film for all times, a thinking man's spectacular, one whose depth of content is matched only by the artistry of its form. It is particularly noteworthy because, while it is based on a superb stage play, it transcends its source and does so as only film and no other art form can. Inspired and brilliant screenwriting by Robert Bolt and production and direction by Fred Zinnemann, an incomparable performance by Paul Scofield and superb support by Robert Shaw and Wendy Hiller—in fact, the entire cast—all combine to make this historic drama of conscience a great motion picture. It is certainly the best film of 1966, but it goes well beyond calendar confines.

The Shop on Main Street, certainly the best foreign film of the year, is almost the other side of the same coin. Here the Czechs, led by director Jan Kadar, have told the apocalyptic tragedy of our times (the extermination of Europe's Jews) in terms that we can comprehend and cope with, and done so with a simplicity and humanism that are soul-searing, an honesty and integrity that are unforgettable. Traditional in technique, albeit outstanding in performance and extraordinary in accomplishment, the film turns a holocaust that beggars the imagination into a story of ordinary people and does so with laughter and tears, scorn and affection and, above all, the simple beauty of truth.

Georgy Girl has rightly been called last year's *Darling*, if only because here too we find contemporary truth about today's young, who have so vivid a sense of self and of an integrity that demands an uncompromising stance against society. Georgy is embodied by Lynn Redgrave, without doubt the outstanding actress of the year, and it is through her chameleonlike qualities, both physical and spiritual, that we learn of the freakishness of being a love-seeker and a giver, with the giving predicated on undemanded response. She is offbeat and kooky and sentimental, and her kitchen-sink-Cinderella film story throbs with vitality, laughter and compassion and a kind of crazy truth that is irresistible.

Compassion is a key word, too, for *Loves of a Blonde*, wherein the young Czech director, Milos Forman, shrewdly aware of the foolish minds and simple hearts he is dealing with but with fondness and understanding tempering that awareness, gives us an unabashedly forthright view of young people in all their vulnerability, their foibles, their frailties and their essential romanticism. Above all, perhaps, he makes unbeautiful and unbright people very real and very appealing.

The Wrong Box is the year's wittiest bit of polished foolery. Adding a dash of Oscar Wilde and a dose of Mack Sennett to a Robert Louis Stevenson story of a tontine that came to flower in

Edwardian times, director Bryan Forbes has set his comedy asparkle by letting masters of the acting craft have a fling, albeit under his own talented supervision. One doubts that Peter Sellers himself will ever outshine his portrait of a medico gone to pot, seed and cats, or that classic comedy can match the encounter in which an ailing and aged John Mills persistently and energetically attempts to slaughter his brother, an unaware and unwitting Ralph Richardson.

Dear John, a lyric and beautiful Swedish film by Lars Magnus Lindgren, is a truly adult story of love, simple in content, subtle in form and remarkably frank, sensitive and sophisticated in its treatment of much that could and, indeed, in lesser hands, has approached the banal and the sensational. With a demanding and artful (but never arty) technique, the director plumbs the very souls of a man and a woman in the process of that mutual discovery that is the basis of love and gives us a romantic experience, a morally contemporary one and an honest one, that deserves indeed to be termed a "mature" love story for adults.

Harper is a stylish return to the great Bogart private-eye tradition, with screenwriter William Goldman, director Jack Smight, and Paul Newman, plus a number of other fine performers, bringing us back to the days when men were not only flesh and blood but men in the fullest sense, and when intrigue and nastiness were personal and professional rather than international and sexual affairs, when a man could like his work and love his wife and know the difference between right and wrong while being aware that neither is quite that simple. Fast-paced, beautifully filmed, finely performed, it is outstanding in itself and in the tradition.

Shakespeare Wallah is a subtle, gently satiric and deeply human exploration of contemporary India by the same American-Indian team of *The Householder*. Producer Ishmael Merchant, director James Ivory and author Ruth Prawer Jhabvala make their perceptive comments on the past and present of a society in flux through the wanderings of a seedy Shakespearean company through the countryside. Touched by brilliance, marked throughout by grace, it is a quiet film that allows one to perceive the ironies and the poignancy of a time of transition.

Our Man Flint flared out at the first of the year as one of the merriest, nuttiest spy spoofs for grown-ups to have come our non-comic-strip way and by year's end still stands as the top entry of its class in a year that seemed for months on end to offer little else but spy spoofs. Beyond a completely irresistible performance by James Coburn, we have a dandy supporting cast and all the gags, takeoffs and imaginative nonsense that a fully packed story and screen could hold, raising the result far beyond a mere parody of Bondism or even "camp" and hurtling it into the top echelon of good inspired fun and filmmaking.

Crazy Quilt is the surprise of the year, a first film that displays a fresh cinematic talent in producer-writer-director John Korty and offers proof positive that low-budget (under one hundred thousand dollars, in this case) films can be done with polish and professionalism and that hand-held cameras can be held steadily and to artistic and intellectual purpose. Relatively unknown actors, Tom Rosqui and Ina Mela, are perfection as the illusionless man and the visionary girl, but it is Mr. Korty's cinematic terminology—narration, sparse dialogue, a beautiful score and his superb photography—that triumphs. The hand of the novice is evident only in the freshness and contemporary tone of the film. It is a charmer in the most sophisticated sense.

There are the ten at the top. The eleventh? Put down *Blow-Up,* of course, *Dead Heat on a Merry-Go-Round, The Shameless Old Lady, Gambit, Alfie, Endless Summer, John F. Kennedy: Years of Lightning, Day of Drums;* for twelfth best: *The Professionals, The Russians Are Coming, King and Country, Funeral in Berlin, A Big Hand for the Little Lady, Khartoum, How To Steal a Million, Flight of the Phoenix.* Let's keep the list growing with *Walk in the Shadow, A Funny Thing Happened on the Way to the Forum, The Sleeping Car Murders, Naked Prey, Up to His Ears.* Make special note of two plays transferred to film, *Othello* and *Who's Afraid of Virginia Woolf?,* noting the first as a record of Laurence Olivier's magnificent and fascinating Moor, and the second as a near-record of the text of Edward Albee's scathing and outspoken drama. And *Grand Prix* should be somewhere simply for its ingenious and stunning cinematography.

Add your choice—top or bottom. And at least the coin-flipping and pots-and-kettles comparisons are over for the year.

Sins of Omission?
January 29, 1967

Let's in this last Sunday of the first month of the year straighten out the record, which suffered a lapse in sixty-six during the four-and-a-half-month newspaper strike. We're not going to go into the concomitants of our Ten Best list again. We're going to go into our sins of omission, however, purely in the interest of point making. Our major sins, it seems, were the omission of *Blow-Up* from the very top of the list, of *A Man and a Woman* and *The Gospel According to St. Matthew* from any mention at all, and of *Who's Afraid of Virginia Woolf?* from the listing other than in the film-record-of-a-stage play, or noncinematic, category.

These four films are "successful"—i.e., at the box office—and more we cannot wish them. They are certainly above the run of the Hollywood mill; *Blow-Up* is 'way 'way up there—and deservedly. It is a strikingly beautiful film (so many films are these days that this is fast becoming no mark of distinction), but more important, it is a provocative and stimulating one, prompting (as I have found to my hoarseness) endless discussions of whether it is just about a fashion photographer or the ultimate comment on our society, whether there is or isn't a murder, whether it is or isn't a cop-out on Michelangelo Antonioni's part. I am of the real-murder school and feel that, for more than half the film, Antonioni was approaching the ultimate comment, brilliantly dissecting contemporary attitudes and for the first time in his hitherto torpid studies of alienation coming to grips with flesh-and-blood humanity, when he suddenly copped out in a welter of indulgent cinematography and mishmashed symbols. Its being condemned by the National Catholic Office for Motion Pictures and denied a seal by the Motion Picture Association (I must go back and restudy the orgy scene that apparently left this truly adult film sealless) certainly isn't harming its local box-office appeal; but neither the foolishness of these censorial gestures nor its success should blind one to the film's imperfections—which stand out so vividly because of the many perfections it has.

A Man and a Woman is also "beautiful," a great plug for color film and its varied uses. But no amount of artiness can cover the banality and slick-fiction accouterments of its romantic little tale nor the frequent lapses into incoherence that pockmark the picture. The director's failure is epitomized for me in his beguilement with that rain-splattered windshield, so great a beguilement that while attempting to show us a growing intimacy between his couple he keeps that splattered windshield between us, adding the wipers for further distraction.

Both *The Gospel According to St. Matthew* and *Virginia Woolf* seem to me to fall into the dancing-dog category. It is not that they are done well from the movie viewpoint; it is that they are done at all as movies that has won them their deserved attention. So sick of spectacular Biblicals are we, so jaded with the monumental banalities and ha'penny religiosities to which even men of George Stevens' and John Huston's stature can reduce *The Greatest Story Ever Told* and *The Bible*, that we leap upon *The Gospel* for its very lack of spectacle, its complete humility and simplicity, the "truth" we find in the unknown faces, the "realism" we find in the untheatrical presentation. Here is the primitivism of Great Art, something that we are only too prone to find in foreign films (that old snobbery of the subtitle). Indeed, we joined the leap initially, stunned by the impact of stark scene and faces from Renaissance master paintings—but so long does director Paolo Pasolini linger on his images that by midpoint we have a surfeit of the unshaven and the snaggle-toothed; so literally does he dramatize the Gospel that by the end we are left with a factual biography that omits the essential—the spirit, the soul, the essence of Christ that made Him more, in His own time and for the millennia, than a philosopher, a radical, a passionate proselytizer and a martyr. On its own, then, without comparison, *The Gospel* stands as a good rather than great film, an honest attempt that did not succeed; even cinematic simplicity, we may well conclude, cannot capture what the simplest of words have created in the minds of men.

Virginia Woolf has the expected fine performance by Richard Burton, the unexpected from Elizabeth Taylor, a remarkable drowned-rabbit portrait from Sandy Dennis; it has retained the abrasiveness of the Albee play. But by its attempt at "cinematic" qualities it has suffered; the artificial opening-up of the set has lost the claustrophobic atmosphere, the empathetic sense of entrapment essential to the horrors of the drama. We need not stay and watch others—and ourselves—being peeled to the inner being if we can go swing on a swing (why a swing? for the nonexistent offspring?) or go roadhousing around; the revolting bedroom interlude becomes just another movie sex scene in silhouette for Peeping Toms. And the bright light of dawn leaves us with the notion that things will be better from here on, whereas the power of the play lay in our sure knowledge that this would happen again and always, so long as there were playmates available. But the language and the fun and games—ah, the dancing dog, the screen star uglied-up for great drama, the unexpected on film—thus we are deluded into the non-critical attitude instead of simply being grateful for the small favors of having the Albee play more or less (less indeed) on the record, of watching Burton subordinate himself, or seeing Miss Taylor give the best performance of her career.

Too many moviegoers, chief among them the advocates of these films, go in for instant-impact judgments these days, so bemused by the dancing dog that they let the choreography go by the board and see only a four-legged Nijinsky or Pavlova.

☆
☆ Part V ☆
......From Georgy
..........to Clyde

Resnais's Courageous
In-Depth Thriller
February 12, 1967

Well, there we were last week, eyes glued to the telly, trying to think back to 1955 and wonder what it was like then. Back then, you see, *Man with the Golden Arm*, about a poker dealer with a monkey on his back, couldn't get itself a seal from the Motion Picture Producers Association of America. And here it was, for popular consumption, with a dope addict now perfectly acceptable right in our own homes.

Times, as we are wont to note perhaps too frequently, sure do change, and let narcotics addiction be the least of the subjects that are practically minimum requirements for commercial success in moviemaking. Not that we're quite ready to have the absolute in sex rampant on the home screen—at the moment, anyway. An absolutely irresistible item in *Variety* reports that production of *On My Way to the Crusades, I Met a Girl Who* . . . (formerly named *The Chastity Belt*), costarring Tony Curtis and Monica Vitti, finally began after the producer, Seven Arts, and "Yank video execs" reached agreement "on moral requirements that would clear the film for home-screen viewing and still bring out sex-happy [sic] filmgoers in prior theatrical release." Meanwhile the Italian director, Pasquale Campanile, was soothing Italian public opinion with assurances that although the film would retain its original title there, "he would treat the belt as a symbol of distaff subjugation rather than an object of bawdy screen entertainment."

There is so little that we are denied on the screen these days, with full approval—let alone qualified approval—from all manner of sources, that it is almost embarrassing to have to come right out and commend a filmmaker for courage. And yet, let us pause and consider the courage of Alain Resnais, whose *La Guerre Est Finie* is in theatrical distribution at long last.

But the apples don't grow dollar-green in Mr. Resnais's orchard. The genius flourishes and the valor is there. The core of the plot is a thriller, but it is surrounded by cogent comment and food for the intellect—and a demand that, like his hero, we pause and reexamine our values and our realities and our dedications. And the irony of this day of enlightenment is that it does take courage even to assume that the sex-happy filmgoer has a mind and to provide it with both food and stimulation. And then, of course, there is the cinematic genius required to do all this in terms of film, in a totally absorbing and satisfying manner.

Resnais, exposing new creative style in each of his films, does so here in a manner that places him so far beyond the current breathless, eye-filling, mind-skipping, whipped-cream school of cinematography that we are left in awe. All that he shows us, every detail, is revealing of the mind; we see the present and we see, in lucid foreflashes, what the mind retains, what it envisions, what it anticipates. The thriller theme becomes a matter of counterpoint to a man's reexamination of himself, his sudden suspicion that all the words and phrases and theories that have been his catechism in a lifetime as a professional revolutionary are child's play; that the exiles in Paris are fighting a war long finished, that they have lost touch with reality. Can one, after a lifetime, give up the comrades, the passwords, the dedication? How can these old men say, as they have for twenty-five years, that every minute counts—and why are these new-generation revolutionists, with their terrorist tactics, so impatient? How long can "patience and irony, mostly patience" remain the virtues of the revolutionist?

It takes courage to cope with this basic political theme of our century and it takes the art of Resnais to consider it in terms of human relations placed in a "thriller" framework. This is the total satisfaction of *La Guerre Est Finie*—surface after surface can be peeled away, the depth of the film increases, surprises and tantalizes; but what Resnais says never eludes one.

How can one be, initially, facetious about the thriller core of the film, and why should one point to the erotic scenes with two women? The sad part is that to say this is one of the most important films of the past several years, that it is one of the most satisfying intellectually, a complete work of art, undoubtedly would lose half the audience, sex-happy filmgoers all, who'd tear off around the corner to see something firmly labeled for those eighteen and over— sure signal that within, at very least, is grinding a high-class grind movie. So let us emphasize that Mr. Resnais's great film boasts thrills and chills and beautiful women—and only whisper about the fine performances of Yves Montand, as the weary courier, Ingrid Thulin as the mature and loving woman whose understanding goes beyond speech; Genevieve Bujold, who is the essence of youth in all its loveliness and passionate infatuations, and a host of others. And we'll speak no more about the depth and content of the film.

The Anti-Establishment Man
February 26, 1967

Trend-spotters take notice:

Item: Dealers in pop-poster blow-ups of movie-star photos report that "the younger crowd," hitherto sold on Brando and Bogey and Belmondo, are starting to switch to W. C. Fields, long an established favorite with "the intellectual Madison Avenue types."

Item: Fields festivals are busting out all over, in museums, revival houses and campus auditoriums, and Fields films on television guarantee a good audience.

Item: Robert Lewis Taylor's biography, *W. C. Fields: His*

Follies and Fortunes, first published in 1949, is now out in a Signet paperback, and the newest in the Citadel pictorial series is *The Films of W. C. Fields*.

Spot something there? Can it be that twenty years after his death, Fields is coming into his own as the foremost American funnyman? Or is it, as those of us who've never had doubts about Fields' status have long suspected, that it is Fields as a social satirist who represents something particularly pertinent to our time?

"Social satirist" is strictly a think-piece term in its application to Fields, who was, if anything, antisocial, as un-American as a deep antipathy toward every revered aspect of middle-class morality and mores could make a native son. The Fieldsian cliché is that "Any man who hates dogs and children can't be all bad." But the glory of Fields is that he didn't just hate dogs and children; he hated doctors and lawyers and bankers and banks, directors and producers and income-tax collectors and all things institutional, from marriage to medicine to Methodists. He was the total anti-Establishment man, the essential con man in a world wherein the honest man could be cheated and the sucker was about the only one who could get an even break.

Consider the pop-poster photo of Fields that you're as likely to find in an executive office as on a dormitory wall. It's a still from *My Little Chickadee*, but it might well be from any Fields period opus in the course of any Fieldsian poker game. In stovepipe hat and pinstripe, with carnationed lapel, one dapperly gloved hand clutching his cards secretively chestward, the other about to make a fatal discard, Fields shifts his eyes craftily on the next man's hand. All the pomposity of the poker ritual, all the fraudulent cogency to disguise the cheat, all of the "con" and all the mistrust of a mistrustful world lie in the frown, the jowl, the shifty eye. And all of us know (shades of *Mississippi*) ; that Fields' basic problem of the moment is how to get rid of that fifth ace he's somehow managed to deal himself. And all of us know (shades of all things Fieldsian) that beyond the moment lies the life of constant conflict with objects inanimate and live, the former to be attacked with all the juggler's perfect skill, the latter with the bombastic amenity and the mumbled insult, and neither to be conquered except by sleight of hand or sheerest accident, and never by virtue.

It is, of course, the lack of virtue that makes Fields a singular clown, that separates him from Chaplin and other greats. He is without pathos or humility; he is unlovable. He is the alter ego of all that is good and pure and noble: he's put upon by society, and he's out to get his by fraudulence, because society is a fraud. And it is all that is cowardly and ignoble and antisocial in us that rejoices in the triumphs, because the windmills he tilts at are blots on our own horizon, and we root for the man who knows that his lance is bound to be out of alignment and the windmill full of secret booby traps but enters the fray unheeding.

Fields—whether as Charles Bogle or Otis Cublecoblis or Mahatma Kane Jeeves or himself—created on screen the family circle as he saw it, one wherein shrewish wives and shrikish mothers-in-law had mouths filled alternately with food and vituperation, wherein small girls had to be brained before they conked their daddies' noggins, and a wise father swiped the baloney from his loving son's sandwich, wherein peace and quiet could come only with cash in large quantities. In the world at large, survival depended on chicanery, success on aggression.

It is Fields as an angry man who delights our souls, for the anger is hidden behind the overblown facade of the innocent abroad, an innocent as truthworthy as his label, whether it is Larsen E. Whipsnade or Egbert Souse (accent grave on the "e," of course) or Professor Eustace McGargle or Cuthbert J. Twillie or The Great McGonigle or Micawber. It is because of his facade that the suppressed un-nice side of our souls can get vicarious pleasures from his outrages, whether it's a matter of booting Baby LeRoy in the behind, conning an innocent into embezzlement, or making sport of a blind man (to be identified, of course, as the house detective of the local hotel). Fields himself knew he was catering to the unkind-of-heart among us. "I like, in an audience, the fellow who roars continuously at the troubles of the character I am portraying on stage," he once wrote, "but he probably has a mean streak in him and, if I needed ten dollars, he'd be the last person I'd call upon. I'd go to the old lady and old gentleman back in Row S who keep wondering what there is to laugh at."

That Fields found so much to laugh at, that he could convert (or sublimate) his bitterness and cynicism into a laugh-producing stock in trade, is remarkable but not quite so paradoxical as his retention of character off-stage as well as on. Taylor's biography is particularly valuable in probing the development of a genuine and dedicated artist and detailing the Horatio Alger rags-to-riches story of a man who simply refused to behave according to Alger's moral ground rules. From a Dickensian childhood and no youth in any tolerable sense of the word, Fields grew to fame and wealth that exceeded even his boyish fantasies, but these did nothing to alleviate his suspicions of the world, his fears of insecurity, his tight hold on the dollar and the martini glass. He was true to the character he created for himself, rooted to the shabby clown-juggler who could justly claim perfection in his art, to the artist who could survive and succeed in the changing professional arenas of the century, going on from road companies to side shows to vaudeville, to Broadway, Hollywood, and radio, indomitably at war with the world.

His was, long before the label and the fashion, a black brand of comedy, an amoral one tinted by the paranoia that is only suggested by Durante's image of being "surrounded by assassins." There were no assassins in Fields' world—only frauds and fools of the Establishment—and it took a genius, in the guise of a fradulent fool, to declare war on behalf of the anti-Establishmentarians. To this Fields dedicated his art and, as Mr. Taylor so skillfully implies in his affectionate but objective dissection of a legend, life has a way of imitating art.

Lost in Translation
March 5, 1967

Go commit yourself. Declare outright that movies is—or are, as the case may be—where the action is. And then spend a couple of nights at the theater, where the action is alive, say, at *Cabaret* or at *Black Comedy*—and discover the stuff that movies cannot be made on.

But more and more theater-based movies seem to be coming our way this season, and once again, much as in the case of the best-seller-reading moviegoer, the dilemma of the theatergoing moviegoer comes to the fore. Time and again we've seen theatrical fluff—be it *Mary, Mary* or *Any Wednesday*—inflated, miscast and distorted into cinematic flug; time and again we've seen the "point" of serious theatrical fare distorted or lost or just abandoned for larger-than-life commercialism. And perpetually one faces the same book-into-movie, play-into-movie dichotomy in judging the result as a film per se, without root, and as a film version, bound in fidelity to its source.

Generalize, then, if you can, from recent experiences. *A Thousand Clowns* and *A Man for All Seasons* stand as perhaps classic examples of stage works enhanced and enriched by their transition to the screen. Can it be, beyond retention of the stars in the major roles and the intelligence of direction and production and so on, that the essence lay in the basic creators, the playwrights, being involved in the screenplays and in the production as a whole? Try the rule; it won't apply to, say, *Becket*, a highly satisfying translation on screen with only the director remaining of the original stage creators.

Perhaps what these three examples have in common is that they were story-telling dramas, hewing close to the truth as it is traditionally seen and therefore akin to the terrible reality that the camera faces and translates into larger-than-life terms. And I suspect, because the terms are indeed gigantic, that certain fluff cannot survive the magnification. Above all, the fluff of absurdity, the symbol that exists because we can imagine its portent only in life-size terms of our own and within the confines of our own imaginations, the special claustrophobic power of the theater by the mere presence of humans on both sides of the footlights—these, we find, do not survive the transition.

Two current examples of the untranslatability of certain stage works are *Oh Dad, Poor Dad . . .* and *Dutchman*, both of which flourished in the intimate confines of Off Broadway, both of which have reached the screen, albeit in almost opposite manner, to disastrous effect. Arthur Kopit's fresh-from-Harvard bit of I-hate-

Momism was given sophisticated and beguilingly fantastic packaging by Jerome Robbins' staging and some impeccable performances, so that the supermonstrosity of Mom became an amusement. But for the screen, the best of everything Hollywood can offer in the way of simplification and vulgarization—sublowbrow commentary, idiot title song, literal but illiterate gaggery—is brought to bear on this fragile little black comedy, and annihilation is inevitable, for theme, performers (Rosalind Russell is Auntie Mame taking a hysterical amateur-theatrical fling at Samuel Beckett; enchanting Barbara Harris is made only an iota less repulsive than the gifted Robert Morse) and audience.

In *Dutchman* the failure is of the medium itself and not the filmmakers, who have attempted the transition with integrity. The bare bones of the LeRoi Jones parable can survive a transition, much as Kopit's creatures, complete with their stuffed corpse and carnivorous plants and coin collection, can literally reach the screen. The white girl accosts the young Negro in a subway, Lilith in her goading and baiting; he turns upon her in a spew of hatred and is destroyed by her; she progresses toward another victim. But put even the same actors—and Shirley Knight and Al Freeman, Jr., enjoyed success in the West Coast stage productions—into the magnified realism of film, make it a real and roaring rattling subway train, and belief is shattered, the essential poetic incoherence of the interaction and response of what are essentially symbols disappear, and we are left with incredibles, in form and content. The girl loses complexity and becomes so much a parody of the apple-munching Evil Eve that the boy becomes gullible rather than vulnerable and his outburst becomes objectively unbearable and easy to reject intellectually rather than a scorching, searing lash that inexorably strikes upon our very souls. And it is the reality of the train, the intimacy of the scene, that vitiates the power of the whole.

What happens to *Marat/Sade* in transition to the screen is particularly interesting in that what happens, what changes, when the Peter Brook stage production becomes the Peter Brook film, happens to and changes for the audience. Some weeks ago Mr. Brook, a seasoned film and theater man (for sheer film, recall his superb *Lord of the Flies*), wrote, "If I say that we set out to make a record of the *Marat/Sade* play, I mean this in every sense of the word. The hope was to capture what it looked like, what it felt like and what it's about." The "what it's about" comes through, in this photographed play-within-a-play, with even greater clarity thanks to the close-up, the ability of the director to block out the rest of the stage physically so that we can concentrate upon the arguments of the Marquis de Sade, the devilish advocate of passivity and indifference and individual gratification in the face of inflexible and destructive nature, and of Marat, the impassioned activist who must call for revolution even in the knowledge that revolutions devour their own and create renewed corruption. The "what it looked like" is there—but cinematically—so that the "what it felt like" has changed for those who felt it in a theater. For, on stage, the vast bathhouse amphitheater of the Charenton asylum resembled nothing so much as a throbbing, buzzing, maggot-covered compost heap that had a rhythmic life of its own apart from the dramatic focus of the moment. Thus this hellish insane world existed as a mirror, and we were too prone to be diverted by its horrible details, to be distracted from the argument by the theatricality of its setting, and this theatricality provided the thrill that transcends the Sundays-at-Bedlam voyeurism because we glimpsed ourselves reflected, and winced in terror at the onmarching horde about to trample us underfoot.

But now, as the orchestration of his stage production would not permit him, Mr. Brook is free to make our eye focus, and each single horror, out of context, is magnified for our study. We cannot empathize as we see in overblown and overwhelming terms the mad eye, the ballooned skull, the catatonic walk, the spastic hand, the drool and the spittle. It is too intimate, too clinical, and the massive surge is gone. It is in its effect an "art" horror film—and despite the clarification of what it's about, it "feels" remote. We are estranged and we are voyeurs; we are where the action is, but we are observers and have lost that sense of participation, of shared human experience that is on occasion uniquely of the theater.

Down South
with Preminger
March 24, 1967

Gather roun' chillun, while dem banjos is strummin' out *Hurry Sundown* an' ole Marse Preminger gwine tell us all about de South.

Tain't de Deep South, or de ante- or post-bellum South. It's de Stereotype South dat you and me done love since ole Massas Caldwell and Faulkner done see all dat decay down yonder past de ole cotton fields. Dere's dem decayin' rich white folks up in de big house, afussin' an' afornicatin' (an' usin' saxophones as highlarious sex symbols) an' betrayin' deir ole mammies an' tryin' to cheat poor folk out of deir land. And dere's dem decayin' un-rich white trash down in de town, cheatin' poor folk an' social climbin' all over an' jest markin' time from one lynchin' bee to de next.

De rich whites dey got marital problems an' retarded children; de white trash dey got red necks an' bratty children—but all God's chillun—hell, baby, dey already got shoes, so now dey got college degrees an' land-owin' ambitions an' Jim Backus to represent them in court an' a banjo handy so that when that lynchin' party is en route they can all gather roun' like de Hall Johnson Choir and sing dat hallelujah title song. Lawsy, chillun, dey ain't been so perspicacious a study of Southern problems since ex-Governor Wallace's last speech on civil rights.

The road to this disaster is, we hasten to note, paved with good intentions (after all, being pro-civil rights is safe box office these days) as well as with tasteless sensationalism and plain and fancy foolishness. Otto Preminger has provided us not only with soap-opera plotting but also with cartoon characters and patronage of Negroes that are incredible in 1967. The whole mélange would be offensive were it not simply ludicrous.

For villainy there's Michael Caine, speaking a dialect that out-Remuses the old Uncle himself, as a sort of sax player by avocation who has married above his station, given his son mental retardation by leaving him alone in a hotel room for a day, and dodged the draft. It's post-World War II in Georgia, and Caine needs two small farms belonging to brave veterans for a big land deal. One farm is owned by a distant relative who has an unretarded son Caine covets, the other by Caine's high-class wife's old mammy and her uppity son, who has a sort of going romance with a school-teacher who is even uppitier because she's been living in Harlem.

Well, Jane Fonda, Caine's wife, is a good kid, fond of her mammy and really pro-Negro and devoted to her retarded son. But she's hung up on Caine, a real love captive melting at his touch, getting all boozed up and stuff—you know how these deca-dent high-class Southern gals are. So she goes along with his attempts to get the veterans' farms with tactics that make Simon Legree look like the soul of subtlety. But then Diahann Carroll, that uppity Harlem gal, corners Jane in the ladies' room for some girl talk and sets her straight.

It's a new Jane, who doesn't even melt when Caine grabs her by the breast and who sets out for the Menninger Clinic to get her son unretarded. Caine, protesting that "It can't end like this" (and indeed only 115 of the film's 146 minutes have droned by), sets out for a last-ditch dynamiting attempt with his redneck chums. And don't think we don't wind up with title-song harmony in the dawn's early light as all God's chillun come marching across the fields to rebuild their white friend's demolished homestead and signify that any small troubles in the South are easy mended— albeit by slickness, soap and slobbery.

This elliptic synopsis doesn't take note of the bigoted old judge, the Negro-loving lecherous sheriff, the dying cotton-wool-headed mammy who asks deathbed forgiveness for being "a white folks' nigger," the husband back from the wars with a nightie "from Paris France," the small boy who denounces Daddy as a "nigger lover." They're all there but, shucks, you got to hear Jane Fonda say "Mind if I crochet while we talk?" to get the flavor.

Those involved in this film deserve better than having their names repeated here. For to say that *Hurry Sundown* is the worst film of the still-young year is to belittle it. It stands with the worst films of any number of years.

Whither Bergman
and the Burtons?
March 26, 1967

It's worry time. All kinds of worries cinemawise. Who wouldn't worry when he finds himself wandering around convinced that there was a murder in *Blow-Up*; that the new Ingmar Bergman film, *Persona*, is simple freshman Freud underneath all the cinematics; and that the Burtons are going to wind up as the Ma and Pa Kettle of our time?

Well, it's a lonely life for the worrier, at any rate. The going thing is to declare, with the happy majority, that *Persona* is simply great—utterly incomprehensible and therefore simply great. I mean, what Bergman has in mind with all those bits of film and symbolism surrounding his film-within-a-film should be beyond the understanding of mortal man, let alone constant moviegoer. If everybody's going to go around digging Bergman, then what's a *cineaste*'s heaven for?

The point of concern here is not a *reductio-ad*-banality of Bergman's complex and uneven study of the public and private personalities of two women. It is the growing insistence on having a perfectly plain piece of sponge cake at the bottom of the whipped cream in the charlotte russe—and having whipped cream galore on the top, for our appreciative and, above all, facile consumption. And if we find the whipped cream not perfectly smooth and the bottom to consist of some sweet-and-sour or lumpy-chewy mixture, we back away, refusing to savor and ponder and let it lie on the tongue for testing. We back away, declaring that the delicacy is so exotic, so complex a concoction, that only the supergourmet can analyze it at first bite.

In effect, the rule of the cinematic day seems to be the less palatable, the more involved—the less comprehensible, that is—the greater the creator. Thus *Persona*, because it is in part perplexing (as well as intellectually complex), in part simpleminded (as well as sophisticated), in part exquisitely clear (as well as obscure) and in part sparkling with truth (as well as befogged by pretension), must be hailed as perhaps one of Bergman's best films. It isn't. It seems—particularly after his *Winter Light* and *The Silence*—almost retrogressive in its reliance on the overt symbol, in its indulgence in cinematics for their own sake, in its underlining and repetition of its obvious points. And yet this very far from least of the Swedish master's twenty-seven films (and the least is so far above the ordinary that comparisons with the work of others is virtually meaningless) stands clear in its central consideration of the relationship of two women and the near-merging of their personalities in the course of one's psychotherapy, the transference of instability from one to the other, the resumption of their places in the world after their purgation by a strenuous love-hate relationship. What surrounds the bare plot lines is the flavoring, the decoration—some of it for consumption, some of it merely for looking at and pondering and some for naught but its own sweet sake. One need not see it all clearly; the quality of a work often lies in its subtlety. But its obscurity is not necessarily a signal of its greatness.

There is, of course, no obscurity in *The Taming of the Shrew*, the movie for which, the ads tell us, the Burtons "were made." Their making of the movie is, in fact, as obvious as the antics of the Paduan whore on display at the film's opening, who takes one breast out of the unconfines of a more than ample decolletage and waggles it at the customers. The Burtons, we can but surmise, are determined to run the gamut of Western culture together, riding high on Elizabeth Taylor's special face and increasingly ample figure, Richard Burton's reputation as a fine actor, and the public's willingness to pay millions of dollars to see them ensemble. They started out with the culture-spectacular of *Cleopatra*, went on to the sophisticated soap opera of the *V.I.P.'s* and La Vie de Bohème California style of *The Sandpiper*, paid tribute to the New Freedom (motion-picture-production-code variety) with *Virginia Woolf* and to the Old Freedom (classic-lusty-bawdy-romp variety) with *Shrew*, wherein they, with their merry romping in excelsis, and director Franco Zeffirelli, with his misty-glow Renaissance decor, manage to smother Shakespeare in pizza-type Sennett.

One can but wonder where the Burtons go from here. Time for heavy drama again—the Macbeths, perhaps, or Medea and mate? Or classic American drama—a bit of Ibsen, perhaps *Ghosts*, mother and son style, as a starter—the mum and dad in *Long Day's Journey* or *Death of a Salesman*? And then something Chekhovian (Mr. Burton seems beard-happy enough in *Shrew*, and one can indeed picture Miss Taylor's dark beauty as she languishes, Masha-like, red rose in hand, longing for Moscow). And having covered all angles, what's left? Min and Bill? I'll vote for Ma and Pa Kettle. And we face the possibility as long as the team keeps going under the delusion that they are onscreen Lunts. Vide *Shrew*!

It's certainly enough to make you worry. Well, laugh your worries away. A couple of fine opportunities are at hand. For just how a play, a musical play, a smash Broadway musical, should be brought to the screen, see David Swift's elegant movie version of *How To Succeed in Business Without Really Trying*. More cannot be said but that this delicious movie, with Robert Morse and Rudy Vallee repeating their stage roles of the lovably vile urchin and the top boob of big business, will make you realize that you'd forgotten how really good the original show was.

A less perfect but equally refreshing diversion can be found in *You're a Big Boy Now*, a half-kooky, half-sweetly-innocent comedy about breaking out of the womb and into the world, in New York, which is wonderfully photogenic from a young director's point of view. Geraldine Page won an Oscar nomination for her weeping-vampire mama role—but equally likely candidates are Peter Kastner as the nineteen-year-old who finally sheds his parents; Elizabeth Hartman as the actress vamp whose hang-ups include a fifty-three-year-old albino hypnotherapist with a wooden leg; Rip Torn as a curator of incunabula; Julie Harris as a landlady who wants home to be ever so humble—and, well, just about everybody, but most especially writer-director Francis Ford Coppola, who shows wit and style and some forgivable first-movie weaknesses, but who's really enough to make one stop worrying.

Antiquing with Charlie
April 2, 1967

They're rushing the season on me. Antiquing time is summertime, when hot August days are to be whiled away in the coolth of abandoned churches, barns and spring houses in search of Shirley Temple mugs and cigar-band ashtrays and cracked Baccarat crystal from the big house. That's my idea of real antiquing—treasures recalling the grandeur of the past.

And here it is, out of season, and Charles Chaplin is taking me antiquing cinemawise, recalling the grandeur of various pasts. It's as bad as a spring tonic of vinegar-and-molasses as an aperitif on Christmas Day or hot buttered rum in the tropics. It puts the time and the digestion out of joint.

Mr. Chaplin, of course, sends one in search of the grandeur of the Chaplin past—not really a search—simply an instinctive conjuring up of all that shaped our concept of what comedy and pathos, of what laughter and tears could mean in cinematic terms. The very least of his films still stood out, supplemented as it was by our empathetic innocence, our willingness to accept the imperfect because it still bore the hallmark of the master. But time passes; it is ten years since Chaplin made a film; it is fifteen since we have seen a new Chaplin work, since we accepted with reservations *Limelight* in 1952. And now we have *A Countess from Hong Kong*—and we'd prefer not to.

It is not a case of denying Chaplin a Homeric nod—in his case a Homeric collapse into primitivism, in form and content, into a drearily unstylish foray into what pretends to be high-winging satire and comedy but wobbles and crashes into flatulent verbiage and inept pseudo-farce. What is painful is that Chaplin has taken this film seriously as a major opus, comparable in his estimation only with *City Lights*. In a lengthy declaration in *Life* magazine, after the film's release in London but before its American premiere, he in effect answered the critics (who had been no kinder in England) and attempted to disarm us all.

Do we find this tale of a stuffy diplomat and rundown stow-away countess complete contrivance? "The *Countess* is the first film I've ever treated completely as a piece of realism with true characterizations. . . ." Do we find Brando ponderous, gross, and grossly inept for a debonair part? "Marlon Brando is so real, so humorous without any sense of humor. Fascinating. I wouldn't have had Brando if he thought he was funny! And because every scene is played with absolute sincerity, the picture is as funny as anything I've ever tried to make. . . ." Do we find Brando and Miss Loren at a loss, obviously bewildered by the mechanics and sin-gular unfunniness of what they are involved in? "I don't think either Brando or Loren understood the value of the script—that it would work so well. I did. I'm an actor. I wrote it. When you've had fifty years' experience, you know something about a script."

Do we find the head-on camera work primitive, to say the most, the sets all too obvious, the editing choppy? Chaplin concedes that "they" say his technique is "old-fashioned." "Well, we don't twist the camera upside down or twirl it around and hurt your eyes—all that sort of jack-in-the-box magic. I just don't choose to. I think that personality, people, the human equation transcend any acrobatics the camera might do. . . . I'm very fond of acting and I don't want the camera to give the performance."

And there, perhaps, we stumble upon the nub of it all. We don't want the camera—or even big-name stars—giving the performance when the material calls out for Charlie Chaplin, for the balletic clown who could make pseudo-Lonsdale drawing-room farce and pseudo-Feydeau chases and pseudo-Sennett social mockery un-pseudo and very stylish indeed. Language is not Chaplin's forte; it was the weakest element in *Monsieur Verdoux* and has now evolved into having Brando gulp out lines like "I wonder what your fate would have been if you had been in similar circumstance?" or, with the music and the soulful close-up and the anguish of an imminent lovers' parting, "You won't believe me when I tell you that this is the first real happiness I've known." We believe it, all right; we just don't believe we're watching a Technicolor talkie in the year 1967, let alone a Charles Chaplin movie. He's taken me an-tiquing, all right—but where's Charlie?

The Agony
Beneath the Skin
April 18, 1967

Accident, the second Joseph Losey-Harold Pinter screen collaboration, is, like *The Servant*, a film to watch with fascination and brood about afterward. And if ultimately we are left to question whether it is worth the brooding, at very least we are left also with the satisfaction of having watched two master craftsmen at work.

In his adaptation of Nicholas Mosley's novel, Mr. Pinter proves his genius for capturing the essence of our society in the small-talk veneer of our lives, in probing to the heart of the matter with needle pricks that barely blemish the skin, in turning the commonplace into a portentous suggestion of all the human agony that feeds on its own secrecy. And the vivid camera eye of Joseph Losey's direction observes, implies and challenges us to see beyond its own visualizations.

The film literally starts off with a bang—the auto accident near the home of an Oxford don. Two of his students are in the car; William, a golden boy, is dead. The don, Stephen, pulls the dazed survivor, Anna, from the wreckage, takes her into his house, lets the police conclude that only the boy was in the car, and then, watching the girl's troubled sleep, recalls the beginning of their relationship.

Conventionally, then, with flashback, we are introduced to those involved with the boy and girl—Stephen, drawn to both by their youth and the malaise of his oncoming middle age, fighting his desire for the enigmatic and exotic girl; Charley, his successful extroverted colleague and friend, whom he envies for his physical, intellectual and sexual athleticism; Rosalind, his sensitive and pragmatic wife, aware of Stephen's vulnerability during her pregnancy with their third child, aware of the pathetic frailties and stupidities of married men of a certain age.

Thrust among the three "mature" adults are the boy, only

vaguely aware of the challenge his youthful prowess and aristo-
cratic background put upon the men, and the girl, sloe-eyed and
impassive, aware of her status as focus of desire but seemingly
devoid of initiative in stimulating it. And in a triumphant sequence
of the film, the five spend a desultory and languid summer Sunday
at Stephen's home, with sports and drink and small talk to hide the
building pyramid of emotion, the smoldering suspicions and re-
sentments and jealousies, the minor wounds inflicted in passing and
quick to fester. These are relatively decent people accidentally—
by pure chance—involved with each other, tearing at each other's
hearts and guts with a "tennis, anyone?" superficiality.

The center of interest is the involvement of the two men with
the girl, an ultimately overt and abandoned involvement on Charley's part. But it is Stephen, an intelligent and considerate and responsible man, a devoted and honest husband, who—by pure
chance, literally the auto accident—can turn to total amorality,
commit an indecent act and leave the surface of his life unrip-
pled.

The outer lushness and surface calm of their lives in Oxford
and its environs are counterpointed with the frustrations of
Stephen's attempts to compete with Charley as a television pundit
or to rekindle an affair with a past mistress, with explosions of
physical violence in sports (with a "traditional" game of indoor
rugby permitting don and pupil to do physical battle for the girl),
with emotional outbursts in the still of night or in the dreariness of
a sodden country garden.

This is the way it is with us, and the stolidity and intelligence
of Dirk Bogarde's Stephen, Stanley Baker's Charley, Vivien Merchant's Rosalind and Michael York's William add conviction. We destroy each other—by accident. We are victims of our instincts, which
are unleashed—by accident. True. Too true, perhaps. So true, in
fact, that we wind up with a suspicion that Messrs. Losey and
Pinter could not be stating the obvious so obviously.

They state it in fascinating cinematic terms, filling the eye,
alerting the ear to every nuance, titillating the intellect. But they
leave the emotions unscathed. *Accident* is for watching, and even
the brooders among us will settle for that on the Losey-Pinter level.

A Trade
Like Any Other
September 1, 1967

With *The Thief of Paris* Louis Malle once again proves himself not only one of the more thoughtful of the New Wave filmmakers but also one of all the more versatile. This picturesque period melodrama goes beyond the limits of eye-filling entertainment to contemporary significance in its stinging social commentary and its portrait of an antisocial antihero who fits neither a fictional nor a Freudian mold.

Thieves, it is noted, "are the moonlight of honest men," and robbery is not a game but "a trade like any other." Thus, from Georges Darien's turn-of-the-century novel *Le Voleur*, Malle and Jean-Claude Carrière have fashioned a nocturnal tale of a Victorian tradesman, a Raffles in suavity, a Bond in his efficiency on the job and in the bed. But Jean-Paul Belmondo's Georges Randall is something more—and thereby hangs the distinction of this immaculately made movie.

Robbery is a dirty business—but a business, Belmondo concedes at the outset as we watch him, bowler-hatted, mustachioed, stiff-collared, portmanteau in hand, burglarize a chateau room by room with cool detachment, appraiser's eye and complete disregard of impediment. How did he get his start? Well-born, orphaned, cheated of his inheritance by his guardian-uncle and frustrated in his love for his beautiful cousin—we are allowed to suspect up to a point that this autobiographical flashback narrative will cling to the romantic pattern.

But has Malle something more in mind? Is the world upside down? The underworld Georges joins—through an abbot who is indeed aware of spiritual values and therefore masterminds a vast criminal operation—is filled with men of principle and women of basic virtue, dedicated to hitting the *haute bourgeoisie* where it hurts, in cashbox, vault, and jewel box. Is it the overworld of greedy businessmen and conniving politicians, of smuggery and venality and social injustice, that is indeed the criminal segment of our society?

You can raise the questions if you wish or settle for the surface, charmingly aglow in *fin de siècle* fashions, with suspense to be drawn from a series of breath-holding burglaries in an age when physical agility and expert cunning, rather than electronic devices and death-dealing gimmicks, were the robber's stock in trade. Or you can revel in the relevancies of a sharp survey of a society whose politicians and moneymen are decrying the nonconformists and denouncing socialists and calling for a return to old-fashioned national virtues, and whose morality does not rise above materialism.

Malle, as always, gathers the strands of his story slowly and weaves a complex black comedy out of reversed values. On the romantic level he lets true love triumph, and as it does, he needles our smuggery with the suggestion that happy endings needn't mean an ever-after happiness; he lets justice—purely personal justice— triumph and then suggests that the man who is against society need not necessarily be *for* anything.

The last suggestion is in Belmondo's captivating portrait of the darkly brooding burglar, an impressive mixture of cynicism and charm. There are other excellent performances: Genevieve Bujold (the lovely ingenue of *La Guerre Est Finie* and *King of Hearts*) lights up the screen as Charlotte, and Julien Guiomar and Charles Denner are outstanding, the former as the abbot and the latter as a master criminal. These are enhancements of the smoothly sophisticated blend of social comment and romanticism that Malle masters once again in *The Thief*.

The Legend of
Bonnie and Clyde
September 15, 1967

With *Bonnie and Clyde* Warren Beatty and Arthur Penn firmly establish themselves as one of the most excitingly creative teams in American moviemaking. In their second joint effort (their first, *Mickey One*, is still a bit ahead of its audience), the young producer-actor and his director have dealt with an American folk legend in almost ballad form and triumphed.

Bonnie Parker and Clyde Barrow have their fact-and-fiction niche in the hoodlum hall of fame of the thirties; where the fact ends and the fiction begins is no longer decipherable or very relevant to the brief history of the couple who drifted together by chance, set themselves up as bank robbers, graduated to gangsterism and murder, eked through their brief and bloody career, and posthumously won folk-hero status. What is relevant is that they were drifters, nobodies, yearning to be any kind of somebodies, rebels with no cause beyond the moment's rebellion. They happened at a time when a third of the nation was rootless but immobilized by the Depression, debilitated and apathetic, and ready to admire in secret the surface derring-do of those who could get away with striking at the Establishment. Thus Bonnie and Clyde and their "gang" cut a swath from Texas through the Dust Bowl of the Midwest to a deadly entrapment in Louisiana with lawmen on their heels and bystanders strangely divided in their ethical loyalties.

It is in retrospect that the pathos of this pair, so much a product of their time and so potentially to be paralleled in ours, is evident—and this evidence provides the particular distinction of what might well have been just another gangster movie, another glorification of violence and rebellion, another bit of lip service to morality. Instead, Beatty and Penn and their associates have given us a portrait of a pair of displaced young people on the run, catapulted from one atrocity to another by their neurotic sensualities, terrifying in their complete dissociation from humanity, their aspiration to nothing beyond the satisfaction of the moment's whim.

Slowly, almost bucolically, Arthur Penn unfolds the boy-and-girl meeting, underlining the sexuality on Bonnie's part, the introverted bravado on Clyde's. The sordidness of their successes, the horror of their prankishness, the sadism of their playtime, and the emptiness of their lifetimes is played out, all to the tangy twang of a banjo, against the rolling expanse of a countryside that has little to offer even the non-misfit.

Warren Beatty, so often merely a promising performer, fulfills himself as Clyde, revealing every inward weakness and outward ferocity of the man for whom weapons and the driver's wheel provide potency; Estelle Parsons is nothing less than brilliant in her screen debut as Clyde's sister-in-law who is hurled into crime; Gene Hackman is flawless as the brother dumbly devoted to his flashier sibling; and Michael J. Pollard is excellent as the near-moronic lad blindly devoted to his leaders. It is a tribute to Faye Dunaway's talents that she blends with the cast as Bonnie, bringing to her role a jittery libido, a rapacity and an intermittent animalism that almost compensate for her immaculate good looks, which provide a Hollywood contrast to the naturalism of the other players.

Naturalism—in characters and background—is the mark of this film in its technical perfections. We are so thoroughly saturated with a sense of time and place that we are, paradoxically, compelled to recognize the universality of the theme and its particular contemporary relevance. And this is the triumph of *Bonnie and Clyde.*

Hold That Tiger!
October 1, 1967

The Tiger Makes Out, the Murray Schisgal-Arthur Hiller screen version of Schisgal's one-act play *The Tiger*, raises a question best broached, perhaps, as a matter of lapidary logistics. How do you handle a flawless gem in order to show off its perfections in a larger and more lasting setting? The question is one for the jeweler, of course, but even we non-Harry Winstons know that the answer is not to smash the jewel into any number of glittery fragments or cut and quarter it and surround it with lesser gems.

Both methods, alas, have been employed by playwright and director in transferring Mr. Schisgal's exquisite thirty-minute two-character playlet into a ninety-four-minute, two-star, four-costar, eight-guest-star film. Pieces of the play are there intact, shards are scattered throughout, and small glittery screen creations have been added. The result? Any number of flawless bits—but gone is the perfection of the original entity.

We ought to be grateful for small savors, considering the vulgar and total devastation of Murray Schisgal's *Luv* in its transition from stage to screen in lesser hands. By serving as his own screenwriter, retaining the brilliant talents of Eli Wallach and Anne Jackson and adding those of several others, Schisgal has done relatively well by us. But he has not enhanced either our pleasures or his own purpose by the cinematic inflation of his original work.

Murray Schisgal is, of course, the laughing troubadour of the absurdity of our theatrical absurdity; his satire target is the total cliché of contemporary cant. *The Tiger* was in effect a preliminary exercise for the cogencies of *Luv*, limited to the ironic frustration of the pismire-turned-predator, ready to rape and ravish in revolt against the birdbrains and Establishmentarians, who is gently tamed into taking a suburban mistress and French lessons.

Inflated into a mad, mad screen comedy, Schisgal's basic thesis is too often reduced to the realities of city streets and offices and suburban houses and crab-grassed environs, inhabited by madmen and comic characters it is true, but a prosaic reality that too often deflects the ridiculous into repetitious nonsense. Its course to absurdity is further diverted on occasion by Arthur Hiller's direction, by set-up slapstick and telegraphed sight gags, camera tricks that lag behind the intellectual pace, and obvious situation-comedy routines. Ultimately the underlining, the emphatic repetitions and the undisciplined approach make it apparent that fragile absurdity does not survive inflation by camera or even creator; the frenzy subsides in an out-of-context conclusion and the tiger returns to the womb.

Surrounded by an obviously hand-picked Broadway-bred cast, Eli Wallach and Anne Jackson are still perfection in their original roles of the meek and frustrated postman-turned-tiger and the suburban housewife who tames him on her own terms. Outstanding among the added cinematic starters are Bob Dishy as the suburban husband who yearns for ironed handkerchiefs, Ruth White and Roland Wood as a chicken-plucking landlady and her husband, Bibi Osterwald as the lady aware of the amenities even when she's trapped in her nightie with her leg through the ceiling. But despite the quality of actors and script, the gems are scattered, the design diffuse, the original brilliance sporadic. The result is an attractive and bemusing piece of costume jewelry—but not comparable to the real thing.

Chills, Thrills and Jitters

November 1, 1967

The autumn cool is being reinforced by a spate of chill-and-thrill films that are enough to give me the critical shudders and intellectual jitters and to put me off my cinematic stride for the season. *Games* and *The Penthouse* represent the pretentiously posh and pointless nonsense that's flooding the market. In one we're offered a cheapjack mélange of *Angel Street* and *Diabolique* in a New York brownstone jammed with Victorian, op and pop art; in the second we're given *The Desperate Hours* reset in a London penthouse. In neither are we provided with the slightest opportunity or provocation to care about who does what to whom and/or why; and without the caring, horror turns to contrivance and suspense to tedium.

In *Games* Simone Signoret is excellent as the mystery woman who foists herself upon a young, feckless and foolish Manhattan couple given to gadgets and games. So dominant a personality is she, however, in the face of the near-birdbrained wife played by Katharine Ross and the ultra bland husband played by James Caan, that there's no doubt about the winner. "Amateurs," Caan says after he has done in Katharine Ross and before Simone Signoret has done him in, "shouldn't play games with professionals." There's built-in criticism if a film ever had it.

In *The Penthouse*, which made a splash at the Berlin Film Festival (if muck can make a splash), a dull real-estate agent and his shopgirl doxy are held prisoner in a borrowed penthouse by a couple of raving maniacs who while away the hours by torturing the bound man with a switchblade and their rantings and by taking their turns in bed with the girl. A woman right out of the pornographic comic books joins them for a finale that is supposed to have made us all wise to the frailty of mankind.

Our Mother's House, Jack Clayton's movie of Julian Gloag's novel, succeeds far better than its source in dealing with a children's world where the innocence and the absolutes and the imaginings of the young can strike terror and evoke tears and touch the heart. Clayton, who showed his directorial magic with children in *The Innocents* and *The Pumpkin Eater*, works it again in this story of seven children who refuse to surrender their mother when she dies. They bury her in the garden and build a tabernacle for "Mothertime" séances, carrying on alone as almost a secret society within the adult world, until one of them rebels and in desperation calls upon their mother's long-lost husband for help. The seduction of the innocents, the shattering of illusion and the inevitable tragedy that leads the youngsters back to society are told with taut truth, with the horrors and atmosphere of *Lord of the Flies* some-how transferred to the softening colors of a middle-class neigh-borhood, to the sharp sights of a schoolyard and to the glow of a household.

There are remarkable performances by Margaret Brooks as the eldest child, with shaggy bangs and grubby hands; Pamela Franklin as the child given to trances and quick passions; Louis Sheldon-Williams as the oversensitive boy—all the children are superb. And Dirk Bogarde creates an unforgettable character as the vulgar, sin-ister and somehow appealing "father" who invades the children's world. Through them Clayton succeeds where the upstarts have failed in capturing the essence of the horror-suspense film—and that is the realization that the monsters among us are human.

More Heart
Than Pelvis
November 15, 1967

In this age of tough chic and even tougher technique, it is aston-ishing as well as refreshing to find a pair of young moviemakers who realize that the heart rather than the pelvis is at the core of human affairs. Even more surprising is that these two men, festival-sponsored newcomers to American screens, come from behind the Iron Cur-tain. They are technical experts, but the distinction of their films lies in their perceptive and subtle viewing of the human condition and their compassionate appreciation of it, a distinction sadly lack-ing now in the work of most young American moviemakers, whose intelligence and sensitivity are all too often obscured by pseudo-stylish cinematography and smash-and-grab emotionalism.

Dusan Makavejev's film shown in Montreal as *Love Dossier* and at the New York Film Festival as *An Affair of the Heart* is being circulated here as *Love Affair . . . or the Case of the Missing Switchboard Operator*. The thirty-five-year-old Yugoslav wrote and

directed this film, which he accurately describes as a collage of all
the elements that enter into a fatal romance between an earnest
and humorless sanitation inspector and a frivolous and determinedly
emancipated young woman. That it has been a fatal romance emerges
slowly as the retrospective account of the affair is interlaced with
illustrated lectures on criminology and sexology by two prominent
Belgrade authorities in these fields.

As a young woman's murder is discovered and resolved by the
police, as sexual practices and mores are pompously probed by the
sexologist, we are given in counterpoint the ordinary relationship
of two ordinary young people. The irony is inescapable, for good
intentions, thoughtfulness and simplicity of mind and motive lead
to tragedy that society somehow labels "everyday."

The silly libidinous switchboard operator and the dull literal-
minded rat exterminator achieve near-classic stature in their personal tragedy, although neither the fates nor the gods nor even
their own weaknesses or flaws catapult them to disaster—but only
life as they live it.

Istvan Szabo's *Father* is less impressionistic in its technique
but even more universal in its theme. The twenty-nine-year-old
Hungarian's film is an exploration of belief (or, allegorically, of religious or political faith) as a factor in a man's coming of age. It
starts out with a little boy's romanticization of his memories of his
father, a doctor who died at the end of World War II. Memory and
longing merge to create both a hero and a crutch for childhood
insecurities. As he grows into young manhood, the boy is finally
able to draw lines between idolatry and affection, to place the past
in perspective, to accept a heritage and to honor it.

With sensitivity but never a hint of sentimentality, Szabo
touches upon the torments and longing of childhood. Through remarkable casting, the film shows the boy become the man, a young
man who, in a society in constant flux (the history of modern Hun-
gary emerges clearly in the background), creates his own permanent values. Szabo is rare among young directors in his probing of
individual guilt for the past, in considering questions of political
loyalty and religious bigotry that are touchy on either side of the
Iron Curtain. In Andras Balint as the young man and Kati Sol-

yom as his Jewish fiancée, the director has two brilliant performers for his premise of humanism in a society many Americans think of as dehumanized, a premise expressed with both lyricism and logic.

Against the Groin
December, 1967

When I was young and moviegoing, the witch in *Snow White* was supposed to give you the screaming meemies and figure in your future analysis; Tom and Jerry epitomized sadism at its apogee, and a fate worse than death (which was doled out only to bad guys by way of a single and markedly undrippy bullet hole that caused immediate dust-biting) was left entirely to an imagination that could go beyond having Jimmy Cagney grind a grapefruit in your face or finding yourself at work in a dance hall owned by Eduardo Ciannelli.

We were, the Pecksniffs and the puritans of my youth complained, hellbent on a ski-slide of cinema sadism and violence, no matter how the unrealities of life were reinforced by the even then antiquities of the Motion Picture Production Code.

Well, now I'm not so young and still moviegoing and the Code has been revised into farcical impotence and the outcry against the current spate of sadism and violence in films is being taken up by a lot of responsible people who are neither Pecksniffs nor puritans nor tennis-shoe-wearing little old ladies. It is an outcry more than justified by the indecencies that we are being subjected to on the big screen (and more and more on the little one at home), by the puddles of blood and piles of guts pouring forth from the quivering flesh that is being lashed and smashed, by the bouncing of breast and grinding of groin, by the brutalizing of men and desecration of women being fed to us by the hour for no possible social, moral or intellectual purpose beyond our erotic edification and sensual delight and, above all, the almighty box-office return.

What marked this new era of cinematic scummery, what

perhaps sounded its keynote, came at the very beginning of this year when the MPAA via its then still glossily new production code gave its seal of approval to *A Fistful of Dollars* and denied it to *Blow-Up*. The traditional Hollywood Establishment (and puritan) preference for blood over body was obvious. It gave approval to a film with no purpose beyond its ninety-five-minute Technicolor close-up portrayals of men being shot, gouged, burned, beaten and stomped to death. It disapproved of a film that in the course of a brilliant depiction of contemporary society and cogent comment thereon, showed its hero with two young girls briefly romping in the buff.

Both films were box-office bonanzas, *Fistful* certainly proving the public appetite for blood and *Blow-Up* hopefully indicating the public's willingness to accept some aesthetic and intellectual substance along with a *soupçon* of nudity. But it is *Fistful* that seems to me to have served far more as standard-bearer for a genre, beyond its own sequel in which some thirty humans and three cockroaches were done away with in gory close-up in two hours. It served to signal 1967 as the year in which the pure-violence film came into its own. Not by itself. Weren't any number of uncritical critics and laymen in large part to blame for its success? Think back to those who found these studied paeans of mayhem and murder "camp," "tongue-in-cheek" spoofs, "fun" fake Westerns. But why beat a dead Italian dog? Let's go back to the Bonds, hailed as adult comic strips (let alone box-office bonanzas) and reveled in as great tongue-in-cheekers, with not much heed paid to the subliminal Freudianisms, to the rather special tortures to which our James was subjected regularly, to the latent homosexuality so apparent in the supermasculinity syndrome that denies kindness or compassion or a near-human approach to people in general and women in particular.

Subliminal, stylish, sophisticated—the Bonds slipped past some of the best of us and proceeded to break down barriers and set standards of acceptability and money-making that heavy hands and vacant heads could then abuse, because all those liberal thinkers had latched on to the "camp" gimmick and the "spoof" excuse.

We no longer need a "moral"; justice doesn't triumph in the

steady sadistic killing of a *St. Valentine's Day Massacre,* wherein
mobster murders mobster ad finitum, with a moll kneeing George
Segal in the groin for variety. It's all blood for blood's sake, right
down to the Lee Marvin manner of *Point Blank,* where crook kills
crook over a share of the loot and Marvin karate-chops a chap in the
groin for variety, with the scene rerun as flashback for added zest.
We no longer need the humanism of a *Desperate Hours* situation
wherein innocents are held in thrall by villains pending a last-
minute rescue. We get instead *The Penthouse,* so that we can get a
zestful variety of kicks out of watching a couple of psychos torture
a slobbish adulterer and double-bang his sluttish mistress. A couple
of psychos and only two victims? Pretentiously you can increase the
odds for *The Incident,* gather a dozen or more ethnic, racial and
sexual stereotypes into a subway car and have the two psychos torment them until a handsome young Aryan type from the Middle
West sacrifices himself for all those crazy, mixed-up, gutless,
homely, un-Aryan city dwellers.

It is this exploitation of perversion and violence for their own
sick sakes that justifies the current outcry and our increasing concern over the license filmmakers are exercising in their new and
hard-won freedom from censorship. Such abuse is not unexpected.
Any student of American mores could have predicted that the too-
long-delayed freedoms which enable us to watch *La Dolce Vita* or
Never on Sunday on television with no or relatively minor expurgation, or see as well as hear Molly Bloom's *Ulysses* soliloquy intact on
screen, would pave the way to excesses—the transformation of our
neighborhood art theater into a grind house courtesy of *I, a Woman*
and its successors, the increasing flood of brutal and brutalizing film
fare.

But we must differentiate, we must examine the nature of the
violence to which we are objecting. We must realize that just as
violence is the last refuge of the inarticulate, so it is also the first
resort of the incompetent, the easy out for the man who is capable of expressing himself only in the most primitive and vulgar of
dramatic terms. He leaves us with only the obscenity of violence per
se—and the pornographer thereof will always be with us, in film
as in any other medium. And so will his audience.

It is violence for its own sake that is the object of protest. And my concern is that we might go overboard in blanket condemnation, at the behest of the perennial decriers, and deny the creative artist the tools and terms he chooses for his work.

Two of the year's finer films have been pilloried by the Pecksniffs, and both seem to me excellent examples of the use of violence for artistic and intellectual purposes. Of course *The Dirty Dozen* involves psychopaths and murderers in a wartime exploit; its theme happens to be that war is a psychopathic and murderous activity, and who better fit to wage it? And incidentally, to get back to that chestnutty argument that violence vicariously observed gives us human animals an empathetic purgation, who dares not confess that watching at least a part of the Nazi high command being incinerated, even fictitiously, provides a momentary purgation for those of us who remember the millions of innocents who were slaughtered and incinerated in real life by real-life Nazis?

The second film denounced for violence, *Bonnie and Clyde*, may well emerge as the most moral, let alone the best, American film of the year. For here we have a pair of young hoods, stupid, sensual, psychotic, not very successful at the life of crime they so fecklessly undertake, who live by the gun and die by the gun. Oddly, in a film so stunningly contemporary in its sights and sound, we have returned to the rather old-fashioned notion that crime does not pay. It's enough to give a pessimist pause!

As always, the filmmaker's intent and purpose must be our touchstone. Both public and producers, it seems to me, have been lax in setting personal standards. Instead, fashions are slavishly followed by both manufacturer and consumer, and fashions, alas, can go low as well as high. At the moment we seem to be approaching dangerous depths. The warnings are up. It's time for the critical eye and the self-censoring judgment—or, heaven help us, we'll have it thrust upon us. Those little old ladies of all sexes are putting on their tennis shoes in the wings.

Great White
Liberals All
December, 1967

There's a hot chance, my Beverly Hills agent in charge of gauging the schmaltz scene tells me, that Katharine Hepburn might well beat out Dame Edith Evans (so superb in *The Whisperers*) as best actress, and the best-actor award deserved by Rod Steiger for *In the Heat of the Night* may go posthumously to Spencer Tracy. After all, *Guess Who's Coming to Dinner?* was their last film together—his last film.

Thus insult would be added to an insulting film that put these two fine performers to shame under endless platitudes. What a pity that in his last film Tracy was reduced to the daddy-is-a-dope television-series stereotype and Miss Hepburn required to do little more for two hours except fill and refill her fine eyes with tears. They're both real pros; they didn't throw up on camera during the filming of this cinematic antique which indicates that Stanley Kramer hasn't seen anything but Stanley Kramer movies for the past twenty years.

It would be easy to accept this film, as thousands of mindless moviegoers are doing, because it is designed to satisfy the smugs in its lip service to decency while it sloughs off our most pressing national problem in frighteningly insidious terms. In essence it says that it's perfectly fine for the slightly silly daughter of a millionaire to marry a Negro provided that (a) he's Sidney Poitier (b) he's the second-smartest scientist in the whole wide world (c) his mother keeps her gloves on while drinking sherry with her prospective in-laws (only the jolly neighborhood Catholic priest is allowed to drink whiskey bare-handed, yet—he's Irish, you know) and (d) the happy miscegenated couple gets the hell out of this country by midnight and spends the rest of their lives peddling medicine to the natives in Africa.

Kramer and writer William Rose have given us a great White

Liberal Household; from the carryings-on (particularly by the comic-relief Negro mammy-turned-housekeeper), it's obvious that no other Negro has ever walked through the front door, and though the jolly priest (I guess Mr. Kramer did see somebody else's movie about thirty years ago) is free to come in and devour the liquor supply, the folks hasten to explain that they're non-Catholics themselves. Of course, to give credit where due, Sam Levene doesn't show up as their jolly neighborhood rabbi. But heck, Daddy, that bumbling, lovable Great Liberal Newspaper Publisher (who seems never to have heard of medical-missionary work before) loves Mommy, that damp-eyed Great Liberal Avant-Garde Art Gallery Proprietress, and Mommy loves her Happy Little Girl—so that solves our race problems and Hollywood can always provide this sort of stuff for the drive-in trade when the summers get too long and too hot.

Three Loves
of Bathsheba
December, 1967

Curled up with any good Victorian novels lately? If in this audio-visual age you're looking instead for a good Victorian movie to curl up with, there's *Far from the Madding Crowd*, a simple, visually beautiful, endlessly descriptive, primary-level-plotted, comfortably and astonishingly old-fashioned movie. The astonishment is there because this film version of the Thomas Hardy novel comes from the Modding crowd responsible for *Darling*. I expected a movie to make me stand up and cheer or at least sit up and take notice. Instead it's curl-up-and-doze-fitfully time.

Is it a Homeric nod, a labor of love that went over the edge into infatuation, or the fallibility of literal time-travel that explains this offering of so little by so many talents? Behind the camera: director John Schlesinger (with *Billy Liar* as well as *Darling* to his credit) and screenwriter Frederic Raphael (who wrote *Two for the Road*). Out front: Julie Christie, Terence Stamp, Alan Bates, Peter Finch—brilliant performers. And what they are offering is a banal "Three Loves of Bathsheba" swamped in the lushest and loveliest of bucolic settings swarming with rustics.

Admittedly Hardy's 1874 story line is hardly one to conjure with. His claim to immortality rests on what once seemed the spareness of his prose, the realism of his settings, and his then untraditional concern with complexities of character set against immutable forces. Take these away, as Schlesinger and Raphael have, and there is left a superficial and tedious tale of a seemingly silly and willful woman who keeps the faithful shepherd Oak and the infatuated gentleman farmer Boldwood in thrall while she has a sensual although marital fling with the caddish Sergeant Troy. To keep things tidy, Boldwood finally kills Troy; and Bathsheba, cozily burying Troy in the grave of his truelove, whom he had left to die in childbirth but trueloved always, marries the sturdy Oak.

Embarrassing even for soap-opera devotees, this plot stands bare in pristine triteness without a hint of motivation to hide its antique mechanics. Julie Christie expresses the appropriate emotions but rarely sustains the emotion beyond its expression. Alan Bates as Oak manages a consistent stance of patient forbearance (whether with the project as a whole or simply Bathsheba is undeterminable); Peter Finch as Boldwood almost but never quite reaches tragic terms; only Terence Stamp, beneath the black-mustachioed bravado of Sergeant Troy, suggests a complex being. He is the heart of the film's few moments of drama.

What has been drawn and drawn out (the film runs two hours and forty-nine minutes) is every physical nuance of Dorset (Hardy's Wessex), an endless feast of fields and forests and coastal vistas, and of the natives in their habitat, all exquisitely photographed, with even a Mod cut here and there. The background wins out. There is more truth in the quavering voice of an ancient joining in a ballad, in the gossipy eye of a housemaid, in the staggering gait of a sodden bumpkin than in the highly skilled histrionics of the protagonists.

John Schlesinger is not, of course, the first director to be beguiled into indulgence and naïveté in his first color spectacular, and certainly he is entitled to a Homeric nod. But not to a three-hour snooze.

1967:
From Top to Bottom

1. *Bonnie and Clyde*
2. *La Guerre Est Finie*
3. *The Graduate*
4. *In the Heat of the Night*
5. *In Cold Blood*
6. *Ulysses*
7. *The Battle of Algiers*
8. *Falstaff*
9. *Father*
10. *The President's Analyst*

It's Ten Best time again, and what makes 1967's list-making chores different from chores past is that this was the year of *Bonnie and Clyde* and *The Graduate*, the year of *Ulysses* and of Expo '67. In short, this was the year of the American film's coming of age (albeit in a bar-mitzvah rather than voting-age sense) or at least showing a resurgence, with seven of the Top Ten home products, and the year when just about every technique that had been developed over the decades was shown in its fullest flower. (Film technology, in fact, has just about reached the hard-top-convertible anomaly, what with the outstanding Expo film, Ontario's *A Place To Stand*, being a single-projection film that gave the impression of being a multiple-projection movie.)

Much in the *Blow-Up* manner, *Bonnie and Clyde* has become the most talked-about film of the year, but in a much broader area than the Antonioni film. Staunch and no longer lonely advocates of the Arthur Penn-Warren Beatty combination in *Mickey One*, a film slowly but surely letting the audience grow up to it, we espoused *Bonnie and Clyde* from its premiere at the Montreal Film Festival as an artistic triumph, a film that came to grips in original terms with both the American gangster mythology and the mystique of mindless youthful rebellion. It is not an easy film for the prudish or for those unattuned to its harrowing contemporary rhythms to ac-

cept; they settle for it as a prettification of criminals and an exploitation of violence. This is the surface misconception; the film, on
analysis, stands as a clear and forthright statement of the pathos of
the purposeless rebellion of the young, of the frustration of the
empty-souled, of society's rejection of the outsider, of the retribution
violence demands from those it serves. It is, in a sense, the most
"American" film since *On the Waterfront*, capturing a national malaise in terms of a folk legend.

La Guerre Est Finie is the most sophisticated work Alain Resnais has yet provided us, perfecting his technique in dealing cinematically with the interrelation of time and place, and never before has he brought such lyricism to the harshness of everyday
living or given such scope to the probing of the inner man—all this
within the framework of a suspense thriller. This politically forthright and thereby controversial film provides an uncompromising
portrait of the professional revolutionary—a man under orders in a
lifetime's cause, but a man who is beginning to doubt his dedication
and question his goals. It will please neither the left nor the right;
Resnais deals in the various shades of truth. Yves Montand is superb
as the revolutionary, creating a universal figure as the political activist who in his maturity finds the courage to make an objective
self-appraisal.

The Graduate presents us with a Holden Caulfield type five
years later, reluctantly facing life in black comedy set against the
lush and colorful context of affluence. The plot (a mixture of satire
and slapstick, with the youth sexually involved with both a mother
and her daughter) does not and should not bear description; it
is a scathing survey of the amorality and hypocrisy of the established generation. What separates it from all the other visually
attractive   anti-Establishment   pro-youthful-inertia-cum-revolt   en-
tertainments is its thesis that although the young can be seduced
by the Establishment and float along passively on its affluence,
they can fulfill themselves only by getting off their inflated pool
pads and actively pursuing their hearts' desire. The cream of the
jest—and the point of the ultimate beau geste—is that the young
may wind up in as much of a mess as their elders, but at very least it
will be a mess of their own making. There are brilliant perform-

ances by Dustin Hoffman, Anne Bancroft, William Daniels and Katharine Ross, among others; stylish (i.e., derived from many styles) direction by Mike Nichols, and a wonderful musical complement by Simon and Garfunkel. This is seriocomic satire at its best.

In the Heat of the Night has a double distinction as a whodunit in which the sociology of its small-Southern-city milieu is a major element in the plotting and as a vehicle for a remarkable performance. On the surface a story of a redneck police chief and the Negro cop from the North whose help he needs to solve a murder, the film is basically an honest depiction of a duel between two natural-born enemies who recognize for a brief but significant moment their common humanity. What is remarkable is Rod Steiger's subtle delineation of a hitherto clichéd character, the authority with which he molds the many moods of a stolid man and the rhythm of his playing against Sidney Poitier's established noble-Negro character. But under Norman Jewison's knowing and at times beautiful direction, Poitier brings new facets to his characterization. The film, however, is Steiger's all the way.

In Cold Blood is an excellent derivation of the Truman Capote book, and the credit goes to director Richard Brooks for providing the authenticity of setting and the documentary aura essential to this true-crime tale. His major accomplishments are the casting of relative unknowns, Robert Blake and Scott Wilson, as the killers; in pacing the narrative in such a way as to do justice to the book and, perhaps most important, treating senseless violence on a mature level.

Ulysses is not only a dazzling and absorbing film but also an accurate translation of James Joyce's masterpiece; so Joycean is the movie, in fact, that one realizes instantly how cinematic is the novel. There has been condensation but no serious omissions from the monumental work and no bowdlerization or expurgation. Perfect casting (Milo O'Shea and Barbara Jefford are unforgettable as Leopold and Molly Bloom) and clean direction make this an adult film in the finest sense.

The Battle of Algiers is remarkable as a re-creation and reenactment of the Algerian fight for freedom. The young Italian creator of this pastiche, Gillo Pontecorvo, has done an astonishing piece of work in directorial technique and technical processing to achieve not merely a newsreel tempo but a grainy realism unmatched by the average news film and all too rarely approached by even the better ventures into cinema verité. What is equally noteworthy is Pontecorvo's objectivity in showing both the exhilaration and the heartbreak of a fight for liberation, with neither the oppressed nor the oppressor able to survive at ease with his conscience.

Falstaff is a testament to the enduring genius of Orson Welles as screenwriter, director and actor. From five Shakespeare plays he has constructed a dramatic history of merry lechers and tosspots grown old. Their games glow in their own memories but are seen for their staleness and crassness through the cool eyes of youth coming to maturity. His Falstaff, a Rabelaisian behemoth, is weighed and found wanting, a player as worthless as his games in the course of a chronicle told in stark and simple terms. The cold truths of history and the chill of time taking its toll are warmed by Welles's magnificent sense of language, of the poetry that is the substance of the drama. In this first of his own films since *The Trial* in 1962, Welles does justice to Shakespeare, to cinema and to his own great talents.

Father is a beautiful and important film, a young Hungarian's revelation of a particular generation in a particular place in our time that emerges as a sensitive and unsentimental exploration of a universal theme. It is an exploration of belief—by analogy, perhaps, of religious or political faith—as it changes from the personal idolatries of childhood to the affections and evaluations of maturity. His hero, making the painful transition from boyhood to young manhood, is in search of permanent values in a constantly changing society, and the film's hallmark is its emphasis on and revelation of a touching humanism in what we too often think of as a dehumanized system. Istvan Szabo's distinction among young directors on either side of the Iron Curtain is his willingness to question and probe into matters of conscience; his art is the blend of sensitivity and logic he brings to the task.

The President's Analyst could rank in the Top Ten on guts alone as that rare American film that dares take on the Establishment (from the CEA to the FBR to the telephone company as arch villain) with a forthrightness heretofore restricted to stage and cabaret. It's free-wheeling, outrageous and very funny, laced with a sophisticated zaniness that is sheer delight. Because of this, because it is filled with superior performances and off-beat actors and gives further and free directorial rein to Theodore Flicker (of *The Premise* on stage and *The Troublemaker* on screen), whatever imperfections it has are minor indeed.

So much for the Top Ten—with *Two for the Road* and *Accident* vying for tenth-and-a-half place, and eleventh potentially filled by *The Joker, King of Hearts, The Whisperers, The Hawks and the Sparrows, Persona, Portrait of Jason, Our Mother's House.* And hard behind come *Cool Hand Luke, The Deadly Affair, Marat/Sade, How To Succeed in Business Without Really Trying, The Big City* (Satyajit Ray's *Mahanagar*), *Bedazzled, The Naked Runner, To Sir, with Love, The Thief of Paris, You're a Big Boy Now, Naked Among the Wolves, Made in Italy, Divorce American Style, The Dirty Dozen, The Tiger Makes Out*—and we undoubtedly are leaving out some goodies along the way.

As to the year's bottom-quality films, let's say simply that it was a broad bottom, with high competition for the nadir spot. Were it not, in fact, for the presence of Katharine Hepburn, Spencer Tracy and Sidney Poitier to give some semblance of feeling, if not dignity, to *Guess Who's Coming to Dinner?*, it might have edged *Hurry Sundown* out of that choice location. The performers pull the film up to second-worst stature, followed closely by *The Penthouse, The Incident, Reflections in a Golden Eye, Tony Rome, The Happening, A Fistful of Dollars, Oh Dad, Poor Dad . . .*, and *Woman Times Seven*. And lots more, for 1967 was a vintage year for muck and mawkishness. But let's not let the memory—or the aroma—linger. More, as always, to come.

Movies: Morals, Violence, Sex—Anything Goes
January 9, 1968*

FADE IN . . . lone stranger . . . mean, ugly, handsome-ugly, lonely stranger . . . skyline . . . mean, ugly, handsome-ugly, lonely skyline . . . out of shadows comes a man . . . pow, bam, sock . . . four-letter words . . . smash to the groin . . . pow, bam, sock . . . lone stranger pulls a gun . . . pow . . . man bites the asphalt . . . bam, sock . . . lone stranger walks on . . . mean, ugly, handsome-ugly, lonely lone stranger . . . out of shadows comes a girl, beautiful-anonymous, big-bosomed boy-body, all hair and mouth, no forehead, no hips . . . pow, bam, sock . . . five-letter words . . . smooch to the groin . . . pow, bam, sock . . . pop-art penthouse . . . bare shoulders, bare thighs, bare everything . . . pow . . . beautiful-anonymous bites the bed sheets . . . bam, sock . . . lone stranger walks on . . . mean, ugly, handsome-ugly, lonely lone stranger . . . wham, crash . . . op-art penthouse . . . six dead bodies and six beautiful anonymouses, and you can't tell the bodies from the anonymouses without six-letter words . . . discotheque . . . writhing, swaying, hyper-hipping and some tripping . . . psyche my delic and call me Vanessa . . . seven-letter words and eight more nudes . . . nine-letter words and ten-

```
letter words and bingo! ... ALIENATION!!!
...zowie... camp and noncommunication and
every man a lone stranger with two cars in
every garage and pot in the pot...
noncommunication...hallelujah...
incoherence...FADE OUT.
```

Thus the age of film has come full century in the sixties, and the optimists among us choose to think that films have come of age as well. *Blow-Up* has exploded in the worlds of Kirche, Kuche and Kinder alike; but we need not despair, because *The Sound of Music* is still the all-time record holder, and throughout the past year, *To Sir, with Love* had the kids in thrall, and *A Man and a Woman* let everyone wallow in a world of *Ladies Home Journal* fiction while keeping *Réalites* on the coffee table. Above all, *Gone with the Wind* is back in contemporary format to reassert the all-time cinematic values that seemed uncertain a while back when the woebetiders were worrying that Andy Warhol might be the Griffith of our day, and the local art house, the stag-movie showcase of our neighborhood. The nicest thing you can say about Lee Marvin is that he has the Humphrey Bogart magnetic meanness, and there are those who maintain that Julie Andrews might well be Mary Pickford with hair-straightener. So who's America's Sweetheart now?

Doris Day isn't, and Rock Hudson isn't, not anymore, and that's what separates the fifties from the sixties, wherein the fuse was finally lit for the rip-roaring explosion that has shattered any delusions about which is the liveliest of the arts and where the cultural action is today—and tomorrow.

The speed of the explosion, even in this age of hypersonics, is amazing. Was it indeed only yesterday—1960—that *Hiroshima, Mon Amour* burst forth with those embarrassment-evoking bare shoulders and interwined thighs to suggest to the American movie audience that perhaps not every woman went to bed, Hollywood-star fashion, with a long-sleeved nightie that tied at the neck and a bow in her carefully coifed curls, and not every man wore pajamas, all two pieces? (We're left to ponder, those of us who are not unaware of the industrial aspects of the "art form" known as movies, whether it was American morality that kept even married folk at sleeptime well clad and in twin beds or whether it was the nightwear and furniture manufacturers.)

Some of us encountered Godard's hand-held camera in 1961's *Breathless*, and Truffaut's sensations-of-Sennett the next year in *Jules and Jim*. But for the non-art-house-oriented among us, the changes in form and rhythm and content really came with *Tom Jones* and *8½* and *Dr. No* in 1963; *Dr. Strangelove* and *The Servant* and *A Hard Day's Night* in 1964; *Darling* and *Mickey One* and *The Ipcress File* in 1965; *Georgy Girl* and *Dear John* and *Who's Afraid of Virginia Woolf?* in 1966-1967—and, with the sizzling and sputtering of a fuse, *Ulysses* and *Blow-Up* and *I, a Woman* and *The Chelsea Girls* and the shattering impact of *Bonnie and Clyde* and *Portrait of Jason*. Above all, there was Expo '67 to demonstrate the excitement of form, the infinite variety of projection and the endless possibility therein.

Well, the more it changes, the more it is of the same old thing. This movie-minded generation, set agog by Expo's films, is much in the position of the pot smoker who encounters De Quincey's *Confessions of an English Opium-Eater* and wonders how long this sort of thing has been going on. Expo offered Labyrinth, more than a year in construction, longer in conception, millions in expenditure, with its wall and floor projection, its mini-lights and music pause for meditation, its five-screen-cross finale; a 360-degree projection for a trans-Canada trip (another version of the trans-U.S.A. trip offered at Disneyland); projection on moving geometrics; multi-multi-multiscreens; and finally, the circle completed at the Ontario pavilion, where a brilliant film was projected in 70mm on a single screen to give one the illusion of multiscreen projection.

The wonder and stimulation are there for the movie-minded, if not for the movie-history-minded. Let James Card, curator of motion pictures at George Eastman House in Rochester, N.Y., point to another Expo, the great Paris Exposition of 1900, where the results of the first two decades of moviemaking were demonstrated. By then, Mr. Card notes, there were sound films, trick films with stop-motion effects and multiple exposures, news features, story films and movies in color, even Cineorama and a sixty-nine-foot-wide screen. At that other exposition, he reports, Sarah Bernhardt and Coquelin spoke from the screen; Raoul Grimon-Sanson's Cineorama, more than twice the size of today's Cinerama, used ten synchronized cameras and projectors (versus today's single projector) and a screen thirty feet high that completely surrounded the spectators with a gigantic color movie. Today's Cinemascope? The Lumière brothers showed their color films on a 48 x 69-foot screen, with twenty-five thousand viewers (four times a Radio City Music Hall full house) seated at a session.

Why, then, the explosion sixty-seven years later? The wonders of film form and shape were tucked away until they became "commercially" feasible or essential for survival. When the public began staying home to listen to radio for free in the twenties, sound (and sound-on-film had been developed as early as 1908) was added for talkies. When the public began staying home to watch television for free in the forties and fifties, out came the expanding screens, the 3-D experiments, the new shapes and forms. And new generations of filmmakers and filmgoers saw a wondrous world unfolding. Certainly, the explosive nature of the Expo films is to be attributed to the entire audiovisual orientation of our society, our growing literacy and awareness of the aspects of the medium, our perhaps diminishing awareness of the importance of the message.

Our eyes have opened to film. In an age of affluence, ten-year-olds make 8mm movies replete with cuts, miniatures and judiciously applied catsup blood to out-Bond Flint; and teen-agers turn out animations that make middle-Disney look like the filmstrip artistry that elementary-school youngsters turn out daily in more progressive art classes. The long-haired lad who, in a recent *New Yorker* cartoon, approached his father at the breakfast table with, "Dad, could I have twenty thousand dollars to make a film?" was speaking for his generation. Where mine intended to write the Great American Novel, today's plans exclusively on making the Great American Movie—that will, of course, be far ahead of the now slightly aging New Wave boys but pay tribute, naturally, to those great camp artists of Hollywood's Magnificent Thirties. Above all, it will have the Truth that one finds in *Blow-Up* and *Bonnie and*

Clyde and that audiences will be finding this year in Shirley Clarke's *Portrait of Jason*, Dusan Makavejev's *Love Affair . . . or the Case of the Missing Switchboard Operator* and Frank Simon's *The Queen*, on the arthouse and campus circuits, and hopefully, in Bergman's *Shame* or Harold Pinter's *The Birthday Party* or John Frankenheimer's *The Fixer* or Mike Nichols's *Catch-22*.

The Truth, of course, is where you find it—and you can find it on occasion in form, but always in content. And so we can go back to Expo and discover how far form without content sticks with us, how much of the freak-show aspect vanishes, how little of substance does evade us. From Labyrinth one recalls vividly the surprising splash of the bread the little girl throws from shore on the wall screen into the water on the floor screen; but how much more vivid is recollection of the eyes of the savage in search of the diabolic crocodile, the eyes of the woman searching for herself in front of her makeup mirror. And these last are on small, square screens, the art in the humanity on both sides of the camera lens, the Truth in the content of the vision. And Labyrinth stays in memory not because of its meditation room and galleries but because, in the midst of a jubilant world exposition, in the midst of affluence and arty sales pitches for the material wonders of the world, one cinematic voice and vision said to us, "Hey, hold on, maybe what's wrong with the world is inside you." And despite all its beautiful and imaginative use of triple screens, the Francis Thompson-Alexander Hammid *To Be Alive!* provided as memorable an experience at Expo as it had at the New York World's Fair, because it had something to say and voiced the truth that life in the world around us is wondrous and good, but only the very young and the very old take the time to observe it.

What, then, of the content of films that are taking every shape and form that technology permits? Without question, almost every film—from the television-oriented quickie (i.e., *Games*, which fades in and out almost by the clock to adapt its piecemeal plotting to the requirements of commercials and station breaks) to the grind-audience special (i.e., *I, a Woman*, a sexploitation film that became socially acceptable because it was foreign-made and boasted English subtitles)—has beautiful scenes or values in musical scoring or film editing. A Hollywood mogul has rightly said that "It's easy to *take* a good picture—the hard part is to *make* a good picture."

Obviously, and to the horror of the puritans and Neanderthals among us, we're in a no-holds-barred era as far as the content of film is concerned. Inveterate moviegoers (and who more inveterate than a see-'em-all movie critic?) are hard-pressed to think of any human aberration, let alone practice, that has not been put on film, with almost as much remaining in the mind, if not the eye, of the beholder (i.e., *Bonnie and Clyde*, wherein, much as in Bergman's *The Silence*, only those who know of certain practices will see them). Sadism? We've graduated from the recurrent spreadeagle torture scenes of the Bond movies to where, in *Point Blank*, for example, Lee Marvin can deliver a karate chop to a chap's groin. "A first for that one," I remarked to a colleague. "Guess you're right," he replied after a moment's consideration. "After all, in *St. Valentine's Day Massacre*, the gal only kneed George Segal." All the varieties of bloodletting have been explored in full and blazing color, and the body beautiful exposed in repose and in motion in a manner to make *Hiroshima*'s shoulders seem wondrously decorous. We're growing up, as are our movie stars. In *The Family Way*, little Hayley Mills, bless 'er 'eart, not only exposed her scrumptious little derriere but did so in a film devoted exclusively to a young couple's difficulties in "consummating" their marriage. Heavens, when we think of what Doris and Rock used to go through just so Doris could emerge *intacta* at fadeout time!

But is it really the nudity *a trois* that made *Blow-Up* perhaps the most talked about if not the best film of the past twelve months? I think not, no more than that the violence was a come-on aspect of *Bonnie and Clyde*. Both films demonstrate the ultimate in cinematic skill, in establishing a milieu, in editing and romanticizing reality for artistic purpose. More important is that young people— and the young lead us more often than not in movie matters, and I do mean far beyond their inspiring the grown-up world to take that reluctant first look at the Beatles—have found their time of day and their message. To the seasoned and sophisticated aficionado, *Blow-Up* is Antonioni at his most watchable, with cinema style derived from Stanley Donen, but the same old Antonioni on alienation and noncommunication in his refusal to come to grips with the flesh and blood of life. To younger and/or fresher eyes, new to this Italian filmmaker, it is "now," in a world of surface living and sensual self-indulgence, where the fine line between reality and illusion is blurred, and you can blow your mind in the coping therewith. *Bonnie and Clyde* is amazing in its morality, its thesis that those who live by violence shall die thereby, its demonstration that the rewards of crime are nil, its depiction of the empty, shallow young psychopaths who captured the imagination of a Depression-ridden countryside. But young people catch its rhythm as a purely American folk ballad underlining the snowballing of wrongdoing, the inability to stop short once one has set out on a path in that fruitless endeavor to "be" somebody, the interdependence of law-breakers and of lawmen, the sordid depravity of two folk "heroes."

Thus the films we are getting and that are to come have no holds barred as far as sex and violence and language go. Shocking? It's time we faced the fact that films, much like literature and drama, come out of our society and mirror it, and that beyond matters of clothing and interior decoration, movies reflect and do not set patterns. At this point, *Virginia Woolf*'s "hump the hostess" sounds meek and mild next to the fond exchange of "bitch" and "bastard" between no lesser stars than Albert Finney and Audrey Hepburn, reverberating from no less a screen than that of Radio City Music Hall in no less a film than Stanley Donen's *Two for the Road*. And there was no bowdlerization of Molly Bloom's soliloquy from the screen version of *Ulysses*, thanks to the wise judge's conclusion more than thirty years ago, in the course of freeing the American publication of the James Joyce classic, that no girl had ever been raped by a book. Or, he might have added, by a movie— albeit rape and seduction and variations of both may be viewed at leisure at your neighborhood theater. And violence. And bloodshed.

But we are grown-ups, and we have seen a man murdered in our living rooms via television (the Oswald-Ruby murder), and we are ready to face the reality on the wide screen that all is not happy endings and twin beds and ultimate virginity. We're ready, then, for Shirley Clarke's *Portrait of Jason*, a 105-minute near-monologue by a Negro male prostitute (with off-screen "interviewing" by the director and needling by a friend or two), a film that demonstrates the difference between an artist (i.e., Miss Clarke) and a commercialist (i.e., Andy Warhol and other recorders of the boring prurience that evolves on the screen in freak-show terms as *The Chelsea Girls*). Jason talks and does his "act" and his "bit"; and through the completely frank and therefore shocking exposure of a desperate human, we get a throbbing and horrifying and compassionate understanding of what society can make of a man. And because the world is our cinematic oyster, the new year offers us a film "collage" by a young Yugoslav, Makavejev's *Love Affair*, an ironic commentary, via the recounting of a fatal romance between a serious man and a surface maid, on the tragic trivia of all lives, let alone on life behind the Iron Curtain. And very much in the tradition of the New Wave, let alone the internationalism of today's moviemaking, we can revel in *Le Départ*, directed by a young Pole, made in Belgium with a sparkling French cast (headed by Jean-Pierre Léaud, the boy of *The 400 Blows* grown to manhood and stylish comedy), and learn to our delight how a young hairdresser can switch his passions from fast cars to one lovely girl.

What we as grown-ups are willing, let alone ready, to face in the name of adulthood is one thing, however, and what the purveyors of films are offering in the name thereof is quite another. Lip service and sign service to the generation gap—the "suggested-for-mature-audiences" bit, the "persons-under-eighteen-not-admitted-unless-accompanied-by-their-parents" dichotomy, the "adults-only" blurb—serve at most to advise the semiconscientious parent that the film so labeled is not a family film. (A "family" film is all too often one designed for the family that is glued together by sentimentality, simplemindedness and a set of values as distinguished by its banality as its vulgarity; but thank goodness we can take grandma and the kids—there are no bare, though bulgy, bosoms and nothing more lecherous than an eight-year-old ogling Brigitte Bardot, Daddy slapping Mommy gaily on the rump or Mommy comically suspecting Daddy of instant adultery with every female within fifty feet of her own split level.) More often than not, however, the adults-only label serves to alert the thrill-seeker and, on rare occasion, deprive the mature adolescent of cinematic experiences that he may be far better equipped to appreciate than are many of his elders.

But how stringent or restrictive indeed is the adult label when just about every film is destined for television, that massest of the media? The purveyors of *The Penthouse*, which epitomizes the current sex-and-sadism-for-voyeurs product, got well ahead of the game in their publicity. Under the title in tiny letters was "s.m.a.," catering to the production code's "suggested-for-mature-audiences" labeling restriction. But in caps as large as the title was the titillating news that this was "THE PICTURE YOU WILL NOT SEE ON TELEVISION." But who's kidding whom? If there were qualitative safeguards on television films, we might not see on the home screen the sick and sickening and utterly pointless ninety-seven minute depiction of two madmen torturing a slobbish adulterer and taking bedroom turns with his sluttish doxy. But quality is not the test; and morally, there are getting to be fewer and fewer holds barred even on the small screen—with forty million viewers on hand for even the dullest of offerings. Let's just say that we may not be seeing *The Penthouse* on television this year. I'd hedge my bets as far as next year is concerned.

This is, after all, the television season that has brought us *Never on Sunday* on a network prime-time basis, so that the kiddies who weren't abed by nine P.M. could get a gander at the happiest prostitute in Piraeus and consider Jules Dassin's dubious thesis that the life of the flesh and the instincts has it all over the intellectual one in any clime. It's the season that's promising us *Tom Jones*, a bawdy, lusty romp no matter how you slice it—and slice and splice the feature films the networks and local stations do to eliminate that bit of breast or bottom that under our mixed-up morality may be seen in the flesh at home but not in the film that is watched there. But oddly enough, on occasion, the slicing and splicing is done with taste and forethought, and, because great and even good films can manage to survive the interruptions for commercials and station breaks, throughout the country, we've been able, courtesy of local stations, to have such truly adult films as *Room at the Top* and *The Pawnbroker* and *La Dolce Vita* come to us with their guts and basic artistry intact.

This year, feature films will make even further encroachments on prime time that television should ideally devote to its own creations, with seven instead of the current six network movies a week on the agenda. The factories are hard at work to provide the product, with filmmakers and, as *Variety* so jazzily put it on one occasion, "video execs" reaching prior agreement "on moral requirements that would clear the film for homescreen viewing and still bring out sex-happy filmgoers in prior theatrical release." But we can rely on television to serve its sex-happy video viewers as well, what with tailored-for-television films (produced directly for television, with no exhibition in theaters beforehand) going on about homosexuality, adultery, drug trips and the other major divertissements of our day. The "moral requirements" of the home or theater screen seem to be getting broader by the season.

Time to view with alarm? Not really. The more it changes . . . We have *Doctor Dolittle* and *Half a Sixpence* for the high-class family trade for the new year, and Claude Lelouch's successor to *A Man and a Woman*, his *Live for Life*, to permit us to wallow again in some schmaltz *à la française* and feel sophisticated about our sentimentality. And lurking offscreen, ready to pop on—beyond the bare bones of Jane Fonda that are getting to be a cinematic staple, beyond the much-anticipated screen debut of Barbra Streisand, beyond the black comedies and sick comedies and tough-guy dramas—there is the great moviemaker. He's a man of any or all nationalities, age or background. It doesn't matter. What does matter is that he is a man with something to say that can and must be said only through film in his very own way and on his own terms. He is the man to move us and the movies up a few rungs of the ladder in our climb to maturity.

We're readier than ever, perhaps, certainly willing and anxiously waiting for him. Let's hope that sixty-eight will be his year. After all, the greatest movie is still unmade.

☆ **Index** ☆

Index

About the Author

A native New Yorker, Judith Crist is a graduate of Hunter College and the School of Journalism at Columbia University. In 1945 she joined the New York *Herald Tribune*, serving successively as a reporter, editor for the arts, associate drama critic and film critic, and continued as film critic for the New York *World Journal Tribune*. Currently, she is an adjunct professor at the Columbia School of Journalism, as well as film and drama commentator on the NBC-TV *Today Show* and is regular film critic for *TV Guide* and for *New York* magazine. She is also president of the Columbia Graduate School of Journalism Alumni Association and a vice-president of the New York Newspaper Women's Club. Her awards include: the George Polk journalism award; Page One Award from the American Newspaper Guild; three New York Newspaper Women's Club "Front Page" awards. Mrs. Crist's favorite companions at New York movie theaters and before the TV set are her husband Bill and son Steven.